the edible garden

▶ by hazel white,
janet h. sanchez,
and the editors
of sunset books

menlo park · california

▶ sunset books

VICE PRESIDENT, GENERAL MANAGER:
Richard A. Smeby

VICE PRESIDENT, EDITORIAL DIRECTOR:
Bob Doyle

PRODUCTION DIRECTOR: Lory Day

OPERATIONS DIRECTOR:
Rosann Sutherland

RETAIL SALES DEVELOPMENT MANAGER:
Linda Barker

EXECUTIVE EDITOR: Bridget Biscotti Bradley

ART DIRECTOR: Vasken Guiragossian

SPECIAL SALES: Brad Moses

▶ staff for this book

WRITERS: Janet H. Sanchez, Hazel White

MANAGING EDITOR: Marianne Lipanovich

COPY EDITOR: Zipporah W. Collins

ART DIRECTOR: Alice Rogers

PHOTO EDITOR: Cynthia Del Fava

ASSISTANT PHOTO EDITOR: Laura Del Fava

ASSOCIATE EDITOR: Carrie Dodson Davis

ILLUSTRATOR: Erin O'Toole

PAGE PRODUCTION: Linda M. Bouchard

PREPRESS COORDINATOR: Eligio Hernandez

INDEXER, PROOFREADER: Rebecca LaBrum

COVER, TOP FROM LEFT: Norman A. Plate;
Arnaud Descat/Mise au Point; John
Glover. MIDDLE, FROM LEFT: Mise au Point;
Thomas E. Fitzroth; Howard Rice/GPL.
BOTTOM, FROM LEFT: R. Todd Davis; David
Cavagnaro.

For additional copies of *The Edible Garden* or
any other Sunset book, call 1-800-526-5111
or visit us at **www.sunset.com**.

design basics 6

contents

design options 24

spring 40

summer *60*

fall and winter *80*

special techniques *92*

edibles a–z *104*

apples·apricots·artichokes·arugula·asparagus·basil·beans·beets
blackberries·blueberries·broccoli·brussels sprouts·cabbage
carrots·cauliflower·celery, celeriac·chard·chinese cabbage·chives
cilantro, coriander·citrus·collards·corn·cucumbers·eggplant
fennel·figs·garlic·geraniums·grapes·johnny-jump-ups, pansies
kale·lavender·leeks·lettuces, salad greens·melons, watermelons
mint·mustard greens·nasturtiums·okra·onions·oregano, marjoram
parsley·parsnips·peaches, nectarines·pears·peas·peppers·plums
potatoes·pumpkins·radishes·raspberries·rhubarb·rosemary
sage·southern peas·spinach·squash·strawberries·sunflowers
sweet potatoes·thyme·tomatoes·turnips·watermelon·zucchini

design basics

- Choose a style, formal or informal—or a little of each.

- Create a path that's comfortable for garden work and pleasing to walk along.

- Build a handsome boundary fence to enclose your garden and provide privacy.

- Place focal points as you would in an ornamental garden; design your own scarecrow.

- Stretch your growing space by espaliering trees, planting intensively in beds, mixing edibles with ornamental plants, getting plants to do double duty.

- In city gardens—make use of every square foot. Stack potted plants, organize plant collections, conjure a sense of vitality and freshness.

formal styles

A formal style emphasizes a sense of order. Rows of vegetables run straight and parallel to one another, a fruit tree sits exactly centered at the end of the path, or a perfectly circular herb garden aligns with the back door. Formality has many advantages; a little of it is useful in almost all gardens.

EASY ON THE EYE An easily recognizable pattern delights the eye, whether it's a checkerboard of plain green and red-tinged lettuces or a series of rectangular raised beds. Repetition is pleasing. If it edges toward predictable, try introducing a little humor, such as an invasion of chives into one side of the checkerboard.

GRAND AS THE HOUSE
Unless your architecture is rustic, vegetables sprawling alongside it may seem far too casual. If you contain them inside trimmed boxwood hedges or sleek steel containers and align their edges with the patio or the house doors, suddenly your vegetable garden serves the architecture well.

YEAR-ROUND STRUCTURE
A formal garden survives hard frost and snow; its patterns and bold lines (its bones) look good throughout the winter. If your vegetable patch isn't hidden by a fence or a hedge when the growing season is over, arrange it so that its shapes please even without plants.

Two lemon trees arranged symmetrically greet you with a touch of formality at the beginning of this path. Imagine the scent of the blossoms and the many times during the long fruiting season that you could invite guests to pick fresh lemons from the trees.

A BETTER FIT In cities and many suburbs, the views out of the house and the garden are composed of geometric lines—from the sidewalk to the skyscrapers in the distance. Creating a pocket of nature complete with natural lines that looks right within such a setting is a hard task; it's easier by far to pick up the lines native to the surroundings. The garden settles in well this way, and the beautiful irregularity of the plants shines in contrast to the geometry.

ABOVE *A play of geometric shapes—circle, octagon, square, pyramid—creates so much liveliness that there's a sense of generosity rather than economy in this small space.*

RIGHT *Loosen its rigidity, and formal geometry can become playful. Classic parterres were not meant to be entered; this wire-framed boxwood woman breaks that taboo. The purple and the variegated green parterre plants are varieties of sage.*

LEFT *Neat trimming increases a formal look.*

9

more formal styles

Set boxwood plants 1 to 2 feet apart, depending on the variety (some grow to 6 inches, others to 5 feet). Use string to guide a straight line. Right after planting, cut the branches back by ⅓; the next spring, cut back again by ⅓, and during the summer trim the side growth several times. Once the hedge has reached the desired height, prune each year after the spring growth flush has stopped.

ABOVE A neatly trimmed boxwood hedge frames a square plot of red cabbage and lettuce, putting the plants on display, just as if they were classic bedding plants like petunias. For an elegant touch, grow boxwood balls on the bed corners: At planting, choose a particularly bushy specimen for each corner, and prune it hard in the first few years to force dense new growth (see left). When the plant is large enough, place a ball-shaped topiary frame over it as a trimming guide. Maintain the shape with frequent light clippings; eventually the plant will hide the frame.

RIGHT These squares of vegetables and herbs read like a giant quilt. The possibilities for presenting different textures and colors are vast; even a few squares of bare, cleared earth would fit perfectly well. Low-growing plants with pretty forms, such as parsley and lettuce with ruffled or red leaves, are excellent choices for patterns.

ABOVE *Uniform beds, placed parallel to one another, provide a pleasing series of lines among a profusion of different edibles and flowers. Some plants, such as marigolds and leeks , hold a tidy form; bushier ones, like fennel and dahlias (and beans and roses overgrowing their supports), soften a formal arrangement; best of all for undermining a too-rigid formality are plants such as poppies and johnny-jump-ups that reseed themselves in the paths. DESIGN: NANCY HECKLER.*

LEFT *Galvanized steel containers set out in neat rows on a rooftop provide a city gardener with a large range of edibles— and a chance to be creative. Each box holds a single plant type or a variety, plants are repeated from box to box sometimes, some are annuals and some perennials: the picture changes throughout the year and from one year to the next.*

informal styles

Vegetables and other edibles can be planted in neat rows without much planning. It takes a sense of purpose, and more thought, to arrange them informally. The motivation for planting edibles informally is usually to integrate them into an existing ornamental garden that has an informal style. You can have fun choosing and arranging edibles in such a garden as carefully as if they were ornamentals. Here are some tips on how to proceed.

BALANCE Balance is the key to successful informal gardens; it leads the eye through the garden delightfully, with a lot less insistence than symmetry does. To achieve balance, imagine a bold plant, say, or a tepee shape, repeated through the garden, the visual weight of it on one side of the path balanced by the next appearance of it on the other side, and so on, farther and farther into the space. For subtlety, you'd have the plant or shape appear less often, and you'd introduce other plants or shapes that are roughly equal in visual weight to your original choices, checking, with each addition, that the composition is holding and becoming more sophisticated. Balance is a skill; experiment a little, and you'll acquire it.

RESTRAINT Until you are pleased with your arranging skills, work with a smallish range of plants, and put in three, five, or seven of each, because odd numbers of plants look more natural than even numbers—and one of this, one of that rarely looks good. Variety of leaf and stalk and fruit color can quickly result in a visual hodgepodge. Whenever that happens, resort to a little formality: corral each type of plant into a row or a square.

LEFT *Consider incorporating natural features such as boulders into a rural garden, and mix just a few kinds of plants in each area, to give a sense of naturally formed communities. Rambling together here are artichokes, cardoon, and lavender. DESIGN: ARTFORMS.*

FACING PAGE, TOP *The eye explores this garden of edibles and ornamentals following a rhythm of blues and slim vertical lines. Note the strong presence of the fig tree in the background and how it is balanced by the twig pyramid and bold foliage in the left foreground. Deeper into the garden is a blue umbrella; the blues that come and go through the seasons always seem to lead there. DESIGN: FEENEY GARDEN.*

Liveliness results from a play of repetitions and contrasts. Here (below, left), the shape of the zucchini flowers is similar to the shape of the nicotiana flowers, while the yellow flower color shifts interestingly to softer hues in the marigolds and nicotiana. The contrast in scale between the zucchini leaves and the ground cover beneath them is bold; so is the contrast of gold and purple. A small pot of edibles (below, right) shows the same exciting mix of repetition and contrast.
DESIGN (LEFT):
BUNNY GUINESS.

A pot anchors this pretty planting of alyssum and herbs. On a larger scale, use a bold plant such as rhubarb or artichoke as an anchor.

paths

A path organizes a journey through the garden; it should be comfortable for garden work and pleasing to walk along. The edging of the path is also a matter of both function and aesthetics.

PATH MATERIALS A firm, flat surface such as brick, cut stone, or concrete allows you to roll a wheelbarrow along easily. These are the most formal materials; they look good close to the house, and they are easily kept clean with a broom or a hose. Dirt paths are by far the simplest choice for an edibles garden, but mud gets tracked about in wet weather. Grass makes a handsome path, but it, too, may become impassable after a storm, and the maintenance is high. Bark gives a rustic look to a garden; plan on replenishing it every year or two when the bark pieces break down. Gravel suits both informal and formal situations; be sure to create a proper base for the path so that water drains off it, and tamp the surface down firmly so that a wheelbarrow runs easily over it.

EDGINGS Edgings help keep soil from the planting beds off the path. They accentuate the lines of the path and give the garden a well-cared-for, permanent look. Almost any material works: bricks, wood boards, metal strips, stones cleared from the garden, or objects such as pots. Pansies and parsley make low-cost, decorative edgings.

A dirt path can look quite attractive, especially if you sweep it. Keep a bale of straw on hand to strew over muddy areas, and look forward to finding plants that reseed, such as arugula and johnny-jump-ups, appearing underfoot.

Place an arch along a path, or build a couple of steps into the pathway, to mark the threshold between one area of the garden and another. A fragrant plant, such as this lemon, also helps to announce an entrance.

A path should have a pleasant destination. To create a sense of arrival, dress up the end of a path with a simple seat and a pot of strawberries or something fragrant.

RIGHT Raised beds have many advantages (see pages 94–95), including edges to lay tools on, even to sit on for a few minutes if you have built them well. Paths between beds need to be 2 feet wide to accommodate a wheelbarrow.

BELOW An herb garden set on the stairs overcomes the separation between garden and house and makes climbing the stairs more pleasant. Select unbreakable, stable containers and plants like mint and sage, which release their fragrance as people brush by them. DESIGN: ROBIN GREEN AND RALPH CADE.

boundary fences

A series of open and closed sections can protect the privacy of your patio and still allow sunlight and air circulation into your edibles garden. Another option is to make some sections of a fence low and others, where you need privacy, high.

The best boundary for an edibles garden allows free movement of light and air while keeping rabbits and puppies out. A post-and-rail fence with wire mesh (or a wood-and-wire fence) is a popular option and relatively inexpensive compared to a solid wood fence. It creates very little shade, and if it is at least 2 feet tall, rabbits can't jump it. Rabbits and puppies do burrow, however, so extend the wire mesh 6 inches or more underground; on a gate, make the mesh 12 inches longer than the gate, and fold the mesh into an L shape at the bottom so that it extends away from the garden; when you close the gate, place a stone or two on the extending mesh to secure it. Deer won't be deterred by a fence unless it's higher than 6 feet (see page 79 for more information on controlling deer and other animal pests).

OTHER BOUNDARY OPTIONS Walls and hedges are beautiful, more permanent options for enclosing an edibles garden. A south- or west-facing wall offers an especially warm place for frost-sensitive fruit blossoms. If you are considering a hedge, boxwood (see page 10) is a conventional choice. For a more informal hedge, plant blueberry bushes about 3 feet apart.

GATES A gate can either match the fence or contrast with it. In a small garden, perhaps make a feature of the gate; for example, paint it, or place an arch over it and grow vines there. A gate is usually hung so that it swings inward, toward the garden. If it's essential that the gate stay closed, install a spring to pull the gate shut automatically after you pass through.

Painting a wood fence gives it weather protection. If you choose white paint, be aware of how it calls attention to the details of the fence, or lack of them, and how much presence the fence has in views of the garden.

This fence isn't as much a barrier as a design element that doubles as support for an espaliered apple. Separating an edibles garden from the main garden gives a sense of privacy, and having two spaces instead of one makes a garden seem larger.

The garden boundary may be a pretty place for a path. Plant screening plants such as peas, so you can stroll along out of sight of the house. Capping the top rail of the fence helps to protect the entire fence from weather damage; a slanted cap sheds water quickly.

A simple wood-and-wire fence can be constructed with 4-by-4 posts set 6 feet apart and lengths of 2-by-4 wire mesh stapled to the posts. The fence here, which faces the street, has a cap rail and decorative post caps.

focal points

To start a scarecrow, build a wood frame. Nail a 4-foot crosspiece, at shoulder height, to a 6-foot stake. For a head, use a bucket, a pumpkin, or a pillowcase stuffed with rags, old clothes, or straw. Tie the clothes to the frame (one leg of the pants hangs outside the frame), and then put stuffing into the clothes.

These scarecrows aren't just for birds. "They make people laugh," says creator Katie O'Hara-Kelly, of Goodyear's Bar, California. A focal point need not be serious or expensive or permanent.

ocal points draw the eye or point the way to the beautiful elements of the garden. Placed well, they ensure that visitors see what you want them to see—perhaps more than is really there. If you want no attention paid to some garden features, such as tight boundaries and dull views, judiciously placed focal points will make visitors look right by them.

Large urns, sundials, fountains, and benches are traditional focal points. They are often placed at the end of a long vista. It's a clever idea, especially in a small garden, to organize a view along the longest possible axis (often a diagonal) and place a focal point at one end, to make the grandest announcement of that view. Set up smaller focal points, such as a water bowl or a chair, at other points of interest. Each focal point, if nicely accomplished, creates a sense of place; the more places you can devise in a garden, the bigger it will appear.

LEFT *All paths lead to this bright seat, which is nestled for comfort between tall cosmos plants. Many garden seats aren't used much, but they extend an invitation, which makes a garden seem hospitable and a lovely place of rest. You or a guest might actually take up the offer, so make sure the view from the seat is interesting at all times of the year.* DESIGN: DEAN RIDDLE.

A birdbath can give a garden a peaceful center, create a special place to which you always return. You might set a seat nearby against a block of tall plants. Keep the water in the bath fresh so that birds come to drink and bathe.

ABOVE *A colorful container planting provides a focal point in a bed of green crops. Choose color that lasts, such as these chard stems and petunia flowers, so you can move the container around during the season, to a bare spot or anywhere that needs something fresh.*

19

stretching space

Grow anything you can—beans, cane berries, cucumbers, grapes, melons, peas, pumpkins, and squash—off the ground. Plant other crops intensively in beds (see pages 47 and 96–97). This U-shaped garden measures 12 by 11 feet. More than two dozen kinds of vegetables and edible flowers are growing here.

A garden rarely has enough space to accommodate our dreams. The ideal kitchen garden surely has a greenhouse, an orchard, and vegetables growing in long rows converging in the distance—oh, and a decent pumpkin patch. Although space limitations may fall away if you do a little concentrated thinking, consider first what matters most to you, what you would have for sure if you did have more space. Maybe an orchard or a pumpkin patch is exactly what would please you most, and therefore you should have it. Allot to that idea whatever space you can muster, and think hard about how to make the idea work. Later, it will be obvious what other delights might fit in around it.

COLONIZE AIR SPACE, WALLS, AND FENCES Fruit trees grow well when espaliered (see page 91) against a wall or fence; pumpkins can be grown on trellises—you need to support the fruit on a shelf, an upturned container, or an old stool. Several other vegetables can be trained up off the ground (see page 27); many thrive in hanging baskets (see page 29).

DOUBLE UP The shade you need over the garden table might be provided by a fruit tree, instead of using space for a garden umbrella. Screens for privacy can be composed of tall edibles such as corn. Edible plants can double as focal points (see pages 18–19), too.

A potager saves space by combining edible and ornamental plants. Plan one carefully (see page 48). Make the path broad enough for strolling, and set a seat against the boundary for the grandest possible view.

ABOVE *Avocados are generally unwise choices for small gardens, because the trees grow large and create dense shade. But a new variety, 'Holiday', grows to only 12 feet tall. Dwarf trees are an excellent option if you want to grow tree fruits in a small space.*

Edibles are often relegated to the back of the backyard. But who doesn't love to see fruit ripening in the sun? Consider placing edibles right out front to delight passersby.

An informal espalier is a simple space-saver. Fasten a trellis or wires to a wall or fence, and set a fruit tree 8 to 12 inches away. As the tree grows, tie the branches to the support, and clip off shoots that jut out too far. Formal espaliers are described on page 91; all the trees listed there can be trained informally.

city gardens

City gardeners appreciate each square foot of the outdoors that belongs to them, and they learn to use space ingeniously. Smallness has the advantage of leaving the gardener more time to plan and then to follow a whim and redo the garden, a process that builds experience quickly. Fine materials and objects may be affordable because the garden requires only a few. The greatest advantage of a tiny garden is its special atmosphere—it's by necessity intimate, and nature's wildness and fertility seem even more miraculous in a pocket-size plot.

SEATING It's tempting to maximize the planting area in a small space by leaving out a path and a proper place to sit. But, if you want the garden to be used and loved, commit yourself to allocating a generous amount of the space to a path and sitting area. Walking through the garden, experiencing it from different viewpoints, through sunlight and shadows, provides a satisfying sense of exploration. And nothing draws visitors outdoors more effectively than the sight of a comfortable, sheltered seat.

COLLECTIONS Collections have a magical quality of plenitude that's especially useful in a city garden. The most successful collections have a theme: the plants are all dwarf citrus trees, say, or the containers of varying plants are all terracotta or all steel. The mind delights in identifying similarities and differences; there's less fun if there are no similarities.

ABOVE *People love a garden—and the whole natural world—because it stimulates the senses. This tiny balcony garden delights all five—taste, touch, smell, sight, and hearing. It also provides the pleasures of watching something grow that you've cared for and of feeling attuned to the weather and the seasons.*

RIGHT *Freshness is an elemental garden pleasure. Make space for fast-growing delicate lettuce, and give water a major presence in the garden. The sink and faucet here are irresistible—guests would surely rush to use them. Consider gorgeous water bowls and watering cans also.*

RIGHT *This roof garden has all the charm of a country living room—and kale, tomatoes, herbs, and figs. A single tomato plant placed next to a fabulously comfortable chair may provide more pleasure than a large, high-maintenance tomato plot in a backyard. Because of their featured role, be sure to keep plants in a small garden healthy and attractive.*

ABOVE *A window box hung on a deck railing, or beneath a window, generates extra growing space. Choose a plastic, terra-cotta, or wooden box; plastic weighs little and lasts well if the quality is good. This box will drain mostly on the deck; if it were mounted outside the railing, it would drip directly on the ground. Planted in the box, from left to right, are curry plant (Helichrysum italicum), sage, variegated sage, and curly-leafed parsley.*

An étagère, or a commercial display rack, can increase planting space by many times its small footprint. Place shade-tolerant plants on the lower shelves, sun-lovers on the top. For a little informality, include trailing plants, such as rosemary or nasturtiums, and vary the pot shapes.

design options

- Make plant supports architectural or fanciful.

- Choose containers that have presence; pack them with bold foliage and sweet fruits; arrange them as objects of interest.

- Have fun creating a garden that works for kids.

- Get a color game going— harmonious or contrasting.

- Plan places of fragrance to reward yourself as you work and to surprise your guests.

- Pick plants that are natural good-lookers; place them so they'll be much admired.

- Don't overlook the charm of a late fall and winter garden. Welcome the cold and the change of pace.

plant supports

Climbing plants need support, but the support need not be plain and merely functional. You can devise your own fanciful structures of prunings or purchased canes and netting, or invest in a piece of permanent architecture that will serve the garden year-round. For more ideas on stakes and trellises, see page 57.

LEFT *Tall crisscrossed bamboo canes lashed together with twine offer scarlet runner beans a decent space to run. Shorter canes help keep tomato plants in order. Using the same type of support for different crops unifies the garden in a pleasing way. Tepees are also pretty when repeated through a garden.*

RIGHT *Supports put together with neatly sawn prunings and uniformly knotted ties suggest that the gardener knows a thing or two about craft. Peas don't need any more support than this; tendrils grow from the shoots and wrap themselves firmly around any fairly slim pole.*

prettiest vining edibles

ABOVE *Like gates and potting sheds, permanent plant supports can be beautiful structural elements of the garden. They lend character to the landscape whether or not you cover them with crops, and they have a particular presence in the off-season, standing tall against the elements after you have cleared the plants that are annuals. Consider them architecture; if you like, paint them to match your house.*

RIGHT *A little architecture elevates an edibles garden into a grander affair. Foreground your carrots and leeks against an obelisk and a clipped hedge, and you might catch visitors talking wistfully of their own desires to grow vegetables. For more ideas on formality, see pages 8–11.*

containers

Any sunny place is a perfect site for containers full of edibles. Try them on steps, the tops of walls, and a bare spot in a flower bed, as well as on the patio and along the garden path. Bring some containers right up to the house doors; you'll be surprised how much interest they arouse, especially near harvest time. More information on growing edibles in containers can be found on pages 58–59.

ABOVE *Crops raised in hanging baskets are out of reach of dogs, rabbits, slugs, and snails. What's more, you can pack a lot of vegetables into a small space by staggering the baskets at different levels. Wire baskets 14 to 16 inches in diameter work best. Line them with sphagnum moss, or use plastic liners. Add a controlled-release fertilizer to the potting soil, and place soil polymer at the bottom of the basket to retain moisture at root level. Choose compact varieties of plants. You can start beans from seed, if you like, but otherwise use seedlings. To keep the growth uniform, rotate your baskets every 3 days.*

Parsley, sage, golden marjoram, and many other herbs and edibles will winter cheerfully in pots on a sunny windowsill. To keep the garden alive in your imagination during winter, fill a matching container or two with hardy evergreens, and leave them in sight outdoors.

Deep containers are not necessary for growing edible crops, particularly lettuce, but large containers have a distinct presence. In a small garden especially (right), make your containers, and the plant arrangements, work as objects of interest. These painted oil drums (below) contain ornamental and edible plants: salvia, spider flower (Cleome hasslerana), nasturtiums, tomatoes, cabbage, and corn. Drums and plants together make a useful tall screen.

BELOW In a small garden, look for "bush" varieties of sprawling plants such as cucumbers and squash (this is 'Salad Bush' cucumber; see page 135), and contain them in a large, broad pot such as a half barrel. Before you fill the pot, place it close to the house, so you won't have to walk far to keep up with watering and harvesting. 'Lemon' cucumbers, which produce small round yellow fruits, do well in containers and are a good size for eating straight off the bush.

productive in pots

Beans, snap, bush or pole (page 113)

Carrots, short (page 124)

Eggplant 'Asian Bride', 'Farmers' Long' (page 137)

Herbs (pages 112, 129, 153, 157, 158)

Lettuce (page 148)

Peppers 'Giant Marconi', 'Habanero' (page 164)

Potatoes, red, 'Buffalo', 'Red La Soda' (page 167)

Radishes (page 171)

Strawberries (page 182)

Tomatoes 'Sun Gold', 'Bush Celebrity' (page 186)

kids' spaces

Creating a garden space for children brings significant rewards. They'll learn to nurture themselves and their environment—and they'll use their senses to figure out a thousand little joyful things about dirt, leaves, petals, and light as they play.

ABOVE *Children enjoy watering. It may be their first interest in gardening—toddlers love pouring water into dirt. Buy watering cans (and other tools) that are the right size for a child; or improvise with measuring cups and spoons or sand toys. Older children may like to press flowers, make a flower wreath, build plant supports or scarecrows (see page 18), and follow the activities of bugs using a magnifying glass. Compost (see pages 98—99) is magical for most kids.*

LEFT *Vegetables such as pole beans, summer squash, and radishes, which grow fast and are easy to harvest, suit children well. Peas and berries make excellent choices because they are sweet and can be eaten right on the spot. For easy sowing, choose big seeds, such as corn and pumpkin, or buy those that have been clay coated. These purple beans are sure to create even more delight when they turn green during cooking.*

BELOW *"People feel as good as their surroundings," says Manuel Jimenez (far right). Jimenez founded and works this community garden in California's Central Valley, with a volunteer crew of 8- to 17-year-olds. Ask your local community garden to set aside a plot for the neighborhood children; or help start a school garden (for information, visit www.kidsgardening.com).*

ABOVE *Give children a place of their own, not just chores. A secret place, with something to sit on, such as a log, is guaranteed to be popular. Set up gardening projects that allow children to make at least some of the decisions. This tepee, for example, could be covered with scarlet runner or pole beans, melons, cucumbers, peas, or squash, in addition to the nasturtiums shown. Kids know how to mix it up.*

kids' favorites

Beans, especially pole beans (page 113)
Carrots (page 124)
Peas (page 162)
Popcorn (page 133)
Potatoes (page 167)
Pumpkins (page 169)
Radishes (page 171)
Raspberries or strawberries (pages 172, 182)
Sunflowers (page 185)
Tomatoes, for pizza topping (page 186)

color

An edibles garden arranged with an eye to color can provide even more pleasure than an ornamental garden. Be sure to consider the colors of the leaves as well as the fruits, and, for the best results, start out with a smallish color range, contrasting or harmonious. The multicolored varieties of ornamental cabbage and chard are fun, but they work best alone or as accents among shades of green.

ABOVE *A pretty edibles garden can be built around harmonious blues and greens. The secrets to avoiding a flat look are to vary the shades of the colors and to add a spot of contrasting color, such as the red here. For beautiful blue-gray color, consider cabbage, artichokes, and sage.*

LEFT *Before the tomatoes gain color, before the nasturtiums bloom, a blue wheelbarrow hung with orange gourds enlivens this edibles garden. Large painted containers and brightly colored seats and plant supports can also color the garden in the green early season.*

RIGHT *Chard swaggers with color and texture. The blood-red-stemmed varieties show off well here alongside sweet peas in red and burgundy hues; the yellow-stemmed chards can be color-coordinated with yellow tulips. Try dark-purple-leafed chard in a pot with pink cosmos or petunias (see page 19).*

most colorful edibles

RIGHT *Lavender and yellow are complementary (contrasting) colors; they are at opposite sides of the color wheel, as are red and green, another striking combination. Later in the season yellow poppies or marigolds might take the place of the daffodils, and purple pole beans or eggplant could take over from the cabbage. Johnny-jump-ups and pansies (see page 145) provide striking color for many months and need very little space.*

fragrance

Pleasing scents can drive our desire to garden as much as the prospect of harvest. We step outdoors in spring with packets of seeds and catch the welcoming smell of the sunshine on the earth; then, as summer comes, we work more and more gladly among sweet-smelling herbs, pungent tomato leaves, and ambrosial ripe melons.

LEFT *Lavender is a must for an edibles garden. You can cook with the flowers, of course (see page 146), but merely gardening near a fragrant bush of it brings sufficient satisfaction. Lavender provides the "body" to many different perfumes. For bees, it furnishes food; they are very loyal visitors to lavender and will help pollinate your other plants. Here, lavender runs between paths of fragrant chamomile.*

BELOW *Fragrance usually increases in response to heat. If you have a warm greenhouse or porch, make a corner for a few fragrant plants. These miniature orange trees have a beautiful scent in winter as the fruit ripens and in spring when the flowers appear.*

scented edibles

LEFT, TOP *Position at least some of your herbs so that you can touch them easily as you go about your garden chores or in and out of the house. The resinous "odor plume" from this topiary rosemary greets anyone passing by. You might also allow rosemary and other herbs to overflow a path, so that you brush against them every day.*

LEFT *The smell of onion tops and freshly cultivated soil on a damp autumn morning contributes significantly to the experience of sowing seeds. Gardening teaches us quickly and well—about weather, seasons, time, and the earth—because it engages our senses.*

ABOVE *Fragrance is a strong component of memory. Gardeners can often remember the weather the previous spring when the apple tree was in exquisitely fragrant bloom or when the fava beans came into flower. This is a "step over" apple espaliered to two low horizontal branches (see page 91, step 1).*

good-lookers

Some plants are naturally handsome and therefore sure bets for making a kitchen garden a pleasurable place to be. Take a fresh look at the beauty of edible plants; consider the shapes of the leaves, and select a range of textures. Arrange the plants ornamentally, and make focal points of your favorites.

ABOVE *Fig trees branch beautifully, and the leaves, with their familiar cutout shape, look lovely from quite a distance. Dwarf fruit trees suit small gardens, because they are space-efficient, but consider the pleasure of being able to stand under a full-size tree, to seek its shelter during a rain shower, or to picnic on a bench in its dappled shade.*

LEFT *Blue plants are always favorites, in flower beds and vegetable gardens. Cabbage also has a sculptural form, making it a popular candidate for contemporary gardens. For more information on using color in an edibles garden, see pages 32–33.*

BELOW AND BOTTOM LEFT *The rows of vegetables in this small garden present a satisfying arrangement of textures, colors, and forms—crinkled, bright or dark green rosettes of lettuce, sleek gray-blue-green shoots of onions, ferny light green masses of carrots, and so on, down the garden path to the stone figure appreciating the prettiness before her. Plants in the allium family—chives, garlic, onions, leeks—are particularly useful if you want to make an aesthetically pleasing edibles garden; they rise slim and tall over lower crops, and they are striking when they go to seed. Some gardeners mix in giant ornamental alliums with huge seedheads.*

edibles with presence

Artichokes (page 109)

Cabbage (page 123)

Eggplant (page 137)

Figs (page 138)

Kale (page 145)

*Onion family members
    (pages 129, 140, 147, 155)*

Parsley (page 158)

Rhubarb (page 175)

Squash (page 180)

Sunflowers (page 184)

LEFT *Large, bold-leafed plants such as these vining cucumbers and sunflowers add drama to an edibles garden. Compact low plants often yield more, but having too many makes a garden look small, so plant one or two tall or large-leafed crops for a lively change of scale. A sunflower is a winning choice; its sunniness is irresistible.*

late fall, winter

Just when it might seem that the garden is done for the year, it starts to assume a different charm. Anything left standing becomes pearled with raindrops or crusted with frost or dolloped with snow. In mild-winter climates, plants may go on producing; but, even if the ground freezes, you can make the garden worth visiting.

ABOVE *In northern California, late fall is a time of easy gardening. The soil is naturally damp, pests and diseases are fewer than in spring, leafy crops grow evenly without bolting, and harvesting goes on right through to spring. See pages 43 and 82–83 for information on cool-season gardening.*

LEFT *Time is a deeply resonant theme in gardens. A plant pyramid left behind in the ice and snow is a reminder of the vine that entwined it and of the summer just gone. Although it's important to clean up the debris of some plants to prevent pests and diseases from overwintering, other plants can be left standing to catch strings of raindrops and icicles. They'll be featherlight and easy to clear by winter's end.*

BELOW *Cold-hardy salad greens can be grown past the normal season in a sheltered spot, especially if you have some straw for a blanket on cold nights. Techniques for extending your growing season are described on pages 102–103.*

cold-hardy candidates

RIGHT *In winter, time seems to stop, giving you a chance just to be in the garden and to reflect upon it. Plants respond to wintertime in different ways: annuals that weren't harvested shed their seeds before they die; hardy perennials live on through the winter, dormant, with or without foliage. This rosemary seems fairly cold hardy; some varieties of the herb withstand freezes much better than others (see page 176).*

ABOVE *An ornamental cabbage in a winter garden provides an excuse to putter outside, enjoying the cold and the fabulous patterns created by ice and frost. Frost heightens the coloring in the leaves of many edible plants and also makes them taste sweeter.*

spring

▸ Prepare soil for spring planting.

▸ Plant cool-season crops by setting out transplants and sowing seeds in the ground as soon as the soil can be worked.

▸ Plant warm-season crops by sowing seeds indoors 6 to 8 weeks before the average last frost date for your region.

▸ Harden off transplants of warm-season crops.

▸ After your last frost date, set out transplants and sow seeds of warm-season crops in the ground.

▸ Prepare to protect plants from late frosts.

▸ Thin overcrowded vegetable seedlings.

▸ Protect young plants from snails, slugs, and cutworms (see pages 75–76).

▸ Stake tall-growing vegetables.

selecting a site

Deciding where to plant your edible crops is the first step in producing healthy, tasty vegetables, herbs, and fruits. Whether you plan to grow edibles among your ornamental plants, in containers, or in a special plot set aside for food gardening—or all three—it's important to select sites that meet certain requirements if you want your vegetables and fruits to thrive. When looking around your garden for suitable places, keep the following factors in mind.

SUNLIGHT Most vegetables, fruits, and herbs need 6 to 8 hours of full sun daily for top production and flavor. (For exceptions, see the tip below.) Select a site that is not shaded by buildings, trees, or shrubs. In addition to blocking sunlight, trees and shrubs send roots far and wide, competing with your edibles for water and nutrients.

AIR CIRCULATION While edibles do not thrive in heavy winds, air flow from gentle breezes helps keep foliage dry, reducing the possibility of diseases. If your garden is exposed to constant winds, consider planting a sheltering windbreak or hedge.

FROST POCKETS Cold air settles in low-lying spots. Plants in such areas may suffer damage from frost in late spring and early fall.

SOIL Most crops prefer well-drained soil enriched with plenty of compost or other organic matter; see pages 49–50 for information on soils and how to improve them. In very poor soil, consider planting in raised beds (see page 94).

IRRIGATION Locate your garden where you can easily reach it with a garden hose. See pages 62–63 for watering methods.

LEVEL GROUND Planting, watering, and general care are easier in a level garden. If you must plant on a slope, run planting beds or rows across the slope, not up and down, to keep the soil from washing away.

CONVENIENCE If possible, locate edibles fairly close to the kitchen door. That way, it's easy to dash out before dinner for a few vegetables or a handful of herbs.

tip EDIBLES FOR PARTIAL SHADE The following vegetables can be grown in partially shaded sites, such as a plot near a fence or building, or in containers on a deck where the sun shines for only 4 to 5 hours each day: arugula, beets, cabbage, chard, collards, endive, kale, leaf lettuce, mustard, onions (bunching), and spinach. Herbs that grow in partial shade include chives, mint, and parsley.

'Winterbor' and 'Lacinato' kale

what to plant

Deciding which edibles you want to plant from among the wide and fascinating array of vegetables, herbs, and fruits can be both exciting and a bit daunting. Keep the following points in mind as you make your selections and decide how much of each crop to plant.

FAMILY PREFERENCES What crops do you and your family really enjoy eating? Will you use the harvest right away, or do you plan to store some food for winter? Beyond the tried-and-true favorites, it's fun to sample a few new varieties each season.

AVAILABLE SPACE How much space can you devote to edibles? In a small garden, for example, sprawling winter squash takes up too much territory for the payback of only a few squashes. In general, it is a good idea to start with a fairly small plot, especially if you are new to growing edibles. That way you won't be overwhelmed with too much work and perhaps far too much produce. Smaller gardens are easier to keep tidy and thus are more enjoyable, as well.

YOUR CLIMATE Consult the maps on pages 44–45 to learn about the length of your growing season and average frost dates. Then check the requirements for the crops you want to plant.

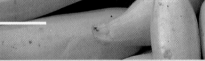

A colorful selection of summer squash.

warm-season and cool-season vegetables

When shopping the produce aisles at the supermarket, you can easily conclude that all vegetables are ready to harvest year-round. You find fresh tomatoes, peppers, kale, and lettuce in both summer and winter. In reality, all these vegetables don't ripen at the same time of year; some need heat, while others grow best in cool weather. Many offerings at the store have been shipped long distances from different climates around the world. Home gardeners celebrate each season through their harvests of truly fresh, seasonal produce.

The traditional crops of summer, such as beans, corn, cucumbers, peppers, tomatoes, and squash, are warm-season vegetables. They need both warm soil and high temperatures to ripen fruit. These plants are killed by frost, so don't plant them until after the last frost in spring, unless you are prepared to give them cold protection (see pages 56, 102–103).

Cool-season crops grow best at temperatures an average of 10 to 15°F/6 to 8°C below those needed by warm-season types. Most will endure short spells of frost. Cool-season vegetables include broccoli, cabbage, cauliflower, kale, leeks, lettuce, peas, and spinach. Success depends on bringing these plants to maturity in cool weather; in hot conditions, they may taste bitter and bolt to seed rather than producing edible parts. Plant them either in very early spring, so the crop will mature before summer heat settles in, or in late summer to early fall, to harvest in fall. In mild-winter climates (indicated on the maps on pages 44–45), many of these crops can be harvested throughout winter and early spring, as well. The listings on pages 106–190 include information on the best season in which to plant each crop.

LAST SPRING FROST

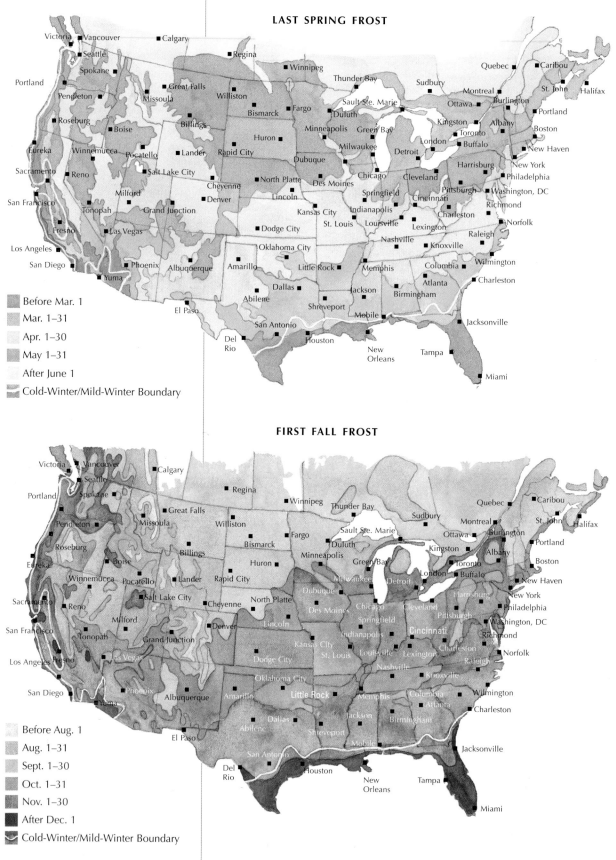

Before Mar. 1
Mar. 1–31
Apr. 1–30
May 1–31
After June 1
Cold-Winter/Mild-Winter Boundary

Victoria · Vancouver · Calgary · Regina · Winnipeg · Thunder Bay · Sudbury · Quebec · Caribou
Seattle · Spokane · Great Falls · Williston · Bismarck · Fargo · Sault Ste. Marie · Montreal · St. John · Halifax
Portland · Pendleton · Missoula · Billings · Huron · Minneapolis · Duluth · Green Bay · Ottawa · Burlington · Portland
Roseburg · Boise · Rapid City · Dubuque · Milwaukee · London · Toronto · Albany · Boston
Eureka · Winnemucca · Pocatello · Lander · Detroit · Buffalo · New Haven
Sacramento · Reno · Salt Lake City · North Platte · Des Moines · Chicago · Cleveland · Harrisburg · New York · Philadelphia
Milford · Cheyenne · Lincoln · Springfield · Cincinnati · Pittsburgh · Washington, DC
San Francisco · Tonopah · Denver · Grand Junction · Kansas City · Indianapolis · Richmond
Fresno · Las Vegas · Dodge City · St. Louis · Louisville · Lexington · Charleston · Norfolk
Los Angeles · Nashville · Raleigh
San Diego · Phoenix · Albuquerque · Amarillo · Oklahoma City · Knoxville
Yuma · Little Rock · Memphis · Columbia · Wilmington
El Paso · Dallas · Jackson · Atlanta · Charleston
Abilene · Birmingham
Shreveport · Mobile
San Antonio · Jacksonville
Del Rio · Houston · New Orleans · Tampa
Miami

FIRST FALL FROST

Before Aug. 1
Aug. 1–31
Sept. 1–30
Oct. 1–31
Nov. 1–30
After Dec. 1
Cold-Winter/Mild-Winter Boundary

climate maps

The maps here give general growing seasons and spring and fall frost dates. "Growing season length" is the number of days between the average dates of the last spring frost and the first fall frost. The length of your growing season determines whether you can grow certain crops successfully. Each vegetable seed packet gives the number of days from seed to harvest. If your season has fewer days, you need to either use season-extending methods to grow that crop (see pages 56, 102–103) or choose another variety.

Spring frost dates help you determine when it is safe to set out warm-season crops. Fall frost dates not only give you an idea of when summer harvest is likely to be finished but also help you plan for fall harvest of cool-season crops (see pages 82–83). For more precise dates for your area, consult your Cooperative Extension Office.

alaska and hawaii

Alaska can be divided into several climate regions. The coldest encompasses most of interior Alaska; the average growing season in Fairbanks is 113 days. The last spring frosts occur in late May, and fall frosts begin in early September. The climate of the Cook Inlet and Anchorage is a bit milder; the average growing season in Anchorage is 138 days. Spring frosts strike until mid-May; fall frosts can be expected in mid-September. The maritime-influenced climate found from Kodiak to Juneau is generally even milder. The growing season runs from 113 days in Cordova to 162 days in Haines; average last spring frost dates range from early to mid-May and the first frosts of fall occur from the end of September to mid-October.

At the opposite end of the climate scale, Hawaii has the only true tropical climate in the western United States. In general, the growing season is year-around, though frosts can occur at the highest elevations.

AVERAGE GROWING SEASON LENGTH

- −60 days
- 60–120 days
- 120–180 days
- 180–240 days
- 240+ days
- Cold-Winter/Mild-Winter Boundary

making a garden plan

Deciding what to plant where is something of a juggling act, because there are so many considerations. It helps to begin planning the layout of your garden by drawing a map on paper. Many gardeners use graph paper, with one square representing 1 square foot. On the graph paper, indicate rows or blocks of plants. Be sure to allow for the spacing between plants suggested in the listings on pages 106–190 and on seed packets. Also allow room for paths, so you can get around in the garden. Place tall crops, such as corn and pole beans, on the north side of the plot, so that as they mature they won't shade lower-growing crops that need sun. Locate perennial plants, such as asparagus and berries, in their own section of the garden. That way you won't disturb their roots when you prepare the soil for annual crops. To help you get started, plans for space-saving gardens and a border featuring both flowers and edibles are given on pages 47–48.

A wide mulched path makes harvesting easy.

Traditionally, vegetable gardens have been laid out in long, narrow rows, with paths between adjacent rows. The width of each row depends on the crop being grown, with somewhat wider rows allotted to sprawling plants such as squash, double rows of beans on a trellis, or tomatoes in wire cages. This arrangement works well if you plan to cultivate between the rows with a rotary tiller. However, it does require a lot of garden ground.

Planting all edibles in wider rows or beds, about 4 feet in width, with paths between them saves space, because less room overall is devoted to paths. Rows of plants are set fairly close together within the beds. These wide beds don't have to be rectangular; you can design curving beds around a circle in the center, triangular beds, or whatever suits your fancy. For other layouts and methods, see raised beds on pages 94–95 and French intensive gardens on pages 96–97.

tip A GARDEN JOURNAL Making a journal about your garden can help you plan what to grow where. Choose one of the journals available at bookstores and through mail-order garden suppliers, which have handy pockets for seed packets and plant labels. Or make your own, using a simple notebook. Store your garden plans in your journal, and keep records of which varieties you plant and how they perform, planting dates, fertilization schedules, and pest-control measures. Learning to grow edibles is an ongoing process. With your journal notes at hand, you can build on past successes—and disappointments—as you plan each season's garden.

small-space gardens

A small garden, if planned and planted carefully, can yield a bountiful harvest. The examples here show ways to organize two small plots—one rectangular, the other square—for maximum productivity and variety.

SOIL AND PATHS For top-notch results in small gardens, be sure to prepare the soil well, adding liberal amounts of compost or other organic matter plus fertilizer (see pages 50, 64–65). In the plans shown here, the central paths are permanent; that is, you don't cultivate them. Instead, mulch the paths to keep down weeds and make the ground easier to walk on, even in wet weather. Plan your paths to let you reach the planted areas easily without stepping on the soil in the garden beds, which compacts it, making it less hospitable to root growth.

CHOICE OF CROPS Select crops that give a lot for the space they occupy, such as tomatoes, bush varieties of zucchini, pole beans, lettuce, eggplant, and carrots. Gardeners short on space usually leave out space-gobbling low-yield crops such as sweet corn.

SPACE-SAVING TECHNIQUES Whenever possible, grow plants vertically. Train trailing types of cucumbers, melons, and squash on an arbor or trellis. Pole beans and peas and indeterminate tomatoes also need to be trained on a structure. See page 57 for more on plant supports.

Plan for succession plantings, so you avoid empty spots in the garden. Whenever one crop (or even part of a crop) is harvested, be ready to set out new plants or seeds. Interplant fast-growing crops among slower-growing ones. Spinach, lettuce, green onions (scallions), and radishes are good rapid choices. Plant cut-and-come-again vegetables—those leafy crops that continue to grow and produce more after you pick some of their outer leaves. Examples include arugula, chard, endive, kale, lettuce, and spinach. For more on succession planting, interplanting, and cut-and-come-again crops, see pages 100–101.

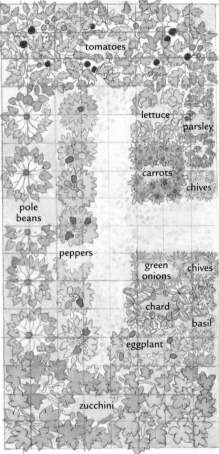

Garden plan scale:
1 square = 1 foot

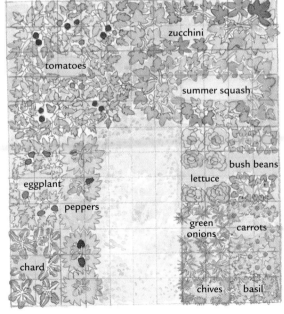

rose
'Joseph's
Coat'

dahlias

pole beans

marigolds

rhubarb

petunias

achillea

peppers

felicia

daylilies

basil

strawberries

Garden plan scale:
1 square = 1 foot

a flower-and-food garden

Planting edibles among your flowers is a beautiful way to save space in the garden. If your front yard is the only sunny spot you have, it may be the best way you can bring in a crop of peppers or strawberries. In addition, a diverse mixture of plants attracts beneficial insects, which prey upon garden pests (see page 73 for more on beneficial insects). The plan shown here gives ideas for mixing vegetables and strawberries with flowering plants in a gracefully shaped border that would look good anywhere.

ORNAMENTAL EDIBLES A huge array of handsome vegetable and fruit plants is available, waiting to inspire your own designs. Many vegetables and herbs feature tinted foliage: chard, lettuces, kale, and mustard greens are just a few. Tomatoes, peppers, and eggplant offer bright-colored fruits. You can find wonderful textures in the vegetable world as well, such as the ferny leaves of carrots and parsley or the bold architectural leaves of rhubarb, artichokes, and zucchini. Vines, such as pole beans, planted on an attractive trellis make a vertical accent. For an unusual effect, choose pole beans with elegant deep purple pods, or scarlet runner beans, which feature showy red flowers followed by green pods. For a list of especially attractive ornamentals, see pages 36–37.

HARVEST FACTORS When planning ornamental and vegetable combinations, keep in mind that some vegetables are a one-shot proposition—you harvest the entire plant. If you use carrots to create a fernlike edge to a bed, you'll lose the effect when you harvest. Parsley used in the same situation for the same effect will last all season, because you harvest sprigs, not the whole plant.

tip **HOW TO PLANT EDIBLES AMONG ORNAMENTALS** When planting vegetables, herbs, or berries among existing flowering plants, pay a little extra attention to soil preparation to give the edibles a good start. Clear an area large enough to accommodate the edibles, and loosen the soil. Then spread several inches of compost or other organic matter, and add a fertilizer, such as 5-10-10 (see pages 64–65 for more on fertilizing). Work these into the soil, and smooth the surface. Now you are ready to set out transplants or sow seeds.

Red-stemmed chard and lettuce mingle
happily with marigolds in this mixed bed.

soil basics

Most edible crops require rich, fertile, well-drained soil to produce healthy, flavorful harvests. Understanding the type of soil that naturally occurs in your garden and finding ways to improve it, if necessary, are basic steps to success in growing edibles.

soil types

All soils are based on mineral particles formed by the natural breakdown of rock. They also contain varying amounts of organic matter, air, and water, as well as numerous living creatures—earthworms, nematodes, bacteria, fungi, and many others. The size and shape of a soil's mineral particles determine its basic characteristics, or texture.

Clay soils, also called *heavy soils,* are made up of very small particles that pack together tightly, producing a compact mass with microscopic pore spaces (the areas between soil particles). Drainage is usually slow, since water and nutrients percolate slowly through the tiny pores. It's not easy for roots to penetrate clay soil, and during prolonged rainy spells (or if overwatered) the soil remains saturated, even to the point of causing root rot. Working clay soil is a miserable job: it's sticky when wet and rock-hard when dry. On the plus side, its slower drainage does allow you to water and fertilize less often.

At the other end of the spectrum are sandy *(light)* soils with large, irregularly rounded particles and large pore spaces that allow water and nutrients to drain away freely. Plants growing in sand are unlikely to suffer root rot, but you need to water them more often to keep their roots moist. The frequent watering leaches nutrients away, so you'll have to fertilize more often, too.

Fortunately, most garden soils fall somewhere between the extremes of clay and sand. The best types for plant growth, referred to as *loam,* have mineral particles in a mixture of sizes. They also contain a generous proportion of organic matter. Adding organic matter improves both clay and sandy soils, making them closer to loam. These materials gradually loosen clay soils, improving drainage; in sandy soils, organic matter enhances moisture retention by wedging into the large pore spaces between soil particles.

soil testing

Before preparing your soil for edible crops, it is a good idea to have it tested. A soil test will determine your soil's pH (see sidebar) and can also reveal nutrient deficiencies and the percentage of organic matter. The simple test kits sold at nurseries give a general indication of your soil's condition; for a more precise reading, have the test done at a laboratory. In some states, the Cooperative Extension Office will test your soil. Or look in the Yellow Pages under "Laboratories—Analytical." The lab will tell you where and how to collect the soil sample to be tested.

tip SOIL DRAINAGE To check drainage, dig a hole 1½ to 2 feet deep, and fill it with water. After it drains, fill it again. If the second filling of water drains away in an hour or less, the drainage is good. If it remains for several hours or more, the soil drains poorly. To help improve drainage, add organic matter—but if drainage is really poor, you may need to plant in a better-drained part of the garden or in raised beds (see pages 94–95).

The acidity or alkalinity of soil is expressed in terms of pH, on a scale from 1 to 14. A pH of 7 is neutral, lower than 7 indicates acid soil, and greater than 7 indicates alkaline soil. The degree of acidity or alkalinity affects whether certain nutrients are available to plants. If the pH is extreme in either direction, key nutrients are chemically "tied up" in the soil and not accessible to plant roots. The ideal soil for most edibles is slightly acid to neutral, but some, such as blueberries, are adapted to more strongly acid soils. Adding lime is recommended to raise pH, while sulfur can be used to lower pH. Follow the testing lab's recommendations for amounts of either lime or sulfur to apply.

tools for soil preparation

Rake with bow head

Tools for spreading organic matter and turning, digging, and smoothing garden soil include a spade, shovel, spading fork, and rake with a bow head. Choose high-quality, sturdy tools that fit your body type. For example, shovels, spades, and spading forks are available with short D-shaped handles or long handles. D handles are best for shorter, smaller gardeners (they're also useful in confined spaces), while taller people are usually more comfortable using long-handled tools. If you have a large plot to cultivate, you may want a rotary tiller in addition to these hand tools.

Left to right: round point shovel, spading fork with short D-shaped handle, spade with D-shaped handle.

organic soil amendments

Adding organic matter improves and enriches any garden soil. Organic matter helps loosen the soil, allowing air and water to penetrate and making the soil more hospitable to plant roots. Organic matter is especially important in improving clay and sandy soils (see page 49). And, as organic matter decomposes, it releases small amounts of nitrogen and other plant nutrients into the soil.

Use generous amounts of organic matter when you prepare soil for edible crops. Begin with a 3- to 4-inch layer of most amendments (except for manure, see below) on a new planting area; add another 1 to 2 inches each time you prepare the soil again for another crop. Each year your soil will become easier to work and will reward you with larger harvests. As a rule of thumb, a cubic yard of organic material should cover 100 square feet of planting bed to a depth of 3 inches. Cover crops and green manure (see page 84) are also excellent sources of organic matter.

COMPOST One of the best soil amendments, compost is easy to make (see page 98). Gardeners often need more compost than they can produce; fortunately, good-quality compost is also widely available from commercial sources.

MANURE Aged or composted manure (such as dry poultry or steer manure) contains more plant nutrients than other soil amendments. However, these manures may have high concentrations of soluble salts, which can harm plant roots, so you need to apply them sparingly. Add about 1 pound of dry steer manure per square foot of soil surface; 1 pound of dry poultry manure is plenty for 4 to 5 square feet. Working manure into the soil a month or so before planting allows some of the excess salts to leach below root level.

WOOD PRODUCTS Sawdust, wood shavings, ground bark, and other wood products are especially useful in clay soils, where they help separate the fine clay particles. However, most wood products take up nitrogen from the soil as they decompose, so you need to add nitrogen along with them to have sufficient nitrogen for plant growth. (For more on nitrogen, see page 64.) Some wood products, such as redwood soil conditioner, can be purchased already fortified with nitrogen; check the label to be sure.

preparing the soil

Getting ready to plant edibles in a new area, such as a former lawn, or in an area that has not been cultivated recently takes some time and effort. But the payoff is soil that is fertile and easy to work, so that sowing seeds and setting out transplants become a pleasure. If possible, prepare the soil a few weeks before planting, to let the soil settle. You can also get a head start on spring planting by preparing your soil in fall, but wait until spring to spread and rake in fertilizer, so it isn't leached away during the winter.

Preparing the soil for planting annual vegetable crops is an ongoing process. Each time you replant a bed with new crops, first rejuvenate the soil by repeating steps 3 and 4 shown here, adding only 1 to 2 inches of organic matter instead of 3 to 4 inches. Preparation will take less time and effort each year as your soil improves.

1 | Use a sharp spade to cut the sod into sections; then push the spade under each section to sever the roots. Lift the sections away with your hands. They can be used to patch other areas of lawn or can be composted. (If you have weeds rather than sod, remove them by pulling or digging.)

2 | Dampen the soil slightly before you start to dig and loosen it; don't try to work soil that's too wet or completely dry. In small areas, use a spading fork; for larger beds, you may wish to use a rotary tiller. Dig to a depth of about 10 inches, breaking up clods of earth and removing any stones and debris as you go.

3 | Spread 3 to 4 inches of organic material over the area. Add fertilizer now, as well. Phosphorus and potassium (two of the major plant nutrients) should be placed near plant roots to have the greatest benefit, so work a fertilizer high in these nutrients, such as 5-10-10, into the soil before planting. Spread the fertilizer over the soil, using the amount indicated on the label. Also add any amendments needed to alter your soil pH (see page 49).

4 | With a spading fork or tiller, incorporate all the amendments evenly into the soil. Then level the bed with a rake, breaking up any remaining clods of earth. Water well, and let the improved soil settle before planting.

starting seeds

Some popular vegetables, such as tomatoes, peppers, and eggplant, need a long, warm growing season to produce a harvest. If you plan to grow your own seedlings, start such crops indoors in early spring in order to have plants ready to set out in the garden when the weather has warmed up. Starting seeds in containers is also a useful way to have plants of cool-season crops, such as broccoli and cabbage, ready to transplant into the garden in early spring or fall.

You can use a variety of containers, including flats or trays (with or without dividers), small individual pots, and cell-packs. If you're reusing old containers, scrub them out, and soak them for half an hour in a solution of one part household bleach to nine parts hot water to destroy any disease organisms.

seeds to seedlings

1 | Fill 4-inch pots to just below the rim with a light, porous seed-starting or potting mix. Moisten the mix, and let it drain. Scatter seeds thinly over the surface. Check the seed packet for the recommended planting depth, and cover the seeds with the proper amount of mix. (As a rule of thumb, cover seeds to a depth equal to twice their diameter.) Label each container with the plant's name and the date. Moisten the soil lightly.

If you are starting heat-loving plants (tomatoes, cucumbers, eggplant, okra, peppers, squashes, or melons), set the containers on a water heater or use a heating mat (see page 53) to keep the soil between 75°F/24°C and 90°F/32°C. (Most cool-season vegetables will germinate at room temperature.) When the seeds germinate, move the pots into an area with bright light and temperatures between 60°F/16°C and 75°F/24°C.

2 | When the seedlings develop their second set of true leaves, it's time to transplant them to individual pots, such as 3- or 4-inch plastic pots. Fill the new containers with potting mix, moisten the mix, and let it drain. To remove the seedlings from their original pots, squeeze each pot's sides, and turn it upside down, keeping one hand around the soil ball. With both hands, carefully pull the soil ball apart, and set it down on a flat surface.

3 | Separate the fragile rootballs of the seedlings from one another with a toothpick or skewer, or tease them apart with your fingers.

4 | Poke a hole in the new container's potting mix. Carefully lift each seedling and its rootball, keeping your fingers under it for support. Place the seedling in its new container, and firm the mix around it. Water immediately, and then set the pots in bright light (but keep them out of direct sunlight for a few days). Feed the seedlings weekly with a fertilizer sold for starting seeds or with a liquid type diluted to half-strength. Harden off the seedlings as described on page 53 before transplanting them into the garden.

aids for starting seeds indoors

Seedlings of edible crops need bright light to develop properly; when grown in conditions that are too dark, the seedlings are spindly and weak. If you don't have a suitable place for your seedlings, try growing them under fluorescent lights. As soon as the seeds sprout, give them 12 to 14 hours of light each day, setting the light fixture 6 to 8 inches above the tops of the plants.

Seeds of heat-loving summer crops need warm soil to germinate quickly and strongly. Thin waterproof heating mats placed under the containers keep the soil 15 to 20°F/8 to 11°C above room temperature.

Nurseries and mail-order catalogs offer both fluorescent light kits and heating mats.

Warm soil and bright lights help seeds to sprout and grow quickly.

hardening off seedlings

Plants you have started indoors and most vegetable starts you buy from the nursery have been raised in warm conditions. To prevent undue stress to these tender seedlings, gradually accustom them to the bright sun and cooler temperatures out of doors. Start the acclimation process, called *hardening off,* about 10 days before you plan to plant the seedlings in the garden. Stop fertilizing, and set the containers outside for few hours each day in a spot with filtered light and shelter from the wind. Over the next week, gradually increase exposure until the plants are in full sun all day. Bring them back indoors whenever cold or freezing temperatures are predicted. After several nights outdoors in their containers, seedlings are ready to transplant. Alternatively, you can harden them off by placing them in a cold frame (see page 103); open its cover a bit more each day. Plant the seedlings in the garden as shown on page 54.

Set seedlings in filtered light to harden them off before planting.

setting out plants

Planting techniques depend on the plant and how it was grown. Seedlings of annual vegetables that you've grown yourself or purchased from a nursery are usually set out from small containers, such as 4-inch pots. During the growing season, larger plants, such as fruit trees and cane berries, are sold in 1-gallon or larger containers. (Many are also sold as dormant bare-root plants; for planting those, see page 88.)

seedlings

Transplant seedlings of warm-season crops after all danger of frost is past, when the soil is fairly dry and has warmed up. Young plants are vulnerable to cold and may perish in a late frost if planted too early in spring. Be sure to harden off all seedlings, as described on page 53. Water the seedlings before transplanting them.

Dig a hole for each plant, making it the same depth as the seedling container and an inch or two wider. Check the listings on pages 106–190 or the seed packet for proper spacing of plants. With your fingers, lightly separate the roots so they can grow out into the soil (see drawing at top left). If there is a pad of coiled roots at the bottom of the rootball, pull it off. Place each plant in its hole so that the top of the rootball is even with the soil surface. (Tomatoes are an exception; they are planted more deeply. See page 187.) Firm the soil around the roots, and then water each plant with a gentle flow that won't disturb soil or roots (see drawing at middle left).

After planting, water frequently to keep the soil moist but not soggy. Protect young plants from frost or hot weather with one of the devices shown on page 56.

container-grown trees and cane fruits

Throughout the growing season, except during the heat of summer, you can set out plants from containers. Be sure to select healthy plants with strong shoots. Avoid root-bound plants—those with roots above the soil level or growing through the drainage holes.

Dig a planting hole with sides that taper outward at the bottom. Make the hole at least twice as wide as the rootball, leaving a central plateau of firm soil at the bottom of the hole on which to set the root system. This prevents the plant from settling too much. Roughen the sides of hole with a spading fork to help the roots penetrate the soil.

Set the plant in the hole, spreading its roots over the plateau of soil. The top of the rootball should be 1 to 2 inches above the surrounding soil. Backfill with the soil you dug from the hole, working in stages and firming the soil around the roots with your hands. Make a berm of soil to form a watering basin. Irrigate gently (see drawing at bottom left). Spread mulch around the plant, keeping it several inches away from the stem or trunk.

sowing seeds directly in the garden

Many vegetables grow best if you plant the seeds where they are to grow in the garden, rather than starting them indoors and then transplanting later. These include root crops (carrots, beets, radishes, turnips, and parsnips) and corn, peas, and beans.

elements for success

Plan to sow seeds after the soil has warmed in spring; if sown in soil that is too cold, most will germinate poorly or not at all. Check the listings on pages 106–189 or the seed packet for optimum sowing time for each crop.

The soil should be loose and crumbly; rake it smooth, so seedling stems can push through the surface. See page 51 for more on soil preparation.

Refer to the listings on pages 106–189 or the seed packet for the proper planting depth; seeds planted too deep will not sprout. In general, seeds should be covered to a depth equal to twice the diameter of the seed.

The right amount of water after sowing keeps the soil moist but not soggy and prevents crusts from forming on the soil surface. Water with a fine mist, so that seeds aren't washed away. In hot weather, covering the soil with damp burlap helps retain moisture. Be sure to remove the burlap as soon as seeds begin to sprout. If you plan to water with basins or furrows, make them before sowing seeds (see page 63).

It is likely that some seeds will not germinate, no matter how careful you are. For this reason, gardeners usually sow seeds close together and then thin any overcrowded seedlings to their proper spacing (as noted in the listings on pages 106–189 and on seed packets) when they are 1 to 2 inches tall.

three sowing methods

1 | Make shallow furrows to sow seeds in rows. Use a trowel or the corner of a hoe to make a furrow the correct depth for the seeds you are planting. Sow seeds evenly, and pat soil gently over them.

2 | Use hills—groups of plants growing in a cluster, often in a low mound of soil—rather than rows for sprawling plants, if you wish. This method is a traditional way to grow squash and melons. Sow 5 or 6 seeds in a circle, and pat soil over them.

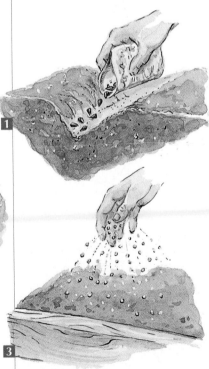

3 | Use broadcasting to sow wide bands of vegetables across a bed. This is a space-saving way to grow smaller crops, such as lettuce, carrots, radishes, or mesclun. Scatter the seeds evenly over the soil. Cover by scattering soil over the seeds or by raking gently, first in one direction, and then again at right angles. Pat the soil to firm it.

how to plant straight rows

To make straight rows, stretch a string between two stakes, and plant beneath it. Or lay a board on the surface of the soil, and then plant along its edge.

55

protecting young plants

Transplants and newly sprouted seedlings are vulnerable both to unexpected late frosts and to hot, sunny weather. Several easy-to-use devices help protect them. For other ways to extend the growing season in spring and fall, see pages 102–103.

1 | Make cloches to fit over the tops of plants, forming miniature one-plant greenhouses, which can save your crops on cold nights. To use a 1-gallon plastic milk jug, cut off the bottom and part of the handle. Place the jug over the plant, and push a stake through the handle to hold in it place. Leave the cap off to allow air ventilation, but recap the jug on frosty nights. Mail-order seed catalogs offer other types of cloches.

2 | Cut out the top of a cardboard box and three edges of the bottom, and turn the box upside down over a young plant. Close the lid at night to protect the plant from cold. Open the lid in the morning.

3 | To protect tender young plants from sudden hot weather and bright sunshine, prop up a piece of plywood or a shingle on the sunny side of each plant to shade it. When the plants are established and growing well, remove the protection.

floating row covers

Made of various lightweight fabrics sold in rolls, floating row covers protect plants from cold temperatures, birds, and many flying insects, including Colorado potato beetles, cucumber beetles, flea beetles, and leaf miners. The covers are permeable to sunlight, air, and water. Three types are available:

✿ *The standard floating row cover serves as an insect barrier and protects plants from frost down to 28°F/–2°C. It allows 75 to 85 percent of light to be transmitted to the plant. Remove the cover when temperatures top 80°F/27°C or else the plants will overheat.*

✿ *The frost blanket offers frost protection down to 24°F/–4°C, with 50 percent light transmission. Since it must be removed during the day when temperatures rise above 32°F/0°C, it does not protect plants from insect pests.*

✿ *Extralight or summer-weight fabric is used as an insect barrier only. It does not retain heat and allows 85 percent light transmission.*

Row covers are designed to be laid directly over seeded beds or plants, though some gardeners support them with stakes. If you plan to leave the covers in place for any length of time, allow enough extra fabric so the plants can push up the cover as they grow. Secure the edges by burying them with soil or placing 2-by-4s on them. This seals out insects, though pests already on the plants may proliferate. If your plants require insects to pollinate their flowers (as melons and squash do, for example), remove the covers when they begin to bloom.

At the end of the growing season, row covers help plants survive the first frosts of fall. This means, for example, that the last tomatoes have a chance to ripen, or that fall-seeded lettuce can be harvested over a longer period.

staking vegetables

Training edibles that grow on vines, such as pole beans, peas, tomatoes, cucumbers, melons, and squashes, to grow up stakes, trellises, or other supports pays off in several ways. It saves space to grow these plants vertically, rather than letting them sprawl across the ground. And you'll harvest more fruits, both because they'll be easier to see and pick and because they won't come in contact with the soil, where they might rot.

Put up your stakes and trellises at planting time. If you try to stake plants after they have begun to sprawl, you risk disturbing the roots and breaking the stems. Train or tie the plants as they grow.

Common materials for vegetable supports are wire mesh, wooden stakes and string, and bamboo, but you can also use rustic twigs, decorative metal or wooden structures, copper pipe, and bent reinforcing bar. For bean tepees, see page 114.

1 │ A weathered ladder in the garden makes a fine support. Sink the legs into 6-inch-deep holes so it won't blow over, and wrap string, wire, or wire mesh around it to help plants such as peas, beans, or cucumbers climb.

2 │ A sturdy frame leaning on a sunny wall makes a trellis for cucumber, melon, or squash vines. Support heavy fruits with netting or cloth slings tied to the trellis (see page 101).

3 │ A wire cage supports a tomato plant; you don't need to tie the stems to it. Buy a 6½-foot length of 5- or 6-foot-wide concrete-reinforcing wire. Roll it into a cylinder 24 inches in diameter. Anchor the cage with stakes.

4 │ A wooden obelisk (purchased or homemade from lumber or tree branches) supports tomatoes and brings height and interest to garden beds. Tie stems to the support as they grow.

5 │ Beans and peas have tendrils, which allow them to climb strings stretched over a wooden A-frame.

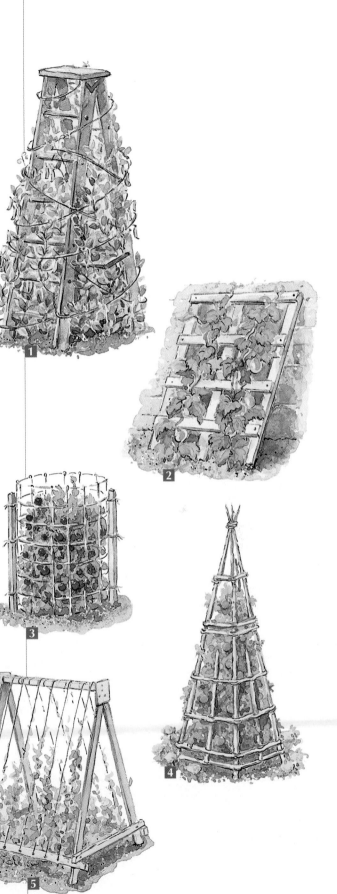

growing in containers

If you have a sunny spot on your patio or deck, along the driveway, or even on a rooftop, you can grow edibles in pots. Vegetables suitable for containers include any salad crop, chard, bush beans and peas, eggplant, peppers, determinate types of tomatoes, and bush forms of cucumbers and summer squash. Even carrots (especially short or round-rooted varieties), radishes, beets, and potatoes can thrive in pots.

For especially attractive containers, mix vegetables with flowers or herbs, such as basil, chives, or parsley. Strawberries are a natural for containers (see page 59), and you could also try blueberries. Dwarf citrus and other dwarf fruit trees offer further opportunities. See pages 28–29 for more ideas and recommended varieties of vegetables, herbs, and fruits that do well in containers.

'Sunburst' squash, 'Early Girl' tomato, and 'Lemon' cucumber thrive in big glazed pots.

elements for success

Large containers, ranging from 18 to 24 inches wide and 12 to 16 inches deep, provide plenty of room for roots and don't dry out as quickly as smaller containers. Plastic, terra-cotta, lightweight fiberglass, and wooden pots all work well, as long as they have drainage holes.

Use a top-quality potting mix, and supplement it with controlled-release fertilizer, following the directions on the label. Root crops, salad crops, peas, beans, and squashes are usually started by sowing seeds in the container; for others, set out transplants you've started yourself or bought at a nursery. If the plants need supports, such as stakes or trellises, install them at planting time to avoid damaging the roots later. Place the pots where they'll get at least 6 hours of sun each day.

Water as often as needed to keep the soil as moist as a wrung-out sponge. In hot weather, edibles in containers may need watering every day. Because frequent watering leaches nutrients from the potting mix, it's a good idea to feed your plants with fish emulsion or a liquid fertilizer. Plan to feed most vegetables every 2 weeks; tomatoes and most fruits need a monthly feeding.

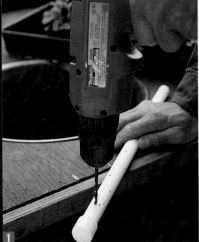

strawberry jars

A strawberry jar provides a harvest of sweet fruit in a small space. Such pots were originally designed to accommodate a few plants in the top, and, as their runners developed, the offspring could be rooted in the pockets protruding from the container's sides. Nowadays, impatient gardeners are more likely to plug small strawberry plants into all the openings to speed up the harvest. Choose a big jar (at least 16 inches tall); smaller ones dry out too quickly. Where winters are severe, cover the entire pot in fall with several inches of straw (use netting to hold it in place), or move the container to a garage or unheated basement.

1 | Make a watering tube from a piece of PVC pipe cut so that the top end is even with the jar's rim when the pipe is set upright in the jar. Cap the pipe on the bottom end. Drill 1/8-inch-diameter holes about 1 inch apart all around the pipe.

2 | Pour potting mix into a bucket, and moisten it. Mix in controlled-release fertilizer in the amount directed on the package. Partially fill the jar with potting mix; then insert the watering tube near the center, taking care not to block the jar's drainage hole. Add more potting mix, loosely filling the jar to the rim.

3 | Working from the bottom up, plant each pocket, pushing the roots firmly into the jar; add potting mix around the roots as needed. Plant the top of the jar.

4 | Water right after planting and whenever the top inch of soil dries out. To irrigate, slip a funnel into the PVC tube, and pour water into it; the holes drilled in the tube will distribute the water evenly. Feed monthly with liquid fertilizer, using the watering tube.

summer

- ▶ Finish planting warm-season vegetables in early summer.

- ▶ Watch for and control pests.

- ▶ Mulch fruit trees, garden beds, and paths.

- ▶ Water, paying special attention to plants in containers.

- ▶ Fertilize.

- ▶ Eliminate weeds before they go to seed.

- ▶ Harvest ripe vegetables and fruits.

- ▶ Thin tree fruits.

- ▶ Pull up spent crops, and plant new ones.

- ▶ In mild-winter areas, sow cool-season crops in containers to set out in early fall (see pages 82–83).

- ▶ In cold-winter areas, plant cool-season crops in the garden for fall harvest (see pages 82–83).

This oscillating sprinkler waters in an arc. Each time you move a sprinkler around the garden, overlap the watering pattern by about a third so that coverage is even.

A drip irrigation system supplies water to a bed of closely spaced garlic plants.

watering

Food crops need a steady supply of water throughout the growing season. If plants are allowed to dry out, they eventually die. Yet too much water, especially in poorly drained soil, deprives plant roots of oxygen, which may also kill them. Figuring out the best ways to water your garden is an ongoing learning process.

how often

Plan to water young vegetable seedlings and transplants frequently—as often as two or three times a day in hot, windy weather—keeping the soil moist but not soggy. As these young plants grow and their roots reach deeper, you can water less frequently. In general, vegetables that are flowering or beginning to set fruit, form heads, or develop edible roots need to be watered more often than older plants. Mature fruit trees and grapes require even less frequent irrigation, because they have much deeper roots than annual vegetable crops. See pages 106–190 for more on the water requirements of each crop.

Your soil type also influences how often you need to water. Clay soils hold lots of water and release it slowly; sandy soils hold less water and release it quickly. Loam soils fall in between, holding less water than clay and more than sand. Clay soils need less frequent watering than loam soils, and loam soils can be watered less frequently than sandy soils. (For more on soil types, see page 49.)

Cool, cloudy weather allows any soil to stay moist longer than hot, dry weather does. Thus cool-season vegetables need less irrigation than those grown in summer.

Mulches slow evaporation and are important aids to water conservation. (For more on mulching, see page 66.)

how much

Once your plants are established and growing well, water them deeply, applying enough water to moisten the entire root zone. This encourages roots to grow down farther, and deeper roots have access to more moisture, which allows the plants to go longer between waterings. Frequent shallow sprinklings are inefficient, because they encourage shallow root growth, which leaves plants subject to stress from heat and drying winds.

How deep a given amount of water will penetrate depends on your soil. On the average, 1 inch of water applied at the surface wets sandy soil 12 inches deep, loam soil 7 inches deep, and clay only 4 to 5 inches deep. To check water penetration in your soil, dig a hole with a trowel after watering.

watering methods

There are several ways to apply water. Throughout the growing season you may want to use more than one method.

Hand watering with a nozzle on the end of a hose or a sprinkling can is useful for newly seeded beds, new transplants, and container plants, since you can apply the water gently and put it exactly where it's needed.

Sprinkling water through a sprinkler attached to the end of a hose is an easy method. Choose a high-quality sprinkler that distributes water evenly. This method rinses away dust and discourages certain pests (especially spider mites). Sprinkling has some disadvantages as well. It wastes water through evaporation, particularly in windy weather. It may also encourage leaf diseases on some crops, especially in humid climates. The best time to use a sprinkler is in the morning (leaves will dry off during the day) and when the air is still.

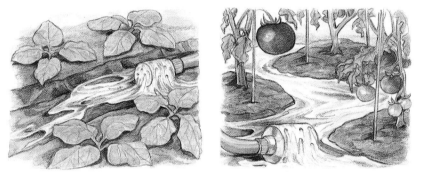

FURROW

BASIN

Flooding the soil around plants with watering basins and furrows is an effective way to apply water to large plants. Basins are used to irrigate trees, shrubby plants, and large vegetables. A basin is a circular doughnut-shaped depression in the soil surrounding a plant; as the plant grows, you need to expand the basin. Furrows, or shallow ditches, dug near plants in rows work well on level ground. Broad shallow furrows are generally better than deep narrow ones: the wider the furrow, the wider the root area you can soak, since water moves primarily downward rather than sideways. Dig basins and furrows when you set out plants or sow seeds, to avoid damaging the roots.

Soil soaker hoses, the forerunners of drip irrigation systems, are useful for slow, steady delivery of water. They are long tubes made of perforated or porous plastic or rubber, with hose fittings at one end. When you attach a soaker to a hose and turn on the water supply, water seeps or sprinkles from the soaker along its entire length. Soakers are ideal for watering rows of vegetables; to water beds, snake the soaker back and forth around the plants. Trees can be watered with a soaker coiled around the outer edges of the root zone.

Drip irrigation is another method of soaking the soil. Water is delivered slowly either by drip emitters that you attach to plastic tubing yourself or by emitter lines—tubes with factory-installed emitters spaced at regular intervals. Emitters operate at low pressure and deliver a low volume of water compared to standard sprinklers. The water is applied only to soil directly over plant roots, much reducing the amount of water needed. This also cuts down weed growth, because most of the soil surface is not moistened. By choosing specific kinds of tubing and emitters, you can tailor drip systems to water individual plants, beds of closely spaced plants, trees, or containers. Drip irrigation supplies and kits are sold by agricultural supply stores, retail nurseries and garden supply centers, and mail-order suppliers.

FAR LEFT *Furrows 3 to 6 inches deep help irrigate straight rows on level ground. The bubbler on the hose end softens the flow of water.*

LEFT *Basins with 3-inch-high sides hold water around large plants such as tomatoes and peppers; they also work well for watering trees. On level ground, link basins to make watering easier.*

A soaker hose lets water ooze slowly and steadily into the soil.

fertilizing

When plants are actively growing, they need a steady supply of nutrients. Though many of these nutrients are already present in soil, water, and air, you generally need to supply others, especially when raising vegetables. Having your soil tested (see page 49) is the best way to determine just which nutrients your garden needs. Your Cooperative Extension Office is another excellent source of information.

plant nutrients

The nutrients plants need in fairly large quantities, called *macronutrients*, are nitrogen, phosphorus, and potassium.

Nitrogen promotes green leafy growth. It is the nutrient most likely to be inadequate in garden soils. Signs of nitrogen deficiency are yellowing and dropping of older leaves and stunted growth. However, if plants get too much nitrogen, they grow so fast that they may become weak and spindly or produce more leaves and stems than flowers, fruits, or edible roots. Excess nitrogen may pollute surface water and groundwater, as well.

Phosphorus promotes strong root growth, flowering, and fruiting. Dull green leaves with a purple tint, stunted growth, and reduced yield are signs of deficiency. Too much phosphorus is not likely to hurt your crops, but it is a serious pollutant of water sources.

Potassium regulates the synthesis of proteins and starches that make sturdy plants. It also increases resistance to diseases, heat, and cold. Symptoms of deficiency include reduced flowering and fruiting, spotted or curled older leaves, and weak stems and roots. Excess potassium can cause salt burn on leaf tips, turning them brown.

Plants also need secondary nutrients (calcium, magnesium, and sulfur) and micronutrients (zinc, manganese, iron, and others). Fortunately, most soils are not deficient in these nutrients.

fertilizer labels

At any nursery you'll encounter a bewildering array of fertilizers in different forms and formulas. To decide which to buy, start by reading the label. Every fertilizer label states the percentage by weight that the product contains of the three macronutrients: nitrogen (N), phosphorus (P), and potassium (K), listed in that order: N-P-K. For example, a fertilizer labeled 10-3-1 contains 10 percent nitrogen, 3 percent phosphorus, and 1 percent potassium. This example is a *complete* fertilizer, because it contains all three macronutrients; it is also a high-nitrogen formula, since it contains relatively more nitrogen than phosphorus or potassium. *Balanced* fertilizers are formulated with equal amounts of each macronutrient, such as a 5-5-5 product; many brands of *all-purpose* fertilizer are balanced.

In contrast, fertilizers formulated with only one or two of the major nutrients are called *incomplete*. An incomplete fertilizer containing only nitrogen, for example, is useful when you want to give crops a supplemental feeding after planting.

Fertilizer forms, from left: concentrated liquid fertilizer, natural all-purpose fertilizer, controlled-release pellets, and chemical all-purpose fertilizer.

natural and chemical fertilizers

You can buy fertilizers in either natural (organic) or chemical (synthetic) form. Natural fertilizers are derived from the remains of living organisms and include blood meal, bonemeal, fish meal, cottonseed meal, and some animal manures, such as bat guano. Most contain lower levels of nutrients than chemical products do. They release their nutrients more slowly, as well: rather than dissolving in water, the fertilizers are broken down by microorganisms in the soil, providing nutrients gradually as they decay. Natural fertilizers are generally sold and applied in dry form; you scatter the fertilizer over the soil, and then dig or scratch it in. A few (fish emulsion, for example) are available as concentrated liquids, which you dilute before applying them.

Many natural fertilizers are high in just one of the three major nutrients. For example, blood meal and cottonseed meal are good sources of nitrogen; bonemeal is high in phosphorus; and greensand is a natural source of potassium. Some manufacturers combine a variety of organic ingredients in pellet form to make a complete fertilizer.

Chemical fertilizers are manufactured from the chemical sources listed on the label. They may be sold as dry granules or as soluble crystals or concentrated liquids to be diluted in water before use. Because their nutrients are for the most part water-soluble, they act faster than organic fertilizers, but most do not last as long in the soil. Liquid fertilizers provide nutrients especially quickly. You apply the dry kinds as you would natural fertilizers, digging or scratching them into the soil. Some chemical fertilizers come in a controlled-release form, which acts over a relatively long period (3 to 9 months, depending on the brand) if the soil receives regular moisture.

when and how to fertilize

Broadcast a complete natural or chemical fertilizer over the soil when preparing a planting bed (see page 51), following package instructions for the amount to use. Work the fertilizer into the soil. This puts nutrients, especially phosphorus and potassium, into the root zone of the plants you intend to grow.

For many vegetables, the fertilizer dug into the soil at planting time will provide sustenance for the entire growing season. But some long-season crops, such as tomatoes, and heavy feeders, such as corn, need supplemental boosts, particularly of nitrogen, during the growing season. (For details, check the individual plant listings on pages 106–190.) Follow-up feedings may also help plants that are growing poorly. Two ways to apply supplemental fertilizer, often referred to as *side-dressing*, are shown at right.

Perennial vegetables (such as asparagus), most berries, grapes, and most fruit trees need yearly feeding. Generally, work fertilizer into the soil around the plant at the start of the growing season. Check the listings on pages 106–190 for recommendations for each crop.

follow-up feeding

TOP *Apply a solution of diluted liquid or water-soluble fertilizer to give plants a supplemental feeding during the growing season.*

BOTTOM *Apply dry fertilizer as a side-dressing during the growing season by digging a shallow trench 4 to 6 inches away from the plants. Scatter fertilizer in the trench, cover it with soil, and water thoroughly.*

mulching

Mulching is the practice of applying organic or inorganic materials to the surface of the soil around plants or on pathways. Mulch reduces evaporation, so the soil stays moist longer after you irrigate your crops. Mulch also helps prevent the growth of weeds and gives the garden a tidy look.

organic mulches

Derived from once-living matter, organic mulches break down slowly, improving the soil and adding nutrients as they decompose. Mulches that work well around plants in garden beds include compost, leaf mold, straw, hay, and grass clippings (be sure to apply clippings in thin layers, letting each layer dry before applying another). For permanent garden paths, choose materials that break down more slowly, such as shredded or ground bark or wood chips.

Nurseries and garden supply centers sell a selection of organic mulches by the bag or in bulk. Farm supply stores offer straw and hay; wood chips are often available from tree maintenance firms.

Organic mulches keep the soil beneath them cool—a bonus in hot weather. This means that you should delay applying them to planting beds until warm weather arrives; soil has to be warm to get most plants off to a good start. Apply organic mulches in a 2- to 4-inch layer, but take care not to cover the plants' crowns (where the stem meets the soil); too much moisture near the crown can cause rot.

plastic mulches

Various sorts of plastic sheeting are useful aids in edible gardening, warming the soil, controlling weed growth, conserving moisture, and keeping developing fruits clean. After preparing the soil for planting, cover it with sheeting; hold down the edges with soil, pieces of lumber, or staples. Cut small holes or Xs when you are ready to set out plants or sow seeds. See page 87 for mail-order sources.

The most familiar sheeting, black plastic, absorbs heat to warm the soil in spring, allowing you to plant heat-loving crops earlier. It also blocks light, so weeds can't grow, and conserves water by reducing evaporation.

Infrared-transmitting (IRT) mulch sheeting is green plastic sheeting that allows infrared light to penetrate. It is more effective than black plastic in warming the soil, increasing early yields of warm-weather crops such as melons, cucumbers, squash, pumpkins, and peppers; it also suppresses weed growth and holds moisture in the soil.

Developed especially for tomatoes and related plants such as eggplant, red plastic selective reflecting mulch (SRM-Red) reflects light waves in the red spectrum up into the foliage, leading to larger plants with increased production, compared to black plastic. It also helps retain moisture and warm the soil but is not as effective at blocking weeds. Strawberries benefit from this mulch, too.

Straw mulch conserves moisture and keeps the soil cool around potato plants.

Red plastic selective reflecting mulch boosts yields of tomatoes and related crops, as well as strawberries.

caring for fruit trees

Summer attention to watering, fertilizing, mulching, thinning, and, in some cases, pruning all lead to better-looking trees and more bountiful harvests this season and in future years.

irrigation and mulch

All fruit trees need regular moisture that penetrates the root zone. Water your trees when the top 2 to 3 inches of soil are almost dry. Methods of watering trees include flooding a basin around the tree's drip line, using soaker hoses, and drip irrigation. See pages 62–63 for more on watering. Dig down with a trowel to check periodically that moisture is penetrating far enough; if necessary, water longer.

Applying a 3- to 4-inch layer of organic mulch (see page 66) helps conserve moisture and reduce weed growth; weeds compete with your trees for water and nutrients. Spread the mulch from just beyond the trunk to just outside the outermost branches. Take care not to let mulch touch the trunk, as it could cause rotting, especially on young trees.

summer pruning

You may associate pruning fruit trees with the winter dormant season when the trees are leafless, but summer pruning can be beneficial as well. Summer pruning reduces vigor, helping to keep dwarf and semidwarf trees smaller—a necessity if you have limited space—and makes fruit easier to harvest. In contrast, dormant-season pruning (see pages 90–91) has an invigorating effect on the tree. Summer pruning should be carried out only on healthy mature trees in a suitable climate. Where frosts come very early in fall, summer pruning is risky, because it leads to some new growth that could be harmed by cold weather. (For information on training and pruning espaliered trees, see page 91.)

A welcome by-product of summer pruning is better fruit color on interior branches exposed to more sunlight by the pruning. Don't remove too much leafy cover in intensely sunny climates, however, or the branches and fruit may suffer sunburn.

To prune fruit trees in summer, cut back some of the new shoots—that is, young branches that grew this year. The best time to do this is when the new growth is slowing down, usually between June and early August.

thinning

Thinning—removing excess immature fruits—in early summer increases the fruit size of the remaining fruits and helps prevent heavy crops that can break tree limbs. Begin thinning apples, stone fruits, and pears when fruits reach about 1/2 inch in diameter. Thin fruits to the spacing recommended for each type in the plant descriptions on pages 106–190. Citrus fruits generally do not need thinning.

Before

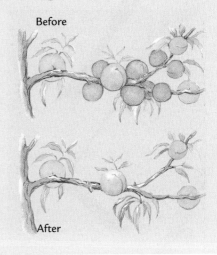

After

FAR LEFT *In summer, prune new growth (here on an apple tree) when the shoot tip or terminal bud is still succulent and the base of the shoot is beginning to harden or become woody.*

LEFT *Starting at the base of the shoot (where it grows from the main branch), count up 2 or 3 leaves above lowest whorl of leaves. Make your cut just above the third leaf; leaving a longer stub invites disease.*

weeding

WEEDING TOOLS

1 | Dandelion weeder
2 | Cape Cod weeder
3 | Swan-necked hoe
4 | Oscillating hoe
5 | Dutch hoe

Weeds are plants growing where gardeners don't want them to grow. Weeds rob your plants of water, nutrients, and sunlight. Some harbor insects and diseases. Most are unattractive, and a weedy garden is uninviting. Despite their undesirable qualities, weeds do have a few redeeming features. An assemblage of weeds can help prevent erosion. Some kinds of weeds provide nectar and shelter for beneficial insects and butterflies. When they die and decompose, weeds add organic matter to the soil. And a few (see page 71) are edible. However, these few positive aspects of weeds do not justify leaving very many of them in the garden. Learning to manage weeds, whether by removing them or preventing their growth in the first place, is an ongoing part of successful gardening.

control methods

Identifying the weeds in your garden is the first step in successful management. Weeds are often classified by the length of their life cycle. Annual weeds grow shoots and leaves, flower, set seed, and die within less than a year. They reproduce by seed, and even a few plants can generally produce lots of seeds. Almost all perennial weeds, which live for several years, also reproduce by seed. Once they mature, however, most produce spreading roots, rhizomes, or tubers as well, making control more difficult. Some common annual and perennial weeds are described on pages 70–71.

Hand pulling or hoeing is your first line of defense against most weeds. If you're diligent for several consecutive years about pulling or hoeing out annual weeds early in the season, before they set seed, their numbers will decline significantly. These methods also help control perennial weeds, as long as you catch the plants while they're young. Once perennials have matured, you usually have to dig out their roots to clear them. If you just pull off the tops, they'll resprout from bits of roots left in the soil. Certain tools are particularly useful for weeding (see photos).

You can compost annual weeds if they don't have flowers or seeds that might survive the composting process. The top growth of perennial weeds that have not yet seeded can also be composted. But the roots of perennials (dandelions and quack grass, for example) and any weeds that have set seed should be tossed in the trash.

Rototilling does the job (at least for a while) when preparing new gardens or working in large gardens with plenty of space between the rows. Weeds that are totally plowed under will decay, but perennials usually sprout again from roots.

Presprouting is a useful technique for preparing planting areas for vegetables. First, add needed soil amendments, and till or dig them into the soil; water the bed, and then wait a week or two for weed seeds to germinate. When they're only a few inches high, scrape them away with a hoe. Then sow or transplant your vegetables, disturbing the soil as little as possible to avoid bringing more seeds to the surface.

Soil solarization (see below) controls many kinds of weed seeds and harmful organisms. It takes 4 to 8 weeks.

Mulching with organic or inorganic materials helps control weeds by depriving their seeds of sunlight. For more on mulches, see page 66.

Herbicides can be useful, if chosen and used carefully. Most gardeners elect not to apply synthetic herbicides in food gardens. However, a couple of natural products can be used. Herbicidal soap is made from selected fatty acids. It kills the top growth of young, actively growing annual weeds less than 5 inches tall. Undiluted white household vinegar (5 percent acetic acid) also kills weeds, if applied during their first 2 weeks of life. Spray herbicidal soap or vinegar when the air is still, taking care not to spray desirable plants.

Trowel, far left; three-pronged cultivator, below.

soil solarization

Solarization traps the sun's heat under clear plastic sheeting to control many kinds of weed seeds as well as harmful fungi, bacteria, and some nematodes. It is done in summer and works best in regions that have hot, sunny weather for 4 to 8 weeks straight; daytime temperatures above 80°F/27°C are ideal. Solarization isn't very effective in areas with summer fog or lots of wind.

Plan to solarize beds you will use for late summer and fall vegetable crops. Follow these steps.

1 | *Cultivate the soil, clearing it of weeds, debris, and large clods of earth. You have to remove growing weeds, because clear plastic—unlike black plastic—doesn't stop plants beneath it from growing.*

2 | *Make a bed at least 2½ feet wide (narrower beds may not build up enough heat to have much effect). Carve a small ditch around the perimeter, and rake the bed level. Soak the soil to a depth of 1 foot. Moist soil conducts heat better than dry soil and helps spur weed seeds to germinate. The heat will then kill any seedlings as well as seeds.*

3 | *Cover the soil with 1- to 4-mil clear plastic; use UV-resistant plastic if it's available, since it won't break down during solarization. Stretch the plastic tightly so that it is in contact with the soil. Bury the edges in the perimeter ditch. An optional second layer of plastic increases the heat and makes solarization more effective; use soda cans as spacers between the two sheets (see inset at left). Leave the plastic in place for 4 to 8 weeks (the maximum for really persistent weeds). Leaving it longer than 8 weeks may harm the soil structure. Remove the plastic, and plant. After planting, avoid cultivating more than the upper 2 inches of soil, since weed seeds at deeper levels may still be viable.*

Bermuda grass

Bindweed

Mallow

Quackgrass

Sowthistle

Spotted spurge

common garden weeds

Use these photos and descriptions to help you identify and manage weeds that show up in your garden.

BERMUDA GRASS (*Cynodon dactylon*). A fine-textured, fast-growing perennial, Bermuda grass is frequently planted as a lawn in warm climates. It spreads by underground stems (rhizomes), aboveground runners (stolons), and sometimes seed. It quickly becomes a hard-to-control weed. If you have a Bermuda grass lawn, use 8-inch-deep barriers or edging to prevent it from advancing into other parts of the garden. Dig up clumps in garden beds before they form sod, being sure to remove all the underground stems; any left behind can start new shoots. Repeated digging is usually necessary to eliminate this weed.

BINDWEED (*Convolvulus arvensis*). Also called *wild morning glory* or *field bindweed,* this perennial forms 1- to 4-foot-long stems that crawl over the ground and twine over and around other plants. The trumpet-shaped flowers are white to pink. Once established, bindweed forms a deep, extensive root system, so hand-pulling seldom controls it—the stems break off, but the weed returns from the root. To kill it, cultivate or hoe every 6 weeks throughout the growing season; this eventually weakens the root system.

CRABGRASS (*Digitaria* species). An annual that grows in spring and summer, this shallow-rooted weed thrives in hot, moist areas. As the plant grows, it branches out at the base; stems can root where they touch the soil. Crabgrass is most likely to be a problem in areas that receive frequent surface watering; infrequent deep watering of established vegetables, berries, and fruit trees can dry out the roots, killing the weed or at least diminishing its vigor.

MALLOW (*Malva* species). An annual (in some climates, a biennial that sprouts in fall and sets seed the following summer), mallow is also known as *cheeseweed,* because of its fruits, which resemble a round of cheese. The leaves have rounded lobes, and the flowers are pinkish white. The plants grow quickly, ranging in height from a few inches to 4 feet tall. They're easiest to pull when young; older plants develop a deep taproot.

QUACK GRASS (*Elytrigia repens*). Also known as *couch grass* or *devil's grass,* this perennial weed can reach 3 feet tall. It produces an extensive underground network of long, slender, branching, yellowish white rhizomes that can spread laterally 3 to 5 feet. Because it reproduces readily from even small pieces of rhizome left in the soil, quack grass is difficult to eliminate. Before planting, thoroughly dig the area, and remove all visible pieces of rhizome; this will slow the weed's growth for a few years.

SOWTHISTLE (*Sonchus* species). An annual weed that grows from 1 to 4 feet high in summer, sowthistle has a stout taproot and hollow stem. A milky sap oozes out when a leaf or stem is broken. The yellow flowers look like those of dandelions. Pull the plants before they flower and set seed.

SPOTTED SPURGE (*Chamaesyce maculata;* also listed as *Euphorbia maculata*). An annual weed that grows in warm weather, spotted spurge is particularly aggressive. Not only does it produce large quantities of seed, but it also sets seed just a few weeks after germination—and the seeds may germinate immediately, producing several generations in one summer. It grows from a shallow taproot and forms a low mat of branching stems that exude a milky juice when cut or broken.

YELLOW NUTSEDGE (*Cyperus esculentus*). This perennial weed resembles a grass, but its stems are solid and triangular in cross section; the leaves of grasses are hollow and oval or flat in cross section. Yellow nutsedge forms small, roundish tubers (nutlets) at the tips of its roots; it spreads by these tubers as well as by seed. Remove plants when they are still small. Older plants are mature enough to produce tubers, and, when you dig or pull the weed, the tubers remain in the soil to sprout.

Yellow nutsedge

Chickweed

Dandelion

Purslane

edible weeds

You can harvest a few kinds of weeds for the table, although this probably won't control them in your garden. Edible weeds have a long history of culinary and medicinal use and are good sources of vitamins and minerals. In fact, seeds of selected varieties of several edible weeds are sold by specialty vegetable seed companies, blurring the distinction between harvesting vegetables and weeding the garden.

CHICKWEED (Stellaria media). This annual weed favors cool weather and appears in very early spring. It is a low-growing plant with smooth, pointed leaves, 1/4 to 1 inch long, bright green on the upper surface and paler on the underside. The slender stems have many branches and a line of white hairs on one side of each branch. Starry white flowers are borne on slender stalks that rise from the base of the leafstalks. Harvest the stems and leaves to add to early spring salads or to make a soothing tea.

DANDELION (Taraxacum officinale). Originally introduced to North America as a food crop, this perennial is a familiar garden weed. The low-growing plants have dark green lobed leaves and a deep taproot; the bright yellow flowers appear throughout the growing season. Dandelions reproduce both by seed and by any fragments of the taproot left in the soil. Management involves pulling young plants before they flower, or taking out the entire taproot of older plants to prevent regrowth. Harvest leaves to eat when they are 3 to 4 inches long; later they're too tough and bitter. Young leaves impart a pleasantly bitter taste to spring salads, and they're also tasty as cooked greens.

LAMB'S QUARTERS (Chenopodium album). Also called fat hen, this annual weed grows in spring and summer. The 1/2- to 4-inch-long leaves are triangular, usually with wavy edges. A white, mealy powder coats the leaves. The plants grow from 1 to 6 feet tall, depending on soil fertility. For the kitchen, harvest the leaves when they are small and tender, and cook them like spinach.

PURSLANE (Portulaca oleracea). A low-growing annual weed with fleshy stems and leaves and small yellow flowers, purslane thrives in moist conditions but can survive considerable drought. The seeds germinate in late spring. Though it's easy to pull or hoe, pieces of stem reroot readily, so be sure to remove them from the garden. The stems and leaves have a tart, lemony flavor. Young shoots enliven salads, while older ones are used in soups, pork stew, and egg dishes.

controlling pests and diseases

Although few gardens escape pests and diseases entirely, the advice and photos in this section can help you prevent the most common problems and, if troubles do occur, assist you in identifying them and taking action. Pests and diseases that harm only one or two crops are covered in the listings on pages 106–190.

prevention

Preventing trouble is the most important step in managing pests and diseases: you won't have to solve problems that don't get a chance to start in the first place. Keep your plants healthy and stress-free. Set them out at the recommended planting time in well-prepared soil, and give them the care they need throughout the year. Whenever possible, select plants resistant to specific pests or diseases. A number of insects and diseases overwinter or spend part of their life cycle on plant debris. Pulling up, shredding, and composting spent plants, and tilling the soil, especially in fall, gets rid of winter hiding places. Don't put diseased or insect-infested plants in the compost pile; discard or burn them.

Mix different kinds of plants in your garden. Expanses of just one sort can draw large populations of pests fond of that particular plant. Mixed plantings of several vegetables, other edibles, and flowers not only discourage large numbers of a single pest but also favor beneficial insects.

management

Check the plants in your garden frequently. A few aphids or chewed leaves are not cause for alarm, and problems often disappear quickly on their own, as pests die out naturally, move on, or are controlled by beneficial insects. However, if you are aware that specific problems may be developing, you can keep an eye on the situation and take action, if necessary.

Physical controls in several forms are useful. The larger pests, such as snails, slugs, grasshoppers, and some beetles and caterpillars, are candidates for removal by hand. Removing infected leaves or even entire branches helps control some pests and diseases. Aim a strong jet of water at plants to dislodge pests such as aphids and mites. Barriers, such as floating row covers (see page 56), exclude many insects, while netting can deter hungry birds.

Biological controls, which rely on living organisms such as beneficial insects (discussed on page 73), are effective. Certain microorganisms are also classified as biological controls. The best-known of these is *Bacillus thuringiensis (Bt)*, a bacterium that, once ingested by caterpillars or larvae, causes them to stop feeding and die. Different strains have been identified, each effective against the larvae of specific pests.

Natural pesticides are derived from naturally occurring organisms or other materials and create minimal environmental hazards. A well-known example is insecticidal soap, which combats various pests. Neem oil or extract, derived from a tropical tree, controls many insects, mites, and some

TOP *Plant collars made from plastic cartons prevent cutworms from reaching vegetable seedlings.* **BOTTOM** *Yellow sticky cards attract and trap whiteflies.*

diseases. Products containing pyrethrins are lethal to a number of pests; the active ingredient is derived from compounds found in a dried flower. Horticultural oils are highly refined petroleum or vegetable oils that smother pests, pest eggs, and disease spores. Sulfur is used in controlling diseases and mites.

Despite their relatively low toxicity, these natural pesticides can kill beneficial and harmless insects. Use them only on plants that are being attacked and only when pests are present, and follow the label directions exactly. The management suggestions given in the pest and disease sections that follow do not include recommendations for more toxic chemicals, since their registration and availability change frequently. If you feel you need stronger controls, consult your Cooperative Extension Office.

Assassin bug

Damsel bug

beneficial insects

Hundreds of species of beneficial insects help gardeners keep pests at bay. Those described here and many others are likely to be present naturally in your garden; some (as noted) can be purchased from nurseries or mail-order firms. To encourage flying beneficials, grow flowering plants that provide the nectar and pollen they need at certain times in their life cycles. Good choices include yarrow, feverfew, coreopsis, cosmos, and sweet alyssum, as well as the herbs cilantro and fennel, among others. In addition to these insects, you can buy beneficial parasitic nematodes. These microscopic worms destroy pests such as maggots and cutworms.

ASSASSIN BUGS *Slim ½- to ¾-inch-long insects; may be red, black, brown, or gray. They feed on a wide variety of pests.*

DAMSEL BUGS *Dull gray or brown, ½-inch-long, very slender insects with long, narrow heads. Nymphs resemble the adults but are smaller and have no wings. Both nymphs and adults feed on aphids, leafhoppers, and small worms.*

GROUND BEETLES *Shiny black insects from ½ to 1 inch long. The smaller species eat other insects, caterpillars, cutworms, and grubs; some larger species prey on slugs and snails and their eggs.*

LACEWINGS *The adults are 1-inch-long flying insects that feed only on nectar, pollen, and honeydew, but the larvae devour aphids, leafhoppers, thrips, and other insects, as well as mites. The larvae resemble ½-inch-long alligators and are commercially available.*

LADY BEETLES *Also known as ladybugs, these beetles and their larvae (which look like ¼-inch-long alligators) feed on aphids, mealybugs, and the eggs of many insects. You can buy lady beetles, but they often fly away as soon as you release them. Freeing them at night or keeping them in cages for a few days may encourage them to remain in your garden.*

TRICHOGRAMMA WASPS *These very tiny parasitoid wasps attack the eggs of caterpillar pests. Commercially available species are adapted for gardens or for fruit trees. Because they are short-lived, repeated releases may be needed.*

Ground beetle

Lacewing

Lady beetle

Trichogramma wasp

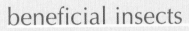

pests

Cabbage aphids

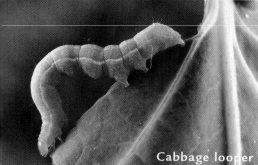

Cabbage looper

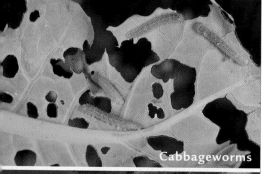

Cabbageworms

Colorado potato beetle

Cucumber beetle

APHIDS Soft-bodied, rounded insects that range from pinhead to match head size. May be black, white, pink, or pale green. They cluster on new growth, sucking plant juices. Some kinds transmit viral diseases.

MANAGEMENT *Use floating row covers. Give beneficial insect populations time to swell and bring aphids under control. Release lacewings and lady beetles. Hose off aphids with a strong blast of water. Spray with insecticidal soap or a product containing pyrethrins.*

CABBAGE LOOPERS Greenish caterpillars, also called *inchworms,* that feed on cabbages and related crops.

MANAGEMENT *Use floating row covers. Handpick adults and small white egg clusters. Release trichogramma wasps, which attack the eggs. Spray with Bt or a product containing pyrethrins.*

CABBAGE ROOT MAGGOTS The larvae of a fly; small, white maggots with pointed heads. They destroy the root systems of cabbage-family crops; plants are stunted and may wilt. Similar maggots attack onions and corn seedlings.

MANAGEMENT *Cover seedbeds or transplants with floating row covers. Place a tarpaper disc around the base of each plant to prevent flies from laying eggs. Remove and destroy infected plants. Release parasitic nematodes.*

CABBAGEWORMS Greenish caterpillars, the larval form of white cabbage butterflies. They eat the leaves of cabbage-family plants.

MANAGEMENT *Handpick adults and eggs, which are yellow to orange, on leaves. Use floating row covers. Release trichogramma wasps, which attack the eggs. Spray with Bt or a product containing pyrethrins.*

COLORADO POTATO BEETLES Yellow-and-black-striped beetles and their reddish larvae. Both eat the leaves of potatoes, tomatoes, and eggplant.

MANAGEMENT *Handpick. Discard infested plants. Spray with Bacillus thuringiensis tenebrionis, the form of Bt that targets this pest, or with neem or a product containing pyrethrins.*

CUCUMBER BEETLES Oval-shaped beetles, greenish yellow with black spots or stripes. They eat all parts of cucumbers, squashes, and melons. The beetles also transmit diseases, such as bacterial wilt, which attacks cucumbers.

MANAGEMENT *Use floating row covers. Discard infested plants; clean the garden in fall to prevent the beetles from overwintering. Release parasitic nematodes. Spray with a product containing pyrethrins.*

CUTWORMS Dull brownish caterpillars that live in the soil and cut off stems of seedlings at ground level. Some kinds climb into plants and eat leaves.

MANAGEMENT Clear and till beds to destroy cutworms. Use protective collars around stems of young seedlings. Handpick at night when the cutworms are active. Release parasitic nematodes.

FLEA BEETLES Very small, shiny, oval, blue-black, brown, or bronze beetles that jump like fleas. Adults chew holes in leaves of seedlings, often killing them. Vigorous older plants usually survive, except eggplant, which may be seriously damaged.

MANAGEMENT Remove dead or damaged leaves and plants. Till the soil in fall. Use floating row covers. Spray with neem.

GRASSHOPPERS Also called *locusts*; adults, 1 to 2 inches long, may be brown, green, or yellow. During their periodic outbreaks, can cause severe damage, defoliating most plants.

MANAGEMENT Cultivate the soil in fall, winter, and early spring to destroy egg clusters. Use floating row covers. Try a biological control, Nosema locustae, *which targets only grasshoppers; it works best when used in large areas, such as a weedy field bordering a garden.*

HARLEQUIN BUGS Black adults with distinctive red markings. They and the wingless immature nymphs suck plant juices from the leaves of cabbage-family plants.

MANAGEMENT Handpick and destroy the bugs and egg masses, which resemble rows of barrels on leaf surfaces. Use floating row covers. Discard infected plants. Spray with insecticidal soap.

LEAFHOPPERS Many species of small green, yellow, brown, or mottled insects that run sideways, hop, or fly. They damage the foliage of many plants and the fruits of apples and grapes. Some transmit plant diseases.

MANAGEMENT Use floating row covers. Release lacewings and lady beetles. Spray with neem.

LEAF MINERS A catchall term for certain moth, beetle, and fly larvae that tunnel within plant leaves, leaving a nearly transparent trail on the surface. They damage leafy crops such as chard and spinach.

MANAGEMENT Plant under floating row covers. Spray with neem to discourage adults from laying eggs; once the larvae are inside the leaves, sprays are not effective. Remove infested leaves.

continued >

Cutworm

Flea beetle

Grasshopper

Harlequin bug

Leafhopper

Leaf miner damage

Mites

Nematodes

Squash bug

Thrips

Whiteflies

Wireworms

MITES Tiny spider relatives found on leaf undersides. Webbing is often present where they live. Mites suck plant juices; the damaged leaf surface is pale and stippled, and the leaves often turn brown, dry out, and die.

MANAGEMENT Hose off plants with strong jets of water. Release predatory mites, which feed on harmful mites; lacewings are also effective. Spray with insecticidal soap, neem, or sulfur.

NEMATODES Microscopic worms that live in soil and feed chiefly on roots of plants. Some kinds cause plants to form root galls. All cause plants to be weaker and less productive. (These are different species from beneficial parasitic nematodes, described on page 73.)

MANAGEMENT Use soil solarization to reduce the population. Plant resistant varieties. Practice crop rotation. Remove and destroy infected plants. Dig in organic matter, which encourages a soil fungus that is a natural enemy of nematodes.

SNAILS AND SLUGS Night-feeding mollusks. Snails have shells; slugs do not. They feast on the seedlings and leaves of many vegetables.

MANAGEMENT Handpick and destroy. Set out containers filled with beer to attract the pests, which fall in and drown. Enclose potted plants and raised beds with copper strips; these give snails and slugs a shock, so they won't cross the strips. Use bait containing nontoxic iron phosphate, which is not hazardous to other creatures.

SQUASH BUGS Dark brown or black adults; smaller, pale green nymphs. Both suck plant juices on the vines and fruit of squashes and pumpkins. The stems wilt and blacken, and the fruits are disfigured.

MANAGEMENT Handpick adults, nymphs, and reddish brown eggs. Use floating row covers. Spray undersides of leaves with insecticidal soap.

THRIPS Near-microscopic insects that feed by rasping soft leaf tissue. Look for small black droppings on the undersides of leaves. Leaf surfaces take on a shiny, silvery, or tan cast.

MANAGEMENT Hose off plants with a strong jet of water. Trap thrips with yellow sticky traps. Release lacewings. Spray with insecticidal soap or neem.

WHITEFLIES Tiny white pests that fly up in a cloud when disturbed. The larvae and adults suck plant juices from leaf undersides. Foliage may show yellow stippling, curl, and turn brown.

MANAGEMENT Trap with yellow sticky cards or traps. For greenhouse infestations, release Encarsia formosa, a predatory wasp. Spray leaves with a strong jet of water, insecticidal soap, or neem.

WIREWORMS Shiny, reddish brown larvae of click beetles. May damage root crops (especially carrots and potatoes). Often found in soil where lawn or pasture was grown.

MANAGEMENT Till the soil deeply before planting root crops. Rotate crops. Trap pests by placing mature carrots in the soil; pull them up after a few days, destroy the wireworms, and repeat.

crop rotation

In general, members of the same plant family are susceptible to the same pests and diseases. So, rotating the locations of the same or related crops in your garden helps prevent a buildup of pests and disease organisms. Try to plan a rotation that allows at least 2 years between related crops. If serious diseases, such as clubroot (see below), strike, a longer rotation is necessary. Noting each season's planting plans in your garden journal will help you keep track of what you planted where and when.

plant families

GOURD FAMILY: *cucumbers, melons, pumpkins, squash*

NIGHTSHADE FAMILY: *eggplant, peppers, potatoes, tomatoes*

GRASS FAMILY: *corn and some cover crops (see page 84)*

LILY FAMILY: *garlic, leeks, onions, shallots*

CARROT FAMILY: *carrots, cilantro, dill, fennel, parsley*

CABBAGE (COLE OR MUSTARD) FAMILY: *broccoli, brussels sprouts, cabbage, cauliflower, kale, mustards, radishes, turnips*

PEA (LEGUME) FAMILY: *beans, peas, and some cover crops*

To make planning for crop rotations easier, group related plants, such as mustards and broccoli together.

diseases

CLUBROOT A fungal disease that causes the roots of many cabbage-family plants to become swollen and twisted. Plant growth is stunted; on hot days plants wilt. Eventually roots rot.

   MANAGEMENT Most common in acid soils; add lime to raise the pH to at least 7.2. If clubroot is present in the soil, do not replant cabbage-family plants there for 7 years. Dig up and discard infected plants, including the roots. Clean tools. Soil solarization helps control the fungus.

DAMPING OFF Various soil fungi that cause seeds to rot in the soil before they sprout or cause young seedlings to collapse at or near the soil surface. Most common in poorly drained or too-wet soils.

   MANAGEMENT Improve drainage, and reduce watering. Do not plant seeds of warm-season crops when the soil is still cold. When starting seeds indoors, use sterile potting soil, and disinfect containers. Thin crowded seedlings to improve air circulation.

DOWNY MILDEW A fungal disease that occurs during cool, rainy, or foggy weather. In most plants, a downy substance appears on the undersides of leaves; yellow to brown spots appear on both upper and lower surfaces.

   MANAGEMENT Plant resistant varieties. Water in the morning, and allow plants to dry. Discard diseased plants. Rotate crops. Spray with neem to help prevent infection.

continued >

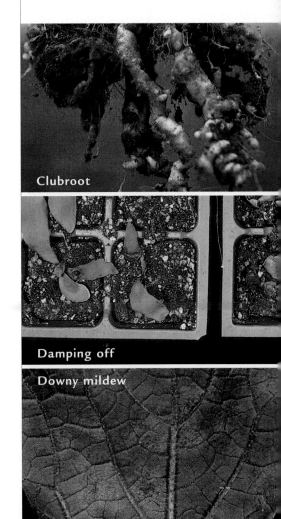

Clubroot

Damping off

Downy mildew

Early blight

Fusarium wilt

Late blight

Powdery mildew

Southern blight

EARLY BLIGHT A fungal disease that causes small dark-brown-to-black spots on leaves; eventually leaves turn yellow and die. Tomato fruits develop dark, leathery spots near the stem. Potatoes, tomatoes, and eggplant are affected.

MANAGEMENT Plant certified disease-free seed potatoes, resistant varieties of other crops. Rotate crops. Avoid overhead watering. Keep plants well fertilized and vigorously growing to resist infection. Clean up and destroy debris after you harvest.

FUSARIUM WILT A disease caused by a fungus that can live in the soil for many years. It invades the water-conduction tissues of plants, occurs commonly in warm temperatures, and affects a number of vegetables. Plants wilt, and the lower leaves turn yellow and die; the whole plant may die.

MANAGEMENT Plant resistant varieties. Fertilize and water to promote vigorous growth. Rotate crops. Discard infected plants. Try soil solarization to help control the fungus.

LATE BLIGHT A fungal disease that affects potatoes and tomatoes. Small dark water-soaked spots appear on leaves and stems and expand rapidly in cool, moist conditions. Tomato fruits are malformed; potatoes rot in storage.

MANAGEMENT Choose resistant varieties. Avoid overhead irrigation. Rotate crops. Discard infected plants and any plant debris after you harvest.

POWDERY MILDEW A fungal disease that causes a powdery white-to-gray coating on leaves, stems, flower buds, and fruits. This mildew is favored by humid weather, poor air circulation, and shade, but (unlike downy mildew) it needs dry leaves to become established.

MANAGEMENT Thin crowded plants to improve air circulation. Plant in a sunny area. Spray with water to wash off fungus. Discard infected plants. Spray with sulfur, copper soap fungicide, or neem.

SOUTHERN BLIGHT Also called *Southern stem rot*, a fungal disease that causes plants to rot at the stem, wilt, turn yellow, and die.

MANAGEMENT Space plants widely to improve air circulation. Rotate crops. Discard infected plants, rootball and all, as well as plant debris. Try soil solarization to help control the fungus.

VERTICILLIUM WILT A fungus that survives in the soil for many years. It affects many vegetables, cane berries, and some fruit trees. Scattered branches on trees may die. On vegetables, plants wilt; their leaves first turn yellow, then turn brown, and finally die. Eventually the whole plant may die.

MANAGEMENT Plant resistant varieties. Rotate crops. Prune out and discard infected growth on trees; discard infected plants. Try soil solarization to help control the fungus.

animal pests

Most gardeners welcome some—though not all—wildlife into their gardens. Certain birds and animals can cause significant damage to vegetables, berries, and fruit trees. Some of the worst troublemakers are described here, with suggestions for preventing damage or controlling the animals.

BIRDS In general birds are gardeners' friends, fun to watch and helpful in controlling insect pests. Some kinds can be a nuisance at certain times, eating tender seedlings and transplants, berries, and fruits. Keeping the birds at bay is the best solution. To protect low-growing plants, use floating row covers (see page 56) or attach screening, aviary wire, or netting to a frame made of wood or plastic pipes. Enclose fruit trees and berry bushes with broad-mesh ($1/2$- to $3/4$-inch) nylon or plastic netting. Plan to protect fruiting plants 2 to 3 weeks before fruit ripens.

DEER Hungry deer can make serious inroads into your harvests in just a few hours. Fencing is the most certain protection. Ideally, a deer fence should be 8 feet high. However, a 6-foot-high fence may suffice if the ground is level or slopes away from the garden on the outside of the fence. Because deer cannot high-jump and broad-jump at the same time, adding a horizontal "outrigger" extension on the top of a fence makes it harder for deer to clear. For the same reason, double fencing works for many gardeners: construct a pair of parallel 4- to 5-foot fences spaced 4 to 5 feet apart. You can plant low-growing crops in the area between the fences. Commercial electric fencing is another useful option.

Commercial deer repellents can work if sprayed often enough to keep new growth covered. Do not apply repellents to edible plants unless the label indicates you can do so.

GOPHERS AND MOLES From tunnels beneath the soil, gophers feed on plant roots. Signs of gopher sabotage include wilted plants that have no roots and mounds of fresh, finely pulverized soil. Moles travel in tunnels that are usually closer to the soil surface than those of gophers. The soil mounds they form are conical in shape. Moles eat earthworms and grubs rather than plants. However, when making tunnels, they uproot young plants.

To protect the roots of individual plants, line the sides and bottom of planting holes with $1/2$-inch mesh hardware cloth. Raised beds lined with hardware cloth are a good solution for vegetables (see pages 94–95).

RABBITS Like deer, rabbits can strip a garden overnight. Erecting a 2-foot-tall fence is the best way to protect your crops. If it's made of wire, use a mesh small enough to keep rabbits from going through. Rabbits are burrowers, so you also need to extend a wire mesh fence at least 6 inches underground. Or fold the bottom 12 inches of a wire mesh fence out away from the garden, making an L shape, and securely stake or weight the foot of the L to the ground; rabbits won't be able to burrow where the mesh covers the ground.

Netting excludes birds.

A handsome wooden deer fence.

Gopher-proof bed lined with hardware cloth.

Wire mesh deters rabbits and birds.

fall and winter

- Set out transplants and sow seeds of cool-season crops.

- Sow cover crops.

- Protect remaining warm-season crops from early frosts (see page 56).

- Give the garden a thorough cleanup.

- Compost spent plants, weeds, and autumn leaves.

- Clean and store tools.

- Protect overwintering crops from freezing.

- Order seeds, supplies, and bare-root stock.

- Plant bare-root stock.

- Train and prune fruit trees.

- Apply dormant-season spray.

planting cool-season crops

Some of the best-tasting vegetables are the cool-season crops you harvest in fall. The combination of warm days and cool nights makes root crops such as carrots and beets crisp and sweet. A touch of frost brings out the mild, delicious flavors of vitamin-rich leafy greens such as kale, cabbage, and spinach. And you can keep your garden alive and producing by replacing spent crops (the ragged-looking zucchini vines, for example) with new ones.

For information on season extenders that help you keep fall crops going longer into winter, see pages 102–103.

best choices for fall

Cool-season vegetables prefer temperatures from 55 to 75°F/13 to 24°C, but almost all can tolerate some frost. This means that you can harvest fresh vegetables up to and even after the first frosts of fall. Favorite fall crops include lettuce, arugula, endive, and other greens; root crops such as beets and carrots; broccoli, cauliflower, and other cabbage-family members. A few extra-hardy vegetables can survive lows down to 0°F/–18°C. These include collards, kale, leeks, and spinach. Garlic and some kinds of bulbing onions are also planted in fall, but they won't be ready for harvest until early the following summer. See the listings on pages 106–190 for more information on each of these crops.

planting a fall garden

Timely planting is the key to a successful fall garden. It's important to start early enough so that the plants have time to grow and produce a crop before really cold weather halts their growth. To decide when to plant each vegetable, you need to know the average date of the first fall frost in your area

Cool-season vegetables, such as cabbages (top) and brussels sprouts (bottom), tolerate frost.

(see the map on page 44). You also need to know the number of days the particular variety needs to reach maturity; add about 14 days to this number to allow for the slower growth of plants during the shorter days of fall. Count back this total number of days from the first frost date to get an idea of when to sow seeds, either directly in the garden or in pots to transplant later. In areas where cold weather arrives fairly early in fall, you actually need to start many of your fall crops in summer.

In most climates, crops that take a long time to mature, such as cabbage and broccoli, are either bought as seedlings from a nursery or sown in containers for later transplanting to the garden (see pages 52–53). To protect them from the heat of late summer, keep the containers in a partially shaded place, such as a porch, while the seeds germinate and grow. Generally, root crops, such as beets and turnips, grow best if they're sown directly in the garden. However, if you want to have seedlings ready to set out in early fall, you can sow seeds in peat pots, made of biodegradable paper pulp. You set the seedlings in the garden, pot and all, minimizing disturbance to the roots. For more information on transplanting, see page 54. Sow seeds of faster-growing crops, such as lettuce and other greens, directly in the garden when the weather has cooled (see page 55).

tip STORAGE IN THE EARTH Carrots and other root crops, such as beets and turnips, can be left in the ground for winter harvest if you cover them with a foot of hay or straw; bags of leaves and bales of hay work well, too. The covering keeps the ground from freezing in all but the coldest climates. You may want to mark the location of mulched crops with tall stakes so you can find them in the snow.

Sow seeds of cool-season crops in peat pots (left), 4-inch plastic pots (center), or nursery flats (right).

protection from heat

If you live in an area where early fall weather is hot and sunny, protect your newly transplanted or seeded cool-season crops until the weather cools. Prop up a piece of plywood or a shingle on the sunny side of individual plants, as shown on page 56. For larger plantings, fasten shade cloth (available from garden supply centers and nurseries) to stakes.

Use shade cloth supported on stakes to protect plants from too much heat.

inoculating legume seeds

Before planting, treat the seeds of legumes (those grown for cover crops as well as garden peas and beans) with an inoculant powder to be certain that Rhizobium bacteria are present. Properly inoculated legumes produce more nitrogen and also grow larger, thus increasing the organic matter they produce. You can purchase the correct strain of inoculant for the legumes you want to plant from seed suppliers. To inoculate your seeds, place them in a bucket and moisten them with a little water. Then sprinkle the inoculant onto the seeds, and mix thoroughly. Plant as soon as possible.

Nitrogen-containing nodules on fava bean roots.

growing cover crops

Also known as green manure, cover crops are legumes (pea-family plants) or grasses planted to improve your garden's soil rather than to harvest. Most cover crops are planted in fall (after the rains begin in mild-winter climates; 6 to 8 weeks before the first frost in cold regions) and dug into the soil in spring. As they decay, they add valuable organic matter to the soil, making it easier to work and helping to retain moisture. They also reduce erosion, choke out weeds, and provide early spring flowers to supply nectar and pollen for beneficial insects.

Legumes such as fava beans, bell beans, Austrian peas, clovers, and vetch also add nitrogen, due to their association with *Rhizobium* bacteria that live symbiotically on their roots. These organisms draw nitrogen from the air and "fix" (concentrate) it in root nodules. When the legumes decompose, the nitrogen is released into the soil. (For information on growing fava beans as a vegetable, see page 116.)

Grasses, such as barley, rye, and oats, don't contribute extra nitrogen to the soil, but they do produce plenty of organic matter. Gardeners often combine legumes and grasses to reap the benefits of both.

Seeds for cover crops, and information on how much of each kind you need to cover specific areas, are available from mail-order suppliers (see pages 86–87) and some nurseries.

timing and steps

Before planting, till or dig the area and rake it smooth. These photos show steps for using fava beans as a cover crop; except as noted, other cover crops are grown in the same way.

1 | Sow fava beans in furrows about 2 inches deep and a foot apart. Cover with soil, and pat down. (Sow smaller-seeded cover crops by broadcasting the seed over the prepared soil. Rake soil over the seeds, and pat it down.) Keep the soil moist.

2 | To produce the maximum amount of nitrogen from fava beans and other legumes, let them grow until after they start blooming in spring. Let grasses grow until several weeks before you want to plant other crops.

3 | Cut or mow your cover crops, by hand or with a heavy-duty mower. Either till, as shown on facing page, or dig the entire mass of stems, foliage, and roots into the soil, or, if that is too difficult, add the cut stems and leaves to your compost pile, and dig just the roots into the soil. Wait 2 to 4 weeks for the cover crop to decompose before planting spring or summer vegetables.

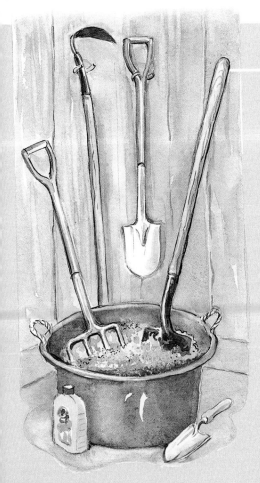

fall cleanup

After you've harvested vegetables and planted cover crops, spending a little time putting your garden to bed in fall will make it healthier and more productive next year. Begin by pulling up all spent plants as well as weeds. This helps destroy any pests that may be lurking among the leaves and also gets rid of winter hiding places. You can add spent healthy plants and any remaining mulch to the compost pile, but plants that are infested with pests or diseases, weeds that have gone to seed, and perennial weeds into the trash instead.

Many gardeners dig or till garden beds in fall, working spent plants and mulch into the soil instead of composting them. This adds organic material to the soil and helps control soil-dwelling pests and diseases by exposing them to cold weather.

Gather together stakes, trellises, and tomato cages, clean them well, so they can't harbor disease organisms, and then store them for the winter. Also store hoses and sprinklers.

This is a good time to care for your gardening tools so they'll be ready in spring. Rub wooden tool handles with linseed oil. To clean and oil the metal parts of digging tools, fill a 16-gallon bucket about 3/4 full with coarse sand. Mix in 1 quart or more of motor oil (used oil is fine). Jab your tools into the mixture until the sand has abraded away the dirt and the blades are coated with oil. Brush off the sand, and store the tools. Oiled sand can be used indefinitely; if you need to discard it, take it to a hazardous-waste disposal station.

ordering plants, seeds, and supplies

As the gardening season winds down, update your garden journal, noting which vegetables and fruits were winners in the past seasons. Begin planning changes you want to make next year. Check your supply of seeds to decide which sorts need replenishing as well as which new vegetables to try. In late fall and winter you can order bare-root cane berries, grapes, and fruit trees for delivery in late winter or early spring. This is also a good time to order products for extending the gardening season and for pest control.

Many mail-order catalogs offer a wealth of information about varieties, cultural methods, and ways to improve your garden and gardening skills. To get you started, here are a few companies that sell fruiting plants, seeds, and gardening supplies.

fruit trees, grapes, and berries

Each of these suppliers offers a wide selection of bare-root plants and trees.

One Green World
28696 South Cramer Road
Molalla, OR 97038-8576
(877) 353-4028
www.onegreenworld.com

Raintree Nursery
391 Butts Road
Morton, WA 98356
(360) 496-6400
www.raintreenursery.com

Stark Bro's Nurseries and Orchards Company
P.O. Box 1800
Louisiana, MO 63353
(800) 325-4180
www.starkbros.com

seeds

In addition to seeds, most of these companies also offer ready-to-transplant seedlings, garlic, seed potatoes, supplies, and tools. As noted, some offer open-pollinated (nonhybrid) seeds; heirloom varieties (interesting, flavorful varieties more than 50 years old); and organically grown seeds (harvested from plants raised without chemical fertilizers or pesticides). Each year more companies pledge not to sell genetically modified varieties (those in which a gene from an unrelated species has been inserted).

Baker Creek Heirloom Seeds
2278 Baker Creek Road
Mansfield, MO 65704
(417) 924-8917
www.rareseeds.com
Has a selection of open-pollinated heirloom seeds from around the world; some are organically grown.

W. Atlee Burpee and Company
300 Park Avenue
Warminster, PA 18974
(800) 888-1497
www.burpee.com
A well-known firm that offers vegetable, herb, and flower seeds; some are organically grown.

The Cook's Garden

P.O. Box 535
Londonderry, VT 05148
(800) 457-9703
www.cooksgarden.com
Offers seeds of vegetables and herbs, with an especially large selection of lettuces and mesclun mixes.

Irish Eyes and Garden City Seeds

P.O. Box 307
Thorp, WA 98946
(877) 733-3001
www.irish-eyes.com
Formerly two separate companies; offers more than 100 varieties of potatoes, seeds for vegetable varieties adapted to areas with short growing seasons, and cover crop seeds. Many are organically grown.

Johnny's Selected Seeds

955 Benton Avenue
Winslow, ME 04901-2601
(207) 861-3900
www.johnnyseeds.com
Offers a wide selection of vegetable, herb, flower, and cover crop seeds, with excellent planting information, as well as tools and supplies for natural pest control.

Nichols Garden Nursery

1190 Old Salem Road, NE
Albany, OR 97321-4580
(800) 422-3985
www.nicholsgardennursery.com
Specializes in herb seeds and plants and vegetable seeds (including many Asian varieties). Also offers seeds of edible flowers, a mix of flowers to attract beneficial insects, and cover crop seeds.

Renee's Garden Seeds

7389 West Zayante Road
Felton, CA 95018
(888) 880-7228
www.reneesgarden.com
Sells vegetable, herb, and flower seeds from around the world (many open-pollinated varieties) through its Web site and at nurseries.

Seeds of Change

P.O. Box 157000
Santa Fe, NM 87592-1500
(888) 762-7333
www.seedsofchange.com
Offers seeds of rare heirloom and traditional native vegetables, including sizable collections of beans, corn, sunflowers, tomatoes, and herbs, all open-pollinated and organically grown.

Territorial Seed Company

P.O. Box 158
Cottage Grove, OR 97424-0061
(541) 942-9547
www.territorialseed.com
Offers an extensive assortment of vegetable seeds and plants, many organically grown, as well as herb and cover crop seeds, seed potatoes, garlic, berry plants, tools, and supplies, including beneficial insects and natural pest-control products.

Vermont Bean Seed Company

334 West Stroud Street
Randolph, WI 53956-1274
(800) 349-1071
www.vermontbean.com
Specializes in seeds for beans (including numerous dried bean varieties); also offers a good selection of other vegetable seeds.

supplies

These firms offer a wide selection of cover crop seeds, inoculants, beneficial insects, natural pest-control products, fertilizers, plastic mulches, compost-making supplies, season extenders (such as row covers), seed-starting supplies, and tools.

Gardens Alive
5100 Schenley Place
Lawrenceburg, IN 47025
(513) 354-1482
www.gardensalive.com

Harmony Farm Supply and Nursery
P.O. Box 460
Graton, CA 95444
(707) 823-9125
www.harmonyfarm.com

Peaceful Valley Farm Supply
P.O. Box 2209
Grass Valley, CA 95945
(888) 784-1722
www.groworganic.com

SETTING OUT
BARE-ROOT STOCK

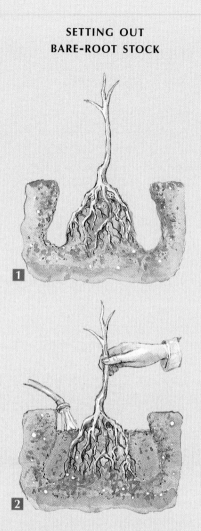

1 | *Make a firm cone of soil in the planting hole. Spread the roots over the cone, positioning them so that the bud union (a slightly swollen area on the lower part of the trunk on grafted trees) is 2 to 3 inches above the ground.*

2 | *Backfill the hole with soil, firming it with your fingers. When backfilling is almost complete, add water. If the plant settles, pump it up and down while the soil is wet to raise it to the proper level. Finish filling the hole with soil, and then water again.*

planting and training fruit trees

During the winter dormant season, you can plant bare-root trees (and cane berries and grapes, as well), carry out formative training of trees (including espalier training), and prune mature trees. This is also the time to spray fruit trees with dormant oil to protect against pests.

planting bare-root stock

If you want to add fruit trees, cane berries, or grapes to your garden, winter is the best time. These plants are traditionally sold bare-root—that is, they are dug while dormant and sold without soil around the roots. Bare-root stock is available in late winter and very early spring from retail nurseries and mail-order companies.

Most fruit trees require some initial pruning at planting time. How to do this depends on the training system you choose; see the descriptions on the next page. Some dwarfing rootstocks for fruit trees result in shallow-rooted trees that require staking as soon as they are planted; check with the supplier to find out if your trees should be staked. Grapes and cane berries are also cut back at planting time; see the listings on pages 106–190 for information on each type.

Before planting, soak the roots in a bucket of water for a minimum of 4 hours (preferably overnight). Just before planting, cut any broken or damaged roots back to healthy tissue; also prune roots that are much longer than all the others. Dig a planting hole with sides that taper outward into the soil. Make the hole twice as wide as the roots of the plant and about the same depth. Roughen the sides of the hole with a spading fork; if the sides are left smooth, it can be difficult for the roots to penetrate the soil. Plant as shown at left.

training young fruit trees

While they are young, fruit trees need training to establish a strong, well-balanced framework of branches that can support future crops. Prune them initially only enough to develop the desired framework: too much pruning delays fruiting.

Two main training systems are used; consult the listings on pages 106–190 for the system recommended for your trees. Central leader training produces a straight-trunked pyramidal tree, with tiers of branches radiating out from the trunk. Such a tree can become quite tall, so this method is best for dwarf and semidwarf trees. An open-center tree, also described as bowl shaped or vase shaped, has several main limbs angling outward from the top of a short trunk. Such a tree can be kept shorter than one trained to a central leader.

In either system, try to select scaffold (primary) branches that meet the trunk at an angle of between 45 and 60 degrees. These are the most fruitful and begin bearing sooner than branches with a narrower angle.

TRAINING TO A CENTRAL LEADER

1 | At planting time, choose the first set of three to five scaffold branches (for simplicity, only two are shown here). Cut off other branches, and cut back the leader to just above buds to get a second tier of branches 18 to 30 inches above the lower set. If the tree is an unbranched whip or does not have good scaffold branches, cut back the trunk to 2 feet above ground level to force branches to grow; plan to carry out this step the next winter.

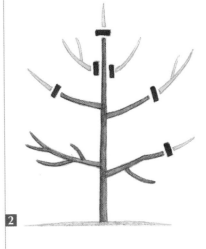

2 | The next dormant season, choose a higher set of scaffold branches from those that grew during the previous summer. Remove unwanted branches, and head back the leader again so that another tier of branches will grow at the proper distance above the previous tier. Also shorten the scaffolds to force lateral (side) branches to grow.

3 | For the next one or two dormant seasons, choose a new, higher tier of three to five scaffold branches. For good light penetration, maintain open space between tiers and keep the branches toward the top of the tree shorter than those toward the bottom. Don't allow fruit to set on the leader, which would bend it over.

TRAINING TO AN OPEN CENTER

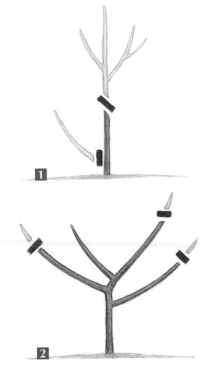

1 | At planting time, head back the trunk so that it is 2 to 3 feet high (even shorter, if desired). New branches will grow from buds below the cut. Remove all other shoots.

2 | The next dormant season, choose three to five scaffold or framework branches. They should spiral around the trunk, with at least 6 inches of vertical space between them. Head back these branches to 2 to 3 feet in length.

3 | The following dormant season, choose two strong lateral (side) branches on each scaffold branch, and cut back the scaffolds to the chosen laterals. Head back the laterals to 2 to 3 feet (if they exceed that), to force additional lateral branches to grow.

TYPES OF PRUNING CUTS

THINNING CUTS open up a tree to sunlight and air circulation and cause the least amount of regrowth. To thin, remove an entire branch, taking it back to its point of origin on the trunk or another branch.

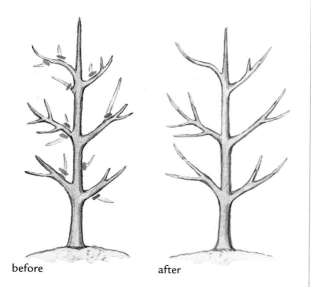

before   after

HEADING CUTS stimulate buds just below the cut to grow, producing clusters of new shoots. In heading, you remove just part of a stem or branch.

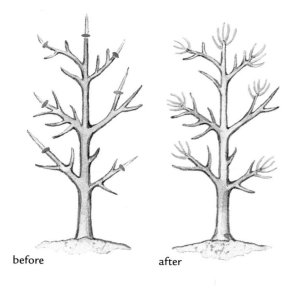

before   after

dormant-season pruning

Most pruning of mature deciduous fruit trees is done during the dormant season. When trees are leafless, you can more easily see the shape of the tree and the positions of branches and buds. In cold-winter climates, wait until late in the dormant season before pruning. East of the Rockies, waiting until spring growth begins can help deter diseases of apricots, plums, peaches, and nectarines. Some pruning of vigorous trees can be carried out in summer (see page 67).

For all deciduous fruit trees, start by removing dead or broken branches. Also remove branches that crowd or cross other branches, suckers (stems growing from the base of the tree or its roots), and water sprouts (upright, overvigorous shoots growing on branches or along the trunk). Then prune to maximize fruit production: remove old growth that is no longer productive, thin out any large limbs that shade other fruit-producing branches, and remove small, shaded branches growing from the lower surface of larger branches. See the listings on pages 106–190 for more on pruning different types of fruit trees.

When removing superfluous branches, it's usually best to use thinning cuts rather than heading cuts (see drawings), to avoid stimulating excessive new growth. When you remove a branch, don't make a flush cut. Position your shears or saw just outside the branch collar, the wrinkled area (or bulge) at the base of the branch where it meets another branch or the trunk. Also take care not to slice into the branch bark ridge (the raised bark in the branch crotch). Leaving these areas intact keeps decay to a minimum.

Use heading cuts (also called heading back) when you want to force new growth, for example, in training a tree initially. Heading cuts are also used when pruning nectarines and peaches. These trees fruit on year-old wood; making some heading cuts encourages the growth of new shoots each year. In contrast, most other fruit trees produce fruit on long-lived spurs, which look like short shoots or stubby twigs; don't cut these off unless they are overcrowded or no longer productive.

tip DORMANT-SEASON SPRAY Apply dormant oil spray when trees are leafless or as buds begin to develop. The oil coats many insects and their overwintering eggs or cocoons, smothering them.

espaliered fruit trees

The art of espalier—training trees to grow in a flat plane—is a time-honored and elegant way to reap a generous harvest of fruit from a small space. You can espalier trees along a fence, on wires fastened to a wall, or over an arbor.

Plant trees in full sun; in hot-summer areas, however, avoid planting against a light-colored, south-facing wall, or you'll cook your fruit. For a row, set trees 4 to 6 feet apart. The tiers of supports are usually spaced 12 to 18 inches apart. Tie branches to the supports with plastic nursery ties or raffia. Generally you need several years of training to develop an espalier pattern fully. Some nurseries sell apple trees already espaliered. Training apples to form a diamond-shaped fence is described on page 107.

The horizontal cordon, a popular pattern, is relatively easy to establish if your tree is already branched. If your tree is an unbranched whip (or has unsuitable branches), cut it back at or just above the lowest support, retaining two buds facing in opposite directions and a third bud to grow vertically. The tree will form branches in the next growing season; begin training the following winter. After you've established the espalier, prune wayward growth often to maintain its shape.

HORIZONTAL CORDON

1 | At planting, select two branches for the first tier (cordon); remove all other shoots, and head back the leader to just above the support wire. Bend the branches gently to about a 45° angle, and tie them to the wire.

2 | During the first growing season, gradually tighten the ties to lower the branches. They should be horizontal by autumn. Keep the leader erect, and tie it to the second-tier wire.

3 | In the first dormant season, head the leader close to the second wire. Select two branches for a second tier, and remove competing shoots. Prune the laterals (side shoots) on the first tier branches to three buds.

4 | In the second growing season, gradually bring the second-tier branches to a horizontal position. Keep the leader upright, and tie it to the third-tier wire. Repeat the process the next year for additional tiers.

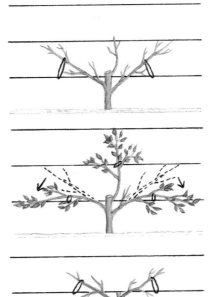

espalier patterns

Semidwarf and dwarf apple and pear trees can be trained to any of these patterns or to the horizontal cordon (see main text). A fan shape is generally best for apricots, figs, plums, peaches, and nectarines. Peaches and nectarines also do well in a Belgian fence.

Candelabra   Belgian Fence

Double U   Fan

special techniques

- Build raised beds to give your edibles better growing conditions.

- Use French intensive methods to make the maximum use of limited space.

- Compost.

- Try succession planting, interplanting, and vertical gardening to save space.

- Extend the season with plastic mulches and collars, crop covers, cold frames, and hotbeds.

creating raised beds

Gardeners favor raised beds for edibles for many good reasons. These beds overcome problems with poor soil (such as compacted, clay, or sandy soils), and they provide the good drainage plants need. The soil in raised beds warms up quickly in spring, so you can plant earlier. Because the soil is usually not walked upon, it remains loose and easier for roots to penetrate. You can fill raised beds with particular types of soil to suit specific plants—acid soil for blueberries, for example—and concentrate water and fertilizer where they are needed. And, as noted on page 79, lining the bottom of the bed with hardware cloth foils gophers.

Plan to make the beds no wider than 4 feet so that you can reach the middle easily. Length can vary, depending on your site and the materials available. Though you can make beds that are only 8 inches deep, a depth of 12 inches allows better root growth. For convenience, make sure the paths between beds are wide enough for you to maneuver a wheelbarrow on them. You can enclose raised beds with lumber, dry-stacked rocks, flagstones, bricks, or interlocking concrete blocks.

Fill the beds with amended native soil or purchased topsoil. In most instances, you can improve native soil by digging in a 4- to 6-inch layer of compost or other organic matter before planting. If your native soil is too hard or rocky to amend easily, bring in topsoil that contains at least $1/3$ organic matter by volume. After filling a raised bed, water well, and be prepared to add a little more soil before planting, because some settling will occur.

an easy-to-build raised bed

For a long-lasting bed with wooden sides, use rot-resistant redwood or cedar, or choose composite lumber, which is made from recycled wood and plastic. Avoid pressure-treated wood containing chromated copper arsenate (CCA) and creosote-treated railroad ties; studies suggest that these are not safe near food crops.

To make the 4-by-8-foot bed shown here, you'll need three boards that are 8 feet long, 1 foot wide, and 2 inches thick (thinner boards are not strong enough). Also have on hand a 4-foot-long 4-by-4 post and about a pound of 12d or 16d galvanized nails. (If you want to make a bed longer than 8 feet, plan to place stakes or posts along the sides to prevent bulging.)

Use two of the 8-foot boards for the sides of the bed; cut the remaining board in half to form the ends. To make the corner posts, cut the 4-by-4 into four segments, each 1 foot long.

Build the bed on a hard, level surface, such as a driveway. To make one side, lay one of the 8-foot boards flat, and place a corner post under each end; fasten posts with four or five nails. Repeat this step with the other 8-foot plank and remaining corner posts.

Next, stand one of the sides on edge and line one of the end boards up with it; fasten with nails. Nail the other end board in place. Then sandwich the remaining 8-foot side between the end boards, and nail it into place to complete the box.

Move the box to its permanent site. Use a carpenter's level to check that the top of the box is level. If not, move it aside and dig trenches to lower the sides that are too high.

applying french intensive methods

Developed by French market gardeners at the end of the 19th century, the French intensive method of growing vegetables makes maximum use of limited space. Its cornerstones include thorough soil preparation, planting in rounded mounds or beds, and close spacing of plants. Once mastered, French intensive methods give impressive harvests from small gardens.

soil preparation

Begin by dividing your planting area into beds running north and south. Plan to make the beds 3 to 5 feet across, so you can reach the middle of each bed easily from the permanent paths around the beds. Remove weeds, and double-dig each bed, as shown at left, to create a light, fluffy cushion of soil, rich in organic matter and nutrients.

double digging

The soil-preparation technique called double digging loosens the soil deeply, incorporates air, and adds amendments. Double-dug soil supports close planting, because roots grow more freely and water can penetrate easily. It's hard work, but the results last for years, especially if you aerate the soil each year (see sidebar, page 97).

1 | *Dig a trench as deep as your spade blade along one side of the plot. Mound the soil from this trench nearby.*

2 | *Loosen soil in the bottom of the trench with a spade or spading fork; mix in several inches of organic matter, such as compost.*

3 | *Dig a second trench one spade-blade deep alongside the first. Shovel the excavated soil from the second trench into the first trench along with more organic matter and a fertilizer high in phosphorus and potassium (such as a 5-10-10 product).*

4 | *Loosen the soil in the bottom of the second trench; mix in organic matter. Continue to dig trenches across the plot in the same way. Fill in the last trench with soil saved from the first.*

After digging, leave the soil rough for several days to settle. Then break up any clods of earth, and rake the surface into a smooth, mounded bed, high in the middle with the edges sloping down to the paths on all four sides. Water the bed, and let the soil settle again for a few days; to avoid compacting the soil, take care not to step on the beds. Then set out your plants or sow seeds.

Before planting subsequent crops, work several inches of organic matter, plus fertilizer, into the top few inches of soil. You can help keep the soil in your French intensive beds loose and fluffy by aerating it once a year (see sidebar at right).

close spacing

In French intensive gardens, plants are spaced more closely than in traditional gardens, which have widely spaced rows. Careful soil preparation allows vegetables to thrive when planted close together, leading to larger yields. At almost all stages of growth, the leaves of vegetable crops shade the soil. This leafy cover acts as a living mulch, reducing moisture loss, slowing the growth of weeds, and preventing fluctuations in soil temperature.

When you sow seeds directly in the garden, scatter most kinds over the bed so that they are about the same distance apart as recommended (in the listings on pages 106–190 and on seed packets) for sowing in rows. Root crops, such as carrots, and salad crops can be sown more closely; begin thinning them when they are quite small, using the thinnings as delicious baby vegetables and for delicate salads. Continue thinning regularly as the plants mature, to give them enough growing room.

Some plants grow so tall or large that solid coverage of a wide mound isn't practical. You can still grow such plants in double-dug mounds (and they'll give a generous harvest), but you plant them in the usual way— clusters (hills) of seeds for melons and squash, and rows for climbing peas, pole beans, corn, potatoes, and tomatoes, spaced in normal fashion.

When you set out transplants, such as cabbage or broccoli, space them so that their outer leaves will touch as they approach mature size.

FACING PAGE *Close planting maximizes growing space in French intensive gardens.*

RIGHT *Set off by feathery fennel, the spreading leaves of cabbage and chard shade the soil.*

soil aeration

Once you've double-dug garden beds, aerating the soil helps keep it loose, making it easy for both roots and water to penetrate. You can do this with a spading fork or a specially designed larger fork, called a broadfork, garden digger, or U-bar; these long-handled tools are 20 to 24 inches wide, with tines 11 to 14 inches long. To use one, hold a handle in each hand, press the tool into the soil with one foot, and pull back on the handles to lift the soil a bit. Then pull the tool out of the soil, move it back a few inches and repeat. You can accomplish the same task with a spading fork, but since it is smaller it takes longer to aerate the same area.

composting with worms

Worm composting, or vermicom-posting, is an efficient way to compost fruit and vegetable scraps from the kitchen in a small amount of space. Red wiggler worms and bins for housing them are sold in nurseries and by mail-order suppliers. Or use a covered homemade wooden bin about 2 feet square and 8 to 16 inches deep; for drainage, drill holes in the bottom about 6 inches apart. Place the bin in a shaded, rain-protected spot where it won't freeze or overheat from sun expo-sure. Fill the bin with bedding made from shredded newspaper. Feed the worms kitchen scraps: 2 pounds of worms can process about 7 pounds of vegetable scraps each week. After 3 to 6 months, you can begin har-vesting the compost (worm castings), which looks like dark, rich, crumbly soil.

composting

Composting is a natural process that converts raw organic material into a valuable soil conditioner you can use to improve the texture of your soil, boost its nutrient content, and help it retain water better.

A pile of leaves, branches, and other garden trimmings tossed in a corner of the garden will eventually decompose with no intervention on your part. However, this simple approach, called *slow* or *cold composting*, can take as long as a year to produce results. With a little effort, you can hasten the process considerably. If you create optimum conditions for the organisms responsible for decay, by giving them the mixture of air, water, and materials rich in carbon and nitrogen that they need, your compost pile will heat up quickly and decompose in a few months. Such *hot composting* also destroys many (though not all) weeds and disease pathogens.

You can make compost in a free-standing pile or use an enclosure (see page 99). Whichever method you choose, the fundamentals of composting are the same.

Making compost recycles garden and kitchen waste to create a rich soil amendment.

GATHER AND PREPARE THE MATERIALS You'll need approximately equal volumes of brown matter and green matter. *Brown matter* is high in carbon and includes dry leaves, hay, sawdust, wood chips, and woody prunings. *Green matter* is high in nitrogen and includes grass, kitchen scraps (do not use bones or dairy products), and animal manure (do not include dog or cat manure). Avoid badly diseased or insect-infested plants, weeds with seeds, and pernicious perennial weeds that might survive composting. The compost will heat up faster if you collect the ingredients in advance and assemble the pile all at once.

Shredding or chopping large, rough materials into smaller pieces allows decay-producing organisms to reach more surfaces, speeding the composting process. Shredder-chippers and lawn mowers are good tools for this purpose; you can also chop the materials with a machete on a large wooden block.

BUILD THE PILE Constructing the pile like a layer cake makes it easier to judge the ratio of brown to green materials. Start by spreading a 4- to 8-inch layer of brown material over an area at least 3 feet square; then add a layer of green material about 2 to 8 inches deep. (Layers of grass clippings should be only 2 inches deep; less-dense green materials can be layered more thickly.) Add another layer of brown material, and sprinkle the pile with water. Mix these first three layers with a spading fork. Continue adding layers, watering, and mixing. To heat up efficiently, the pile should be about 3 feet tall and 3 feet wide, giving it a volume of about 1 cubic yard.

TURN THE PILE In just a few days, the pile should heat up dramatically. In time, it will decompose on its own, but you can hurry things along by turning the contents to introduce more oxygen. Using a spading fork or pitchfork, restack the pile, redistributing it so that the materials originally on the outside are moved to the pile's center, where they'll be exposed to higher heat. If necessary, add water; the pile should be as moist as a wrung-out sponge. Turn the pile weekly, if possible, until it is no longer generating internal heat and most of the materials have decomposed.

USE THE COMPOST Finished compost is dark and crumbly, with a pleasant, earthy aroma. Mix it into your planting beds or use it as mulch. If some of the material is coarser than you like, incorporate it into your next compost pile. To obtain a fine-textured compost to use as potting soil, sift the finished compost through a screen with $1/2$-inch mesh.

tip **COMPOST TEA** This nutrient-rich brew is easy to make and use. Half-fill a burlap bag (or, for smaller batches, an old nylon stocking) with finished compost or worm castings. Place the bag in a barrel, large bucket, or watering can, and fill the container with water. Let the brew steep for several days. Sprinkle the resulting brownish liquid around your plants. Do this several times during the growing season to give plants a quick boost. Some mail-order suppliers offer compost tea machines that aerate and stir the brew, increasing the number of beneficial microbes it contains.

composting systems

You can make compost in a freestanding pile or in a homemade structure; various plastic composters are also sold at garden centers.

FREESTANDING COMPOST PILES

An unenclosed pile should be at least 3 feet high and wide; at this size, its mass is great enough to generate the microbial activity needed to heat the materials. The upper size limit is about 5 feet high and wide; a larger pile may not receive enough air at its center. When siting the pile, allow space alongside for turning the compost.

WIRE CYLINDERS OR HOOPS

For a wire-enclosed system, use welded wire, chicken wire, or snow fencing, supported with stakes, if necessary. The cylinder or hoop should be about 4 feet in diameter and 3 to 4 feet tall. To turn the pile, lift the cylinder and move it to one side; then fork the materials back into it.

THREE-BIN SYSTEMS
Three compost bins in a row make a more complex system than a single pile or cylinder, but they offer a convenient way to handle compost sequentially. The left bin holds new green and brown material; the center one contains partly decomposed material; the right bin holds nearly finished or finished compost. Turn the materials in each bin weekly, moving decomposed material to the right. The center and right bins will be empty at the start. In the design shown here, the side boards are spaced to allow air circulation, and they slide out to make turning and removing the compost easy.

4-by-4
1-by-1
2-by-6

2-by-2 spacer between 2-by-6s

saving space

Reaping the maximum yield from a small garden is a challenge. Learning a few special tricks and techniques can make a big difference, allowing you to harvest a wide variety of vegetables over a long season. In addition to the ideas on these two pages, consider French intensive gardening (pages 96–97), raised beds (pages 94–95), and container gardening (page 58) for saving space. Raising cool-season crops (pages 82–83) and protecting plants from cold weather (pages 56 and 102–103) are other ways to make full use of your garden.

succession planting

Some vegetables grow so fast that you can plant another crop as soon as the first one is finished. For example, in the space where you've harvested an early spring crop of lettuce or radishes, plan to dig in compost and a little fertilizer and sow bush beans. In late summer, when those crops are finished, succeed them with cabbage seedlings or spinach for fall harvest. In other words, don't let valuable garden space lie empty and unproductive: be ready to plant something new throughout your growing season. It helps to keep a few vegetable seedlings on hand, ready to transplant when even a small bit of garden ground becomes available.

Another type of succession is also useful: you stretch the harvest period by planting seeds or young plants at roughly two-week intervals. The successive plantings, each in a relatively small plot, produce a continuous supply rather than one big harvest all at once. This technique works especially well for bush beans, lettuce and other salad greens, scallions, and radishes. For some crops you can stretch the harvest by planting early-, mid-, and late-

cut-and-come-again crops

Gardeners often think of vegetable harvests as a one-time proposition. And this is true for plants such as corn and melons: once the ears or fruits are picked, that's it. However, you can cut leaves as you need them from many greens and salad crops, and the plants will grow more leaves for future harvests. Such cut-and-come-again crops save you space—and time and effort, as well. Depending on the crop, you can harvest leaves when the plants are only about 4 inches high or when they are more mature.

Mesclun, a mix of salad ingredients (see page 149), is grown closely spaced and harvested when very young. Gather the leaves by snipping them all off with scissors when they are only a few inches high, leaving 1 to 2 inches of stems to regrow. Various leafy greens can be harvested the same way as baby greens. Leaf lettuces, arugula, and mustard greens (such as mizuna and 'Red Giant') are good choices. Keep cutting until the greens bolt (go to seed) or become bitter or tough.

Many greens will keep producing for a long time if you pick the outer leaves as they become large enough to use, leaving the plant to grow more. Besides leaf lettuce, arugula, and mustards, you can harvest chard, leaf chicory, endive and escarole, kale, bok choy, and spinach this way.

TOP *Even a wooden crate can produce several cut-and-come-again harvests of salad greens.*

RIGHT *This early-spring crop of peas will be harvested and out of the way before the young beans in front need more space.*

season varieties of the same crop all at once. Try this method to harvest sweet corn over a long period.

When you plan any sort of succession planting, check the listings on pages 106–190 and on seed packets for information on how many days each crop takes to mature. Also keep records in your garden journal to inform your future plantings.

interplanting

Also known as *intercropping,* interplanting is the practice of growing two different crops in the same spot. Some vegetables, such as cabbages and tomatoes, grow fairly slowly. Around or alongside them, you can plant a fast-growing crop that will be ready for harvest before the slower crop needs the entire space. Fast-growing crops for this technique include radishes, turnips, lettuce, and many other salad plants and greens.

For another sort of interplanting, try growing small, compact crops, such as beets, parsley, and basil, close to tall crops (such as corn, pole beans, or tomatoes trained on a trellis) or around fruit trees. The smaller plants appreciate the shade created by the larger ones. A classic example of interplanting is pole beans grown so that they climb and twine around sturdy cornstalks. Plant the beans after the corn has become established.

vertical gardening

Whenever possible, use vertical supports such as stakes, frames, tepees, and trellises (see page 57). Plants trained to grow upward take much less ground-level space than those allowed to sprawl. In addition to pole beans, peas, and tomatoes, you can train vining varieties of cucumbers, summer and winter squashes, and melons to grow on supports.

Tall and thin, scallions take up little space planted among low-growing lettuces.

ABOVE *Use netting or old nylons to support the heavy fruits of melons (and winter squashes) as they mature.*

RIGHT *Save valuable garden space by training squash to grow on a tepee.*

extending the season

In cold-winter climates, finding ways to extend the growing season—that is, keep plants a bit warmer in early spring, in late fall, and even in winter—significantly increases your overall harvest. Even in the mild climates of the Pacific Coast and the South, some forms of climate modification are useful, especially in getting warm-season crops started. For protection that lasts many weeks, try various plastic products or cold frames. For short-term frost protection for small plants, see page 56.

One way to get a head start in spring is to pre-warm the soil. Spreading either black plastic or special infrared-transmitting plastic mulch over your planting beds 1 or 2 weeks before you sow seeds or set out transplants warms the soil; it also helps to dry soil that is too wet. This allows you to plant heat-loving crops such as corn, melons, squash, tomatoes, and peppers earlier. For more on plastic mulches, see page 66.

Gardeners use clear plastic, as well, to extend the growing season. You can make a low tunnel greenhouse to protect seedlings in spring by stretching clear plastic over a framework of wire hoops or PVC pipe. Some kinds of floating row covers serve similar purposes (see page 56).

Mail-order companies offer a product designed especially for tomatoes: small, hollow plastic cylinders are connected to form a tepee-shaped collar, which you place over a tomato plant. Then you fill the cylinders with water. The collars trap a great deal of heat, boosting growth and providing frost protection, so you can set out the seedlings a month or more earlier than you would unprotected plants. These devices are tall enough to be left in place until the weather is thoroughly warm.

a cover-up for winter vegetables

Falling somewhere between raised beds with fitted covers and large cold frames, the arrangement shown above is designed specifically to protect cool-season crops, such as arugula, lettuce, greens for cooking, and root crops. The covers should be placed over the beds before the first frosts strike in fall and may extend your harvests well into winter. (For more on growing cool-season vegetables, see pages 82–83.)

These beds are edged with 2-by-10s. Each arched cover is formed from three half circles of plywood topped by horizontal lath strips, with ultraviolet-resistant plastic sheeting stapled over them. Hinges fasten the covers to the wooden edging. At 2 feet tall, the covers allow enough headroom for taller crops, such as kale and chard. For ventilation, prop the covers open during the day when the temperature is above freezing.

Make your own cold-protection for tomatoes by fastening clear plastic sheeting around a wire tomato cage. In spring, leave the plastic in place until warm weather has arrived. In fall, you can put the plastic on again to prolong your tomato harvest.

cold frames and hotbeds

Basically a box with a transparent lid, a cold frame acts as a passive solar energy collector and reservoir. During the day, the sun's rays heat the air and soil in the frame; at night, the heat absorbed by the soil radiates out, keeping the plants warm.

Cold frames have many uses in edible gardening. In very early spring, sow seeds of cool-season vegetables directly in the frame, and grow the plants there until it's time to transplant them to the garden. Later in spring, use a cold frame to harden off seedlings of warm-season crops started indoors (see page 53). For fall and winter harvests in cold climates, plant cool-season vegetables in a cold frame base. Put on the cover before freezing weather arrives.

Orient your cold frame to face south or southwest, so that it receives as much sunlight as possible. Choose a location protected from harsh wind by a wall or hedge.

how to make a hotbed

Seeds germinate quickly in the warm soil of a hotbed. To convert your cold frame to a hotbed, add an electric soil-heating cable. You can buy cables with built-in thermostats; most models turn on when soil temperature falls below 75°F/ 24°C. Be sure to use a weatherproof GFCI-protected outlet. Make a bed for the cable by digging out 2 to 3 inches of the soil below the cold frame; fill the hole with sand. Lay the cable in loops, spaced 6 to 8 inches apart and 3 inches away from the sides of the frame. Add another inch of sand and then a sheet of window screen or hardware cloth to protect the cables. Finish the bed with a 4-inch layer of sand in which to sink planted pots. If you intend to plant directly in the hotbed, spread about 4 inches of potting soil, instead of sand, over the screen.

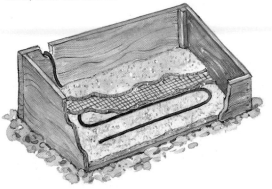

how to build a cold frame

Ready-made cold frames are sold by mail-order suppliers and some nurseries, but it is not difficult to make your own.

1 | *Plan to make the frame about 3 feet wide, so you can reach the plants inside easily; it can be as long as you need. Use rot-resistant lumber, such as redwood or cedar. Cut the sides so that the frame slopes from about 1½ feet high at the back to 1 foot high at the front; this captures more heat and allows rainwater to run off. To give strength, reinforce the corners of the box with vertical posts.*

For the cover, use a recycled window, or staple plastic sheeting to a wooden frame. If the cold frame is longer than about 4 feet, make the cover in sections, so it won't be too heavy to lift. Apply weather stripping around the top edges of the box, and attach the cover with galvanized steel hinges.

2 | *Provide ventilation to prevent overheating. A minimum-maximum thermometer is useful for keeping track of temperature fluctuations. Plan to prop open the cover when the temperature reaches about 70°F/21°C. Close the cover in late afternoon to trap heat. If you won't be around during the day, install a nonelectric vent-controller that automatically opens and closes the cover at a preset temperature. On very cold nights, drape the frame with an old blanket or piece of carpet to provide extra insulation.*

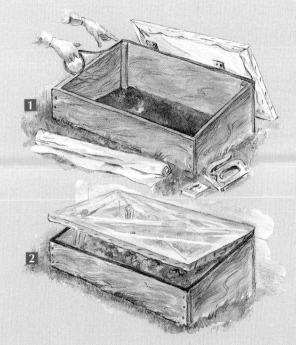

edibles a–z

- Choose from 15 fruit crops, apples to watermelons, including, of course, raspberries and strawberries.

- Select vegetables for spring and fall planting; take a look at more than 40 kinds.

- Plan an herb garden: start at basil, purple-leafed or plain green; thumb through to thyme, common or lemon.

- For fun, grow edible flowers such as Johnny-jump-ups, lavender, and sunflowers.

- At harvest time, make basil or lavender lemonade, berry sherbet, stir-fried garlic lettuce; check out the many recipes included here.

- And see the projects in sidebars: Build an apple fence or a bean tepee. Plant citrus, herbs, peppers, potatoes, and tomatoes in pots and grapes on an arbor. Grow a colossal pumpkin.

apples

Deciduous tree, 5 to 16 feet tall, depending on whether dwarf or semidwarf.

Colonnade apple trees fit easily into the smallest gardens. They grow to 8 feet tall but only 2 feet wide. In summer, prune long stems back to three leaves.

You don't need a big yard to grow apples; dwarf and semi-dwarf trees stop growing at a manageable height. You can also espalier a dwarf apple tree—train it so that the branches grow horizontally along a fence or wall. Other space-saving options are a small "multiple-variety" tree that has three to five varieties grafted onto it or a colonnade tree. If you have just a deck garden, plant a dwarf tree in a half barrel or large pot. Most apple varieties need long, cold winters. Many apple trees won't bear fruit without cross-pollination, so choose at least two varieties that flower in the same period (early, midseason, or late).

POPULAR VARIETIES 'Fuji', late season variety, excellent flavor, stores well; 'Gala', early to midseason, beautiful red-on-yellow skin, yellow flesh; 'Liberty', midseason, disease resistant, red-flushed fruit tastes sweet-tart and is good for pies. *For mild-winter regions:* 'Anna', early season, large pale green fruit blushed with red, bears reliably every year; 'Dorsett Golden', early, progeny of 'Golden Delicious', good fresh or cooked; 'Winter Banana', late midseason, pale yellow fruit blushed with pink.

BEST SITE Sunny, with deep, well-drained soil.

PLANTING AND CARE Container-grown trees can be planted anytime except during extreme summer heat; for planting information, see page 54. Plant bare-root (dormant) apple trees in winter or early spring; for planting information, see page 88.

To train a tree during the first few years, see pages 88–89, 91 (use the open-center or central-leader system, or espalier).

Water consistently, especially while fruit is developing. The soil should always be moist (but not soggy) to a depth of at least 1 foot. Periodic deep soakings are best.

Feed with a low-nitrogen complete fertilizer at the start of the growing season; follow the directions on the bag, reducing the amount while your tree is young or if you have a dwarf tree. Too much nitrogen produces a big tree with smaller fruit yields.

Thin heavy crops when the fruit is small, to prevent branches from breaking and to keep trees fruiting well (heavy crops deplete the tree's reserves and may cause a very light crop the following year). Be especially careful not to let a new tree bear a heavy crop; severely thinning the fruit will allow the tree to establish more strongly.

During winter, remove any weak, dead, or crossed branches (see page 90) to create a healthy, well-shaped tree; if necessary, remove branches or twigs growing toward the center of the tree, because crops are heavier and disease incidence lower when some sunlight can reach the middle.

To restrict tree growth in a small garden area, practice summer pruning (see page 67).

The main insect pests are codling moth, and, east of the Rockies, apple maggot and plum curculio. All three infest the fruit with larvae (causing wormy apples); to control codling moth and apple maggot, hang sticky insect traps in the tree (see drawing). To control plum curculio, spread a cloth beneath the tree just after the blossoms drop, shake the branches, collect the fallen adults, and discard them; or spray with a natural pesticide (see pages 72–73) at that time, following label directions. Leafhoppers (page 75) may also trouble apples.

Many diseases, including apple scab, cedar apple rust, fireblight (see Pears, page 161), and powdery mildew (see page 78), also plague apples, particularly in regions east of the Rockies; choose disease-resistant varieties, and thoroughly rake up and discard fallen leaves and fruit, so spores (and insects) do not overwinter. A dormant-season oil spray (see page 91) applied just when the buds are showing green also helps prevent trouble. If cedar-apple rust is a problem in your area, be sure not to grow eastern red cedars, the other host it needs in order to reproduce.

Set out a codling moth trap just before blossoms open, and replace it after 9 or 10 weeks.

tip If exposed to harsh summer sun, the tree's thin bark can suffer sunburn. To prevent this, whitewash the trunk (with commercial whitewash or white latex paint) or wrap it in burlap. If you have a choice of planting spots, choose an east-facing one.

HARVEST July to early November, depending on the variety. Yields vary, depending on the size, age, and variety of the tree. When picking, keep stems on the apples, but take care not to damage the "spurs"—the short, knobby branches that produce the fruit. To store, wrap apples in paper, and keep in a cool, frost-free place.

FOR THE TABLE Thinly slice ¼ apple into a cheese sandwich (perhaps Swiss cheese on walnut bread spread with honey mustard) and toast it.

apple fence

This 6-foot-tall lattice apple fence consists of bamboo poles and dwarf apple trees. To create the grid, tie bamboo poles in a diamond pattern; the diamonds measure about 2 feet on each side. Plant dormant bare-root dwarf apple trees (see page 88) 2½ feet apart, slanting them 45° to line up with the diagonal grid. Loosely tie the trunks to the poles. Remove the poles in a few years when the tree trunks are larger. For pruning information and other espalier ideas, see pages 89–91.

apricots

Deciduous tree, 6 to 20 feet tall, depending on type and whether dwarf or semidwarf.

With its glossy leaves and froth of white or pink blossoms in early spring, an apricot tree makes a handsome small shade tree or an espaliered fan on a house wall. Smaller, shrubby Asian apricot varieties also make a fine hedge.

Because apricots flower so early, their tender buds and blossoms are susceptible to frost damage; the problem is especially significant in regions prone to surprise late spring frosts. Extrahardy varieties are available for cold-winter areas (but the blossoms may still be damaged by a late frost), and some varieties tolerate humidity well. Most varieties are self-pollinating, but some require a second variety as a pollenizer. Choose varieties carefully; consult a regional nursery or your Cooperative Extension Office for the most successful selections in your area.

POPULAR VARIETIES 'Harcot', self-pollinating, cold hardy and good for areas with late frosts, resistant to brown rot; 'Moongold', needs a second variety, such as 'Sungold', to pollinate it, very cold hardy and very resistant to disease; 'Royal Blenheim', self-pollinating, grown widely in California.

BEST SITE Sunny and sheltered; avoid ground that has grown other crops (eggplant, tomatoes, peppers, potatoes, raspberries, and strawberries) that are susceptible to verticillium wilt (see page 78).

PLANTING AND CARE Container-grown trees can be planted anytime except during extreme summer heat; for planting information, see page 54. Plant bare-root (dormant) apricot trees in winter or early spring; for planting information, see page 88.

To train a tree during the first few years, see pages 88–89, 91 (use the open-center system, or espalier). To restrict tree growth in a small area, practice summer pruning (see page 67).

If your tree is coming into bloom or blooming and a late frost is forecast, you can help protect the blossoms by throwing a light sheet over the tree.

Water consistently from bloom until harvest; deep soakings are best. Feed with a low-nitrogen complete fertilizer in early spring; apricot is a naturally vigorous tree, so it doesn't usually need much nitrogen.

To get a good crop of large apricots and prevent branches from breaking under too heavy a load, thin fruits when still small but after the natural fruit drop, leaving 2 to 4 inches between individual apricots. Be especially careful not to let a new tree bear a heavy crop; severely thinning the fruit will allow the tree to establish more strongly.

Prune every year (see page 90), but only moderately. Wait until the tree has bloomed; dormant pruning may prompt it to flower even earlier. Keep enough new growth for a satisfactory crop, and remove old growth that is no longer producing fruit (spurs produce fruit for only about 4 years).

Brown rot and bacterial canker are serious diseases affecting apricots. Choose resistant varieties; clean up well in fall, so brown rot fungus does not overwinter on fallen fruit; inspect your tree carefully, starting in early spring, and prune out affected twigs and branches, sterilizing your shears with rubbing alcohol after each cut if you suspect canker. Verticillium wilt may also be a problem (see page 78).

HARVEST Midsummer, when fruit is slightly soft. Yields vary, depending on the size, age, and variety of the tree.

FOR THE TABLE Combine with fresh cherries in a fruit tart or crumble.

> **tip** To make a garden talking point, plant an aprium next to your apricot. Aprium is a hybrid between apricot and plum; it tastes only a little like plum. Treat it just as you would an apricot tree.

---

artichokes

Cool-season perennial or annual; needs frost protection.

Bristly thistle relatives, artichokes have tender, delicious hearts and leaf bases inside their big round buds. They aren't easy to grow unless you live in a region with cool summers and mild winters such as coastal California. There, they are perennials, producing reliably for several years. In areas where winter temperatures drop below freezing, with a little fuss you can grow them as annuals.

POPULAR VARIETIES 'Green Globe', for mild coastal areas; 'Imperial Star', best for growing as an annual; 'Violetto', purplish elongated buds.

BEST SITE Sheltered, with rich, well-drained soil.

PLANTING AND CARE To grow as perennials in a mild-winter climate, set out young plants (root divisions) in winter or spring when they become available at nurseries. Place them 4 to 6 feet apart, with growth buds or shoots just above the soil surface.

To grow as annuals in cold-winter climates, sow seeds in flats or pots indoors (see page 52) 8 to 12 weeks before the last frost. Transplant outdoors after the danger of frost has passed.

Water plants weekly, more frequently in hot climates—dryness makes artichokes tough. Apply mulch (see page 66), especially in hot-summer areas, to keep the soil cool and moist. Watch for slugs; see page 76 for nontoxic treatments.

An artichoke plant is so handsome you might place one in a flower bed.

'Violetto' artichoke

Artichoke plants are killed by temperatures below 28°F/–2°C. Help protect the roots by applying a thick mulch in fall. Feed perennial plants once a year, in spring or fall.

> **tip** The soil must drain well, so, before planting, dig a 3-inch layer of compost or rotted manure into the top foot.

HARVEST Summer. Cut buds while they are still tight, including 1 to 1½ inches of stem. Expect 12 or more buds per plant, fewer if grown as annuals.

FOR THE TABLE Make a dipping sauce with crushed garlic and melted butter or mayonnaise.

arugula
(roquette, rocket)

Cool-season annual; withstands light frosts.

Arugula is often a component of mesclun, a mix of tasty young lettuces and piquant greens.

This fast-maturing, very easy-to-grow salad green has a spicy tang somewhere between cress and horseradish. Get it going early in spring so you can harvest it before warm weather makes it "bolt" into flower; or sow it in late summer, when the weather is growing cooler. Arugula reseeds itself around the garden if you let it flower. (For other peppery salad greens, see Lettuces, Salad Greens, page 148, and Nasturtiums, page 154.)

BEST SITE Sunny or partially shady, with fertile soil.

PLANTING AND CARE Sow seeds ½ inch deep and 2 inches apart in rows 16 inches apart, or scatter them in a patch. When the seedlings have 4 or 5 leaves, thin the plants to 6 inches apart (eat the thinnings). Sow in early spring and late summer, even into fall if your winters are mild. Keep the soil moist. Weed regularly. Arugula is not prone to pests or diseases.

HARVEST From 25 to 40 days after sowing. Pull up the entire plant when leaves are still young and tender (if you let the plants shoot up and bloom, you can eat the flowers and flower buds, but the leaves will be too tough and sour). Alternatively, harvest only young leaves from the plant center, leaving the plant to produce a second crop of new young leaves. A 10-foot row should give enough leaves for a family of four.

tip To extend your harvest, sow small amounts of seed every 2 weeks, and also practice "cut-and-come-again" harvesting—snip off all the leaves about 1 inch above the crown, and wait for new leaves to grow (see page 100).

FOR THE TABLE Mix arugula with lettuce leaves to reduce its peppery bite. Or serve it straight, with a simple dressing of vinegar or lemon juice and oil.

asparagus

Cool-season perennial; very cold-hardy.

An asparagus bed is an investment. It takes some work to get it going, and you won't harvest even a tiny crop until the second year, but thereafter the plants will produce bright green succulent spears during a 2- to 3-month period every spring for perhaps 20, or even 30, years.

POPULAR VARIETIES Male hybrids 'Jersey Giant' and 'UC 157' (male plants produce more, and larger, spears).

BEST SITE Sunny, with well-drained, rich soil free of weeds. If drainage is poor, build a raised bed (see pages 94–95).

PLANTING AND CARE Start in winter or early spring with 1-year-old crowns. Dig a trench 8 to 12 inches deep (deepest in the coldest-winter regions) and 12 inches wide. If you're planting more than one row, space rows 3 to 6 feet apart. Pile the soil to one side. Put a 2- to 3-inch layer of well-rotted manure into the trench, and sprinkle in a complete fertilizer. Don't stint on the manure or fertilizer; asparagus needs fertile soil. If the pH of your soil is below 6.0, add lime as well. Mix manure and fertilizer with the loose soil in the bottom of the trench, and mound the soil about 2 inches high in the trench center.

Along the top of the mound, space the crowns 15 inches apart, spreading the roots of each crown over the sides of the mound. Partially fill the trench with loose soil, from your soil pile, until the crowns are covered with 2 inches of soil.

As the shoots emerge, fill in soil around them, but be careful not to cover the tips of the shoots. The crowns should eventually be covered with 6 inches of soil, more if you made a deep trench; and the bed should mound at least a little above the surrounding soil so that water doesn't collect on it.

The first year, let all the shoots grow up and leaf out (don't cut any); the feathery foliage nourishes the growing roots and strengthens the plant for next year's crop. Keep the bed well watered during the first year. Apply a thick mulch (see page 66) to help keep the soil moist and reduce weeds.

Remove the foliage at the end of the year or when it dies back in fall. Cultivate gently around the crowns in the dormant season to remove weeds if necessary. Apply a high-nitrogen complete fertilizer in spring before spears emerge and again after harvest.

Aphids, asparagus beetles (which chew and twist spears), and rust beset asparagus plants. Choose varieties resistant to rust. Discourage beetles by removing all debris from the bed in fall; handpick any adult beetles or larvae in early spring. To control aphids, see page 74.

| **tip** | Weeds, especially perennial ones such as grass, can become rampant in asparagus beds after a few years, so start with a perfectly clean bed, and remove weeds as soon as they appear. |

HARVEST The spring of the year after planting you can harvest the first few spears that are as thick as a pencil. Cut or snap them off when they are 5 to 10 inches long, leaving white stubs on the plants. When emerging spears begin to look spindly, let them grow up and leaf out. By the third spring, the spears will appear in full force, and you can cut them over a long season (8 to 12 weeks). Always stop harvesting when the spears become spindly. Yields are typically 3 to 4 pounds per 10-foot row.

FOR THE TABLE Steam lightly and drizzle with butter.

After the harvest season, uncut spears produce delicate ferny foliage.

basil

Fragrant herb, perennial in mild-winter climates but usually grown as an annual; frost sensitive.

There are more than two dozen varieties of basil.

BASIL LEMONADE

MAKES 4 SERVINGS

All basils add fragrance to lemonade, but colored and scented varieties

contribute extra personality. Dark purple basils tint the lemonade a pretty pink but have a milder flavor than green varieties. Lemon basil adds a lemon-drop essence. Cinnamon and Thai basils contribute spicy overtones.

You can make the lemonade and then cover and chill it for up to 1 day.

In a 1½- to 2-quart glass measure or bowl, combine ½ cup lightly packed **fresh basil** *leaves and 3 tablespoons* **sugar**. *With a wooden spoon, crush the leaves with the sugar until the leaves are thoroughly bruised. Add 4 cups* **water** *and ½ cup freshly squeezed* **lemon juice**. *Stir until the sugar is dissolved, 1 to 2 minutes. Taste, and add more sugar if desired. Pour through a fine strainer into ice-filled glasses. Garnish with sprigs of* **fresh basil**.

PER SERVING: 44 CALORIES, 0% (0 CALORIES) FROM FAT; 0.1 G PROTEIN; 0 G FAT ; 12 G CARBOHYDRATE (0.1 G FIBER); 0.4 MG SODIUM; 0 MG CHOLESTEROL.

Sweet basil, the Italian type with large leaves, is the most popular, especially for making pesto. Purple-leafed basil has more ornamental value; you can mix it with flowers, green basils, and other herbs to make a handsome container planting. Less well known are Thai basil, lemon basil, lime basil, and the mini- and crinkly-leafed basils. The small-leafed kinds make fine edging plants.

POPULAR VARIETIES Italian green types such as 'Genovese'; purple-leafed 'Purple Ruffles' and 'Red Rubin'.

BEST SITE Sunny, with well-drained soil.

PLANTING AND CARE Sow seeds in the garden from midspring through early to midsummer. Place them ¼ inch deep, 2 to 3 inches apart, in rows 18 inches apart. Thin seedlings to 1 foot apart. For an early crop, start seeds indoors (see page 52) 4 to 6 weeks before the last frost date, and plant outside 1 week after all danger of frost has passed. Water as needed to keep the soil evenly moist. Watch for slugs and snails; for nontoxic treatments, see page 76.

 Pinch off branch tips and flowers to keep leaves coming.

HARVEST Early summer to first frost. Pick leaves whenever you need them. Four to six plants are sufficient for most gardeners.

FOR THE TABLE Scatter whole leaves on a salad of sliced tomatoes and mozzarella; add salt, pepper, and olive oil.

What takes the most effort in growing beans? Some people think it's deciding which kind to grow. There are snap beans (your regular bush beans and pole beans), and beans for shelling when the seeds are full-size but still green, and beans to dry and store, plus lima beans, soybeans, and fava beans. Once you've decided, you can relax: they don't need to go in early, and they grow fast. Yields vary depending on the type and variety.

▶ *For asparagus beans, see Southern Peas, page 178.*

BEST SITE Sunny, with well-drained soil.

tip For bumper crops of beans, buy "inoculated" seeds, meaning seeds inoculated with *Rhizobium* bacteria, which help the plants fix nitrogen from the air and store it in their roots. Or inoculate the seeds yourself by rolling them in legume inoculant powder, which contains the bacteria (see page 84).

snap beans
(green beans, string beans)

Snap beans come in two forms—bush and pole—and a choice of colors—green, yellow (wax), purple, and striped. Bush beans are compact plants, 1 to 2 feet tall; pole (climbing) beans grow 8 feet or more and need support. Bush beans bear 10 to 14 days earlier than pole beans, but the crop is smaller.

POPULAR VARIETIES 'Blue Lake' and 'Kentucky Wonder', the classics, available as bush or pole; 'Emerite', French filet pole bean; 'Provider', bush, good resistance to disease; 'Romano', bush or pole, a flat wide Italian bean; 'Royal Burgundy', bush, purple flowers and beans (beans become green when cooked); 'Tricolor', blend of three colors of beans, ideal for small spaces, bush or pole.

tip The pretty flowers of the scarlet runner bean are edible. It's not a true pole bean, but grow it as if it were.

PLANTING AND CARE Plant in spring, but wait until the weather warms. The rule is that late-leafing trees such as oaks, hickories, and pecans should be unfurling new foliage; if you sow earlier, the bean seeds just sit there and may rot. Don't bother presoaking the seeds. But moisten the soil thoroughly before sowing, and do not water again until seedlings emerge.

Sow seeds of bush varieties 1 to 1½ inches deep and 2 inches apart in rows 2 to 3 feet apart; thin the seedlings to 4 to 6 inches apart. Or sow in wide bands with seeds about 6 inches from one another. Bush beans are determinate, which means that the pods on each bush tend to mature together, over a 1- to 2-week period. For continuous harvesting, sow small batches every 2 weeks.

Before sowing pole beans, decide on or build a support for them; the plants may grow 8 feet tall or more, but you can use a shorter structure and pinch out the tips when they reach the top. Consider an existing trellis or

beans

Warm-season annual; damaged by frost, except for the fava bean, which is cool-season.

'Northeaster', an early pole bean.

beans, continued

fence, or run string between posts. Use bamboo poles 8 feet tall to create a tepee or a double row joined to a cross-pole at the top. (For more ideas, see page 57.) Sow the seeds next to the support, 1 to 1$\frac{1}{2}$ inches deep. Space them 6 inches apart; if you are using poles, space the poles 12 to 24 inches apart, and sow 1 or 2 seeds either side of each pole. Space rows 2 to 3 feet apart.

bean tepees

If you choose climbing beans, you can build simple ornamental structures for them, with sticks and poles, netting and twine.

For small tepees like these, space three sticks 1$\frac{1}{2}$ to 2 feet apart. Push the bottoms of the sticks into the ground a few inches, and tie the tops together with twine. Wrap the tepee with netting for a dense cover of leaves.

To make a grand tepee and children's playhouse, arrange eight 6- to 8-foot bamboo poles in a circle 6 feet wide. Leaving an opening between two of the poles for a door, wrap the tepee with netting, or run twine around the base of the tepee, and attach strings from the base twine to the top of the tepee.

Keep the soil moist, especially when the plants begin to flower and while they are forming pods. Occasional deep soaking is preferable to frequent light sprinklings, which may encourage mildew. Pull weeds—don't hoe, because beans have shallow roots. While beans are in flower, apply a low-nitrogen complete fertilizer.

Mexican bean beetle is a common pest in some areas; it looks like a ladybug, yellow when young, then coppery with dark spots. Remove the yellow larvae and clusters of yellow eggs on the undersides of leaves in spring; in summer, shake the adults off the plants onto a cloth, and destroy them. If plants become infested, apply a natural pesticide (see pages 72–73), following the directions on the label. Beans also attract aphids, cucumber beetles, leafhoppers, and mites (see pages 74–76). Leaf diseases include downy mildew (see page 77); to avoid spreading diseases, work around beans only when the foliage is dry.

HARVEST Early summer on, 50 to 65 days after sowing. Pull pods from plants carefully, before the seeds are bulging against the pod. Pole beans produce for a 6- to 8-week period if you keep picking.

FOR THE TABLE Steam for 3 or 4 minutes, and serve with a vinaigrette.

shellies

Beans for shelling from their pods while the beans are still green (green-shelling) are sometimes called *horticultural beans,* or, in the South, *shellies* or *shuckies.* All the varieties listed below grow on bush-type plants like snap beans. Grow them just as you would bush snap beans, described earlier.

POPULAR VARIETIES 'Borlotto', red-and-cream pods; 'Chevrier', a French flageolet bean; 'French Horticultural', classic variety. All these varieties are also delicious if allowed to dry, as described later.

HARVEST Early summer on, 65 to 75 days after sowing. Pick when the pods are full and still green; shell the beans, and discard the pods.

FOR THE TABLE Boil beans in salted water, and dress simply with butter, salt, and pepper.

dried beans

Growing beans for drying is simply a matter of letting the bean pods keep growing past the snap bean stage, past the shellie stage, and into complete maturity. What it takes is a long growing season. When the pods dry on the plant and begin to split, bulging with beans, you harvest them. Beans that taste especially good when cooked after drying include navy beans, pinto beans, and kidney beans. Seed catalogs offer lots of heirloom dried beans with beautiful names like 'Midnight Black Turtle' and 'Dalmatian Bean'. Grow dried beans just as you would the bush type of snap bean, described earlier.

POPULAR VARIETIES 'Great Northern White', also good as a shellie; 'Jacob's Cattle', white beans splashed with maroon; 'Vermont Cranberry', red beans speckled with brown. See also the popular varieties of shellies, described earlier.

HARVEST Summer, about 90 days after sowing. Pick the pods or pull up the whole plant. Spread the pods on racks or screens in a warm, well-ventilated area for a couple of weeks at least, so that they dry completely. Thresh the beans out of the pods: crush the pods with your hands or put the pods in a bag, tie the opening, and walk over or jump on the bag. Before storage, spread the beans on trays and bake them in the oven at 175°F for 15 minutes. Store the cooled beans in airtight jars.

FOR THE TABLE Dried beans make beautiful soups with winter greens such as chard; serve with parmesan and country bread brushed with olive oil and toasted.

'Anasazi'
dried beans

lima beans

Limas are grown for shelling when they are green and also for drying. They don't do well in wet weather or extremely dry, hot weather, and they need a longer growing season than snap beans. If your season is short, choose the varieties that mature earliest, such as the "baby" limas. Like snap beans, limas come in either bush or pole form. Grow them as you would a snap bean, but wait for warmer weather to sow; soil temperature needs to be at least 65°F/18°C.

POPULAR VARIETIES 'Fordhook 242', bush type, heat tolerant; 'Henderson Bush', bush type, small beans, good for a short season; 'King of the Garden', pole type, large flavorful beans.

HARVEST Summer and early fall, 65 to 100 or more days after sowing, depending on the type and whether for shelling or drying. For shelling, pick when the beans are young for best flavor. To harvest when dry, see Dried Beans, earlier.

FOR THE TABLE Serve cooked beans with a tomato-garlic-onion sauce and lamb.

continued >

'Christmas' lima bean

beans, continued

ABOVE *'Green Pearls' soybean*
RIGHT *Fava beans*

soybeans

Edamame is what the Japanese call shelled green soybeans. They are delicious and very high in protein. The South and Midwest are the best growing regions; the beans like warm, humid climates and do poorly in most dry climates. Grow soybeans as you would a bush snap bean. Black-seeded varieties are usually grown for drying.

POPULAR VARIETIES 'Early Hakucho', green-seeded, early, heavy crop, 1 foot tall; 'Envy', green-seeded, early, 2 feet tall.

HARVEST Summer, when seeds have reached full size and pods are still green. Pour boiling water over the pods to soften them before shelling. Soybeans can also be dried; for harvest information, see Dried Beans, earlier.

FOR THE TABLE Steam soybeans lightly in their pods and cool; they make a nutritious snack.

fava beans
(broad beans, horse beans)

Favas are a cool-season crop and take a long time to mature. For drying, they are ready in 120 to 150 days, depending on the temperature, but you can harvest the pods much earlier, when the beans are still green, for delicious shellies. A cautionary note: A very few people have a genetic enzyme deficiency that can cause severe—even fatal—reactions to the beans and the pollen.

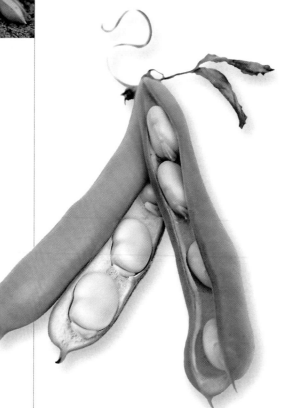

POPULAR VARIETIES 'Broad Windsor', classic variety.

PLANTING AND CARE In cold-winter areas, plant in early spring, as soon as you can work the soil. In mild-winter climates, plant in fall for late winter or early spring crops. Sow seeds 2 inches deep, 4 to 5 inches apart, in rows 1 1/2 to 2 1/2 feet apart. Thin seedlings to 8 to 10 inches apart. Plants grow 2 to 4 1/2 feet tall and may need staking. For general care information, see Snap Beans, earlier.

HARVEST Pick when pods are young, for delicate-tasting green shellies. For drying, see Dried Beans, earlier.

FOR THE TABLE Lightly steam small, shelled green favas with fresh shelled green peas, and serve with a pat of butter.

beets

**Cool-season annual;
tolerates light frost.**

Beets have come back into fashion. Now the leaves are harvested as nutritious baby greens, and the roots are smaller and sweeter than older varieties generally were. For color, choose golden, white, or candy striped, as well as plain red. Those with dark red leaves or bright red leaf stems and veins look handsome in flower beds or mixed vegetable-and-flower pots.

POPULAR VARIETIES White 'Albina Verduna'; red-and-white-striped 'Chioggia'; 'Detroit Dark Red', an old favorite; yellow 'Golden'; 'Red Ace' and 'Cylindra', with long, slim roots.

BEST SITE Sunny or partially shaded, with rich, well-drained soil free of rocks and lumps.

PLANTING AND CARE Sow either in spring for an early summer harvest or in August (September in mild-winter climates) for a late fall harvest. Spring-planted beets often suffer problems with insects and are likely to bolt in summer heat. Beets planted in late summer fare much better, and the cool weather makes the beets sweeter.

Place seeds ½ inch deep, 1 inch apart, in rows 1½ to 2 feet apart. Or broadcast the seeds in wide beds. Cover the seeds with a ¼-inch layer of sand or screened compost to improve germination, which takes up to 3 weeks. Keep the seedbed moist. Thin seedlings to 2 to 3 inches apart when they are 3 inches tall.

Continue to water well so the beets will be tender. Mulch to help keep the soil moist and cool. Weed regularly.

Beets may attract flea beetles, leafhoppers, leaf miners, nematodes, and wireworms (see pages 75–76). Rotate crops (see page 77) to reduce problems.

HARVEST Harvest the first greens as you thin the seedlings. Thereafter, take only the outer leaves. Start pulling the roots 45 to 65 days after sowing, when the beets are 1 inch wide. Roots may also be left in the ground for winter harvest (see page 83). Yields are about 8 to 10 pounds per 10-foot row.

FOR THE TABLE Roast beets with other root vegetables, such as parsnips, onions, turnips, and carrots.

TOP *'Golden' and 'Albina Verduna', center, make a colorful salad with regular red beets.*

BELOW *Cool weather makes beets taste sweet.*

blackberries

Deciduous perennial shrub or vine; fairly hardy, depending on variety.

BLACKBERRY SHERBET
MAKES ABOUT 1 QUART; 6 TO 8 SERVINGS

Berry sherbet is a cool way to bring home-grown blackberries to your table when the bushes are drooping with fat, gleaming berries.

In a blender or food processor, whirl 3 cups (about 1 pound) blackberries, 1¼ cups sugar, 1 tablespoon lemon juice, and ⅛ teaspoon salt until smooth. Press through a fine strainer into a bowl; discard the seeds. Taste, and add more sugar (up to ¼ cup) if desired. Stir in 1½ cups half-and-half (light cream). Cover and chill until cold, about 1 hour. Pour into an ice-cream maker (1½-quart or larger capacity), and freeze according to the manufacturer's directions until the mixture is softly frozen. Serve soft, or freeze in an airtight container until firm, about 3 hours, or up to 3 days.

Included in the blackberry category are cane berries known as dewberry, loganberry, boysenberry, youngberry, and olallieberry. Berries range in color from jet black to red and in taste from sweet to tart. Varieties typical of the West Coast are trailing; they grow long, vinelike canes that need to be trellised. Blackberries of the Midwest and East grow erect, on shorter canes; they can be tied to wire, but they don't need support. All blackberries bear fruit in summer on second-year canes—the first year, the canes have leaves but no fruit. For the best varieties for your area, check with a local nursery or your Cooperative Extension Office.

POPULAR VARIETIES *Trailing types:* 'Boysen', large reddish sweet-tart berries, delightful aroma; 'Cascade', classic wild blackberry flavor, for the West; 'Logan', light reddish berries tarter than 'Boysen', for the West; 'Triple Crown', thornless, large black sweet berries, heavy crop, cold hardy. *Erect types:* 'Apache', thornless, large berries, late fruiting; 'Arapaho', thornless, large firm berries, disease resistant, good for the South; 'Navaho', thornless, firm sweet fruit ripens late, disease resistant, well suited to the South.

BEST SITE Sunny, with rich, well-prepared, deep soil. To avoid verticillium wilt, don't plant where you have raised potatoes, eggplant, peppers, raspberries, strawberries, or tomatoes in the last 3 years.

SUPPORT For trailing blackberries, set up a sturdy 5-foot-tall trellis as a support. Use 3-by-3s or 4-by-4s for the posts; or use round posts 3 or 4 inches in diameter, made of rot-resistant wood such as redwood or cedar. Anchor the posts well. Then string 10- or 11-gauge smooth galvanized wire between them (see drawings on next page).

PLANTING AND CARE In cold-winter climates, plant in early spring before new growth begins. In mild-winter climates, plant in autumn or early spring.

Set the plants into the ground 1 inch deeper than they grew at the nursery (look for the soil mark). For information on planting a dormant, bare-root plant, see page 88; for a container-grown plant, see page 54.

Space trailing blackberries 5 to 8 feet apart in rows 9 to 10 feet apart. Space erect types 2 to 2½ feet apart in rows 6 to 10 feet apart. Don't stint on the spacing; the more sunshine the canes receive, the more fruit they'll produce and the lower the risk of disease. After planting, cut back all canes to 8 to 10 inches long.

Keep the soil moist during the growing season, until the harvest is complete; avoid overhead watering, which can encourage leaf spot and other fungal diseases. Watch for cane borers—larvae boring through the canes (the first indication of trouble is wilting cane tips); cut off canes 6 inches below dying tips and discard them. Aphids, mites, and verticillium wilt (see pages 74–78) may also trouble blackberries.

Weed regularly. At the end of winter, before the new buds swell, mulch around the plants with compost or well-rotted manure.

TRAINING AND PRUNING TRAILING TYPES For trailing blackberries, let the canes grow unpruned along the ground the first summer. In fall, if your winters are cold, cover the canes with mulch to protect them from freezing. If your winters are mild, no mulch is needed. At the end of winter, when growth begins, tie the year-old canes to the trellis, either cutting off their tops at 5 feet or weaving longer canes onto the trellis (see drawings below). Remove weak, dead, or diseased canes.

After the harvest is over, in spring or summer, cut to the ground the old canes, the ones that bore fruit. Let the new canes grow along the ground.

'Chester' blackberry

PRUNING TRAILING BLACKBERRIES

In early spring, when growth begins, prune weak and diseased canes to ground. Tie the year-old canes to the trellis and either prune them to 5 feet (left) or wrap the long canes over the trellis wires (right).

PRUNING ERECT BLACKBERRIES

In early spring, when growth begins, trim side branches to 12 to 15 inches long, and completely remove any dead or diseased branches.

TRAINING AND PRUNING ERECT TYPES For erect blackberries, in summer cut the tops of the new canes down to 2 to 2½ feet to promote branching. In early spring, as new growth starts, cut back the side branches (see drawing at right). After the harvest, cut to the ground the old canes that have fruited.

HARVEST Spring or early summer, when berries are full size and fully colored. Yields vary, depending on the type and variety.

FOR THE TABLE Sprinkle lightly with sugar, refrigerate for several hours, and then serve with whipped cream. If you have rose geranium (see page 141), pick some leaves, crush them, and layer them among the berries, removing them just before serving.

tip Crosses between trailing and erect types are called *semierect*. Train and prune semierect blackberries as you would trailing types.

blueberries

Deciduous shrub; hardiness varies by type.

Blueberry bushes are handsome: blue berries among green foliage in summer, yellow or red fall leaves, many white-pink urn-shaped flowers in spring. They must have very acid, well-drained soil; grow plants in containers or raised beds (see pages 94–95) if your soil conditions aren't right.

There are highbush, lowbush, and rabbiteye blueberries. Highbush varieties grow to 7 feet tall; lowbush are generally less than 2 feet tall; rabbiteye are the tallest, to 10 feet or more. Which varieties you can grow depends on your climate. Don't anticipate a harvest the first year, and be prepared to tend the bushes carefully in the early years.

POPULAR VARIETIES *Highbush for northern regions:* 'Bluecrop', large flavorful berries, ornamental shrub; 'Patriot', large tasty berries, big crop. *Highbush for southern regions:* 'Sharpblue', very early berries, ornamental plant. *Lowbush for northern regions:* 'Northsky', medium-size sky-blue berries, ornamental plant. *Rabbiteye for the South and West:* 'Climax', early, large berries, tall spreading plant; 'Premier', early, large light blue berries. Rabbiteyes need to be cross-pollinated to bear fruit, and other types fruit better if cross-pollinated, so plant at least two different varieties together.

BEST SITE Sunny, with well-drained, very acidic soil (pH between 3.5 and 5.0) that is rich in organic matter.

PLANTING AND CARE Plant 2- or 3-year-old bushes in fall or winter if your winters are mild, otherwise in early spring (see page 88 for planting bare-root bushes, page 54 for container-grown plants). Before planting, prune the bushes to three or four of their strongest shoots, to promote good growth.

Space bushes 4 to 6 feet apart, in rows 8 to 12 feet apart; allow the most space for the most vigorous varieties. After planting, put down a thick mulch around each plant to help shallow roots retain moisture and to keep down weeds.

'Bluetta' blueberry

During the first 3 years, blueberries need 1 inch of water per week in the growing season. Avoid overhead irrigation, which can encourage mildew on leaves and botrytis (gray mold) on fruit. Fertilizer can stress the plants. Don't fertilize at all the first year, and fertilize only lightly the second and third years. After that, apply fertilizer each year just once in early spring. Use a fertilizer formulated for azaleas and rhododendrons.

Before berries begin to ripen, cover the plants with netting to protect them from birds. Watch for powdery mildew (see page 78) on leaves.

PRUNING Prune to prevent overbearing. Plants often produce so many fruit buds that berries are undersize and plant growth slows. Keep first-year plants from bearing any fruit by stripping off the flower buds after planting. This helps the roots establish well and produces a healthier, stronger plant and bigger yields in following years.

After the first year, during early spring, remove low canes, drooping stems, and crossing branches. After 3 years, also cut back the tips of vigorous canes, leaving six to eight buds, to promote side branching, and cut back long stems so that you can harvest the fruit easily. Once the bushes are 5 years old, to keep them fruiting well, remove one or more of the oldest branches every year, and keep the most vigorous new branches that grow from the roots (see drawing at right).

HARVEST Late spring or summer, depending on variety, when berries are entirely blue and taste sweet. Yields vary depending on the type and variety.

FOR THE TABLE Add blueberries to buttermilk pancake mix before cooking; sprinkle more berries on the pile of finished pancakes.

tip Blueberries make a beautiful hedge. Or grow some in a shrub border with their relatives azaleas and rhododendrons.

pruning blueberries

Remove old and crossing branches; shorten vigorous growth.

Italian gardeners are transforming how we think of broccoli. Their 'Romanesco', with its striking spirals of chartreuse florets, is the most photographed vegetable since pear tomatoes. You could grow it just for display. Also consider broccoli raab or rabe, which offers gourmet piquant-flavored greens with button-size florets. Sprouting broccoli is better known; it produces many small florets, not as small as buttons, instead of one tight head; there are green and purple types—the purple turns green when cooked.

Broccoli prefers a cool growing season. If the temperature goes too high it will bolt—into flower stalks that bloom and go to seed before you can pick them. That said, broccoli is one of the easier-to-grow members of the cole family.

broccoli

Cool-season annual; tolerates frost but not hard freezes.

POPULAR VARIETIES 'Green Comet', regular broccoli, matures early, easy to grow; 'Premium Crop', regular broccoli, large compact heads, tolerates heat well; 'Purple Sprouting', lots of side-shoots, tender, sweet tasting; 'Romanesco', beautiful chartreuse heads, slow maturing; 'Spring Raab', broccoli raab, big plants.

BEST SITE Sunny, with fertile soil. Practice crop rotation (see page 77).

PLANTING AND CARE Like other cole crops, broccoli tends to bolt when temperatures are high, so plant it to mature during cool weather. In mild-winter climates, sow seeds or set out plants in late summer

ABOVE *Broccoli raab*
LEFT *'Romanesco' broccoli*

121

broccoli, continued

and autumn for winter and early spring crops. In cold-winter areas, set out young plants in early spring, 2 weeks before the last frost date; or start seeds indoors (see page 52) 4 to 6 weeks before the setting-out date.

Set plants 15 to 24 inches apart in rows 2 to 3 feet apart. (Close spacing results in more sideshoots and smaller main heads.) Or start from seeds sown $^1/_4$ to $^1/_2$ inch deep and 1 inch apart, in rows spaced as above. Thin seedlings to 15 to 24 inches apart.

Keep the soil moist. Feed with a high-nitrogen complete fertilizer before heads start to form. Weed regularly. Broccoli, like its relative cabbage, is prone to pests and diseases. To be fully prepared, see pages 74–78 on how to prevent or minimize damage from aphids, cabbageworms, flea beetles, harlequin bugs, clubroot, damping off, downy mildew, and fusarium wilt.

HARVEST From 50 to 100 days (most popular varieties mature in about 60 days) after setting out plants, before broccoli heads open into yellow flowers. Cut the stem 6 to 8 inches below the head; when side branches grow, harvest them, too. Yield is approximately 4 to 6 pounds per 10-foot row.

FOR THE TABLE Stir-fry broccoli raab with minced garlic and chili flakes; add a little water, cover the pan, and simmer until done.

---

brussels sprouts

Cool-season annual; tolerates frost but not hard freezes.

Brussels sprouts look like miniature palm trees with lumps growing on their trunks. The lumps—sprouts—have the flavor of sweet, tiny cabbages. Unlike palms, they prefer cool weather and taste best after a frost.

POPULAR VARIETIES 'Jade Cross' and 'Oliver' produce early crops.

BEST SITE Sunny, with fertile, well-drained soil. Practice crop rotation (see page 77).

PLANTING AND CARE In cold-winter climates, set out plants or sow seeds in midsummer. In mild-winter climates, set out plants or sow seeds in late summer and autumn. Place plants 15 to 24 inches apart in rows 2 to 3 feet apart. Or sow seeds $^1/_4$ to $^1/_2$ inch deep and 1 inch apart, in rows spaced as above. Thin seedlings to 15 to 24 inches apart.

Keep the soil moist. Weed regularly. Like several members of the cole, or cabbage, family, brussels sprouts are somewhat prone to pests and diseases. To be fully prepared, see pages 74–78 on how to prevent or minimize damage from aphids, cabbageworms, flea beetles, harlequin bugs, clubroot, damping off, downy mildew, and fusarium wilt.

HARVEST From 80 to 100 days after setting out plants, when the big lower leaves start to turn yellow. Harvest sprouts from the bottom of the stem to the top, snapping off firm green sprouts that are slightly smaller than a golf ball. Remove any side leaves growing below the harvested sprouts. More sprouts will grow at the top of the stem as the plant matures. Approximate yield is 3 to 5 pounds per 10-foot row.

FOR THE TABLE Instead of boiling or steaming sprouts, braise them in a frying pan with 1 tablespoon olive oil and $^3/_4$ cup water.

cabbage

Cool-season annual; tolerates frost but not hard freezes.

For an attractive cabbage patch, combine different shapes—round, pointy, and flat—of smooth green cabbage with crinkly, deep green savoy cabbages and red cabbages that have blue-green leaves and purple veins. Add ornamental flowering cabbage, if you like, with its showy leaf marbling and white, cream, rose, or purple edges.

▶ *For Chinese cabbage, see page 128.*

POPULAR VARIETIES *Early:* 'Early Jersey Wakefield', delicious small pointy heads; 'Ruby Ball', red cabbage, heat tolerant; 'Stonehead', firm head, develops well in hot weather. *Midseason and late:* 'Danish Ballhead', keeps well, good for sauerkraut; 'Savoy Chieftain', handsome crinkly blue-green leaves, large heads.

BEST SITE Sunny or partially shaded, with fertile, well-drained soil. Practice crop rotation (see page 77).

PLANTING AND CARE Cabbages mature best during cool weather, so, unless your summers are cool, start early in spring with an early variety, which will mature quickly and taste tender. You can set out purchased transplants 3 weeks before the last frost date or start seeds indoors (see page 52) 4 to 6 weeks before your planting date. In summer, plant or sow another crop directly outdoors, for fall harvest; consider, then, the midseason and late varieties that grow large and keep well. In mild-winter climates, you can also set out plants or sow seeds in fall for winter and early spring harvest.

Set out transplants 12 to 24 inches apart in rows 2 to 4 feet apart. Sow seeds ¼ to ½ inch deep and 1 inch apart, in rows 2 to 4 feet apart; thin seedlings to 12 to 24 inches apart.

Keep the soil moist; cabbages need plenty of water. Feed with a high-nitrogen complete fertilizer once during the growing season. Weed carefully, because cabbages have shallow roots.

Like other cole crops, cabbages are susceptible to a wide variety of soil-borne diseases. On avoiding problems with aphids, cabbage loopers, cabbage root maggots, cabbageworms, flea beetles, harlequin bugs, clubroot, damping off, downy mildew, and fusarium wilt, see pages 74–78.

HARVEST From 50 to 100 days after setting out plants; cut heads before they split or crack. To store, keep cool and damp. Yields are 10 to 25 pounds per 10-foot row.

FOR THE TABLE Stir-fry sliced green cabbage with chopped garlic, shallots, and fennel; sprinkle with grated parmesan before serving.

tip Ornamental flowering cabbages are edible, too. Pot them singly or in groups, or set them out among your flowers or vegetables 15 to 18 inches apart. The "flower" color is most dazzling after the first frost.

TOP *'Julius' savoy cabbage*
ABOVE *Red cabbage*

carrots

Cool-season annual; tolerates light frosts.

Growing crisp, sweet carrots can be child's play once the ground is free of clods and stones. If you find it too time consuming to sift soil to a fine texture so the carrots can grow 12 inches long and perfectly tapered, grow a short variety of carrot—in a heart, finger, or golf-ball shape if you like. Or grow short or "half-long" carrots in a container filled with potting soil.

POPULAR VARIETIES *Extralong (10 to 12 inches):* 'Imperator', tapered, deep orange. *Half-long (6 to 8 inches):* 'Bolero', 'Danvers Half Long', sweet, cylindrical, blunt-tipped Nantes types, store well; 'Touchon', great for juicing. *Short, suitable for heavy soils and containers:* 'Royal Chantenay', deep orange, crisp; 'Short 'n' Sweet', 4-inch, wide-shouldered and tapered; 'Thumbelina', 3-inch balls.

BEST SITE Sunny, with deep, fertile, fine-textured soil.

PLANTING AND CARE In cold-winter climates, sow seeds in early spring for a summer crop and in late summer for a fall crop. In mild-winter climates, sow seeds in spring for a summer crop; for autumn, winter, and spring crops, sow 30 to 80 days before you'd like to harvest.

A few weeks before sowing, prepare the soil. Break up lumps and remove stones to at least the depth to which the carrots will grow, because when the roots meet an obstacle, they fork or detour around it. Work aged compost and well-rotted manure into the soil, to improve its texture.

If preparing an entire planting bed is too big a job, dig a V-shaped planting trench 2 to 3 inches wide at the top and 4 to 12 inches deep (depending on the length of your carrots). Fill the trench with fine soil mixed with fine-textured well-rotted compost (not fresh manure, which will make the roots twist). Or grow your carrots in containers.

Sow the tiny seeds as evenly as possible ¼ deep in rows 1 to 2½ feet apart, or broadcast them in a wide bed. Cover the seeds with ¼ inch of fine soil. Keep the soil moist for the 2- to 3-week germination period. In hot weather, cover the bed with moist burlap to keep the soil from drying out; remove the burlap once the seedlings sprout.

Start thinning the seedlings when they are 1 inch tall. Eventually, the carrots need to be 2 inches apart in the rows or 4 inches apart in a wide bed; thin regularly, eating the delicious thinnings, tops and all, until you reach the final spacing.

To prevent bitter-tasting green "shoulders" on your carrots, cover the root tops with soil or mulch.

Water consistently throughout the growing season. If carrots dry out while growing, their flesh hardens; then, when water is restored, their roots tend to split. Remove weeds while they are small.

Carrot rust flies and carrot weevils are annoying pests. They lay their eggs in the young leafy tops or in the soil, and the larvae burrow into the carrots. Rotate your carrots (see page 77); if you continue to have problems, keep the adult pests out with row covers (see page 56) from the time you sow until the plants are 6 to 8 inches tall. Wireworms and nematodes may also be problems (see page 76).

ABOVE
'Nantaise' carrots
RIGHT
'Thumbelina' carrots

HARVEST Start with thinnings, as described earlier. Harvest the remaining carrots when they reach your favorite eating size—for baby carrots, 30 to 40 days after sowing; for mature carrots, 50 to 80 days. Carefully pull or dig them up with a garden fork. In very cold-winter climates, harvest all your carrots before hard frosts occur. Where winters are not severely cold, you can leave carrots in the ground for storage; after the first hard frost, cover the tops with a foot of shredded leaves, hay, or straw, and harvest the carrots as you need them.

To store, remove the tops and keep the carrots cool and damp. Yields are about 7 to 10 pounds per 10-foot row.

FOR THE TABLE Chop finger-long baby carrot thinnings, tops and all, into green salads. Don't bother to peel young carrots, just brush them clean.

tip To keep a child's interest in a carrot crop, sow a mix of carrot seeds and radish seeds together. Radish seeds germinate very quickly; carrot seeds may take 21 days. The radishes also help the tiny carrot seedlings emerge by breaking up the soil crust for them.

Cauliflower is the most demanding of the cole crops (cabbage, broccoli, brussels sprouts, kale). It's best suited to cool, humid growing conditions and needs to keep growing with no glitches, such as a water shortage, or it'll produce premature undersize heads. If you're expecting snowy white, high-quality heads like the ones you see in the supermarket, either blanch the heads (described later) or choose self-blanching varieties.

POPULAR VARIETIES 'Fremont', self-blanching, good fall variety; 'Snow King' and 'Snow Crown', classic fast-maturing varieties for spring or fall; 'Violet Queen', self-blanching, more dependable as a fall crop, purple heads fade to green when cooked.

BEST SITE Sunny, with fertile, well-drained soil. Practice crop rotation (see page 77).

PLANTING AND CARE Cauliflower can be started in early spring (late winter in mild-winter climates) or summer. A late sowing stands a better chance of success, because cauliflower matures much better in cool weather. For spring plants, get going extra early by sowing seeds indoors (see page 52) 4 to 6 weeks before the setting-out date.

In cold-winter climates, set out plants or sow seeds for a fall crop in midsummer. In mild-winter climates, set out plants or sow seeds in late summer.

Place plants 15 to 24 inches apart in rows 2 to 3 feet apart. Sow seeds ½ inch deep and 1 inch apart, in rows 2 to 3 feet apart; thin seedlings to 15 to 24 inches apart. Keep the soil consistently moist. Weed regularly. Apply a liquid fertilizer regularly during the growing season.

To blanch the head (stop it from yellowing and developing an "off" flavor), when it's about 2 inches wide, fold the large outer leaves over it, and secure them with twist-ties, clothespins, or elastic bands. On self-blanching varieties, the outer leaves naturally grow up and over the head.

continued >

cauliflower

Cool-season annual; tolerates light frosts.

cauliflower, continued

Cauliflower has the cole crops' susceptibility to pests and diseases, which is the reason members of this family should be rotated (see page 77). To arm yourself with knowledge about aphids, cabbage loopers, cabbage root maggots, cabbageworms, flea beetles, harlequin bugs, clubroot, damping off, downy mildew, and fusarium wilt, see pages 74–78.

HARVEST From 55 to 100 days after setting out plants, before buds open. Check every 3 or 4 days around harvest time; the heads mature quickly during hot weather. Yields are about 8 to 10 pounds per 10-foot row.

FOR THE TABLE Toss cauliflower florets in olive oil and salt; then roast until browned on the edges and tender.

celery, celeriac
(celery root)

Cool-season annual; tolerates light frost.

These two relatives need a long (4-month), cool growing season, so if you live where summers stay cool, you can grow celery and celeriac to perfection. Blanching is necessary to produce celery that is pale green, mild tasting, and crunchy, but you don't have to fuss with celeriac's stalks—it's grown for its delicious knobby root.

POPULAR VARIETIES *Celery:* 'Golden Self-Blanching', naturally semi-blanched, short stalks; 'Tall Utah 52-70 Improved', long, dark green stalks; 'Tendercrisp', pale green stalks. *Celeriac:* 'Diamant'.

BEST SITE Sunny, with rich, recently manured soil.

PLANTING AND CARE Growing celery and celeriac from seed is a little tricky and slow; if you want to try it, start seeds indoors (see page 52) 10 weeks before your last frost date.

In cold-winter climates, set out young purchased plants (or your own, grown from seed) in spring after the last frost. In mild-winter climates, set out plants in fall, winter, or early spring; be mindful that night temperatures must be above 55°F/13°C. Place the plants 6 to 10 inches apart in rows 2 feet apart. Keep the soil moist. Apply liquid fertilizer regularly.

ABOVE *Celeriac*
RIGHT *Blanching celery.*

Blanch your celery stalks 3 to 4 weeks before harvest. Tie the tops of the stalks together, and then do one of the following to shut out sunlight: mound garden soil over the stalks, or slip large coffee cans or milk cartons with both ends removed, clay pipes, or rolled newspaper over the plants. Don't cover the leaves.

Aphids, cabbage loopers, leafhoppers, nematodes, fusarium wilt, and blights may be problems (see pages 74–78). Some varieties are resistant to fusarium and blights. To help keep plants healthy, ensure that your soil is moist and fertilized.

HARVEST *Celery:* Remove the blanching soil or sleeves, and cut off the entire celery plant just below the base, where all the stalks come together. Or cut individual stems where they meet the base of the plant. *Celeriac:* Dig up the roots when they are at least 2 inches wide. Yields are 12 to 20 plants per 10-foot row.

FOR THE TABLE To make a celeriac salad, peel the root, and cut it into matchstick-size strips. Parboil for 2 or 3 minutes, and toss with a mustard vinaigrette.

tip Unblanched celery is stronger tasting and greener; it is also more nutritious. Perhaps leave a couple of plants unblanched to see what you think.

Celeriac has a delicious root.

Easy-to-grow chard is a delicious, nutritious vegetable and also, because of its bright-colored stalks and dark green crinkled leaves, a beautiful plant for a mixed flower-and-vegetable garden. It rarely bolts to seed in warm weather, so it's a better choice than spinach and many other leafy crops for fresh summer greens.

POPULAR VARIETIES 'Bright Lights', a multicolor mix; 'Fordhook Giant', broad white stalks; 'Lucullus', yellowish green leaves and yellowish white stalks; 'Rhubarb', crimson stalks and red-veined leaves.

BEST SITE Sunny or partially shaded, with fertile, deeply cultivated, well-drained soil.

PLANTING AND CARE Sow seeds in early spring (late winter in mild-winter climates) 2 to 4 weeks before the last frost date. In mild-winter areas, you can sow again in late summer for a winter harvest.

Plant the seeds ½ inch deep and 2 inches apart, in rows 1½ to 2½ feet apart. Thin seedlings gradually until the remaining plants stand 12 inches apart (cook the thinnings as delicious baby greens).

Keep the soil moist. Weed regularly. Watch for aphids, flea beetles, and leaf miners; see pages 74–75 for suggested controls.

HARVEST About 8 weeks after sowing. Cut off outer stalks near the base, allowing the center stalks and leaves to keep growing. Alternatively, harvest all the leaves at once, cutting them off about 2 inches above the ground; the plant will eventually sprout new leaves. Yields are about 8 to 12 pounds per 10-foot row. *continued >*

chard

Cool-season annual; tolerates light frost.

'Joseph's Coat'

chard, continued

chinese cabbage

Cool-season annual; tolerates light frost.

FOR THE TABLE Cut away the stalks for steaming separately, because they take longer to cook than the leaves. Sauté the leaves in a little olive oil with slivers of garlic.

tip **Varieties with crimson, orange, yellow, or white stalks look superb in flower beds and mixed container plantings. Plant them with pansies and violas or with chives and parsley.**

The large, tall cylinders of densely packed, pale green, crisp leaves are the Napa type of Chinese cabbage. The other main type includes bok choy and pak choi, which have loose, darker green leaves and white stems.

POPULAR VARIETIES 'Jade Pagoda', similar to Napa type, late season, sturdy heads, crinkled leaves; 'Joi Choi', pak choi hybrid, early, bolt resistant; 'Minuet', Napa type, early, slow to bolt, small heads, sweet taste.

BEST SITE Sunny, with fertile, well-drained soil. Practice crop rotation (see page 77).

PLANTING AND CARE Start in spring, once night temperatures are at 50°F/10°C, with an early, bolt-resistant variety. Or, much more reliably, sow in late summer for a fall harvest.

Sow seeds ¼ to ½ inch deep, 1 to 2 inches apart, in rows 1½ to 2½ feet apart; thin seedlings to 8 inches apart for bok choy or up to 18 inches apart for other Chinese cabbages.

Keep the soil moist. Feed with high-nitrogen complete fertilizer once during the growing season. Weed regularly.

Chinese cabbages, like other cabbages, are susceptible to a wide variety of soilborne diseases, which is why they must be rotated (see page 77). For information on avoiding problems with aphids, cabbage loopers, cabbage root maggots, cabbageworms, flea beetles, harlequin bugs, clubroot, damping off, downy mildew, and fusarium wilt, see pages 74–78.

HARVEST When Napa-type heads are full-size, cut with a sharp knife. Snap off individual outer leaves of bok choy, or cut the entire plant. Harvest fall crops before the first hard frost. Yields vary depending on the type and variety.

FOR THE TABLE Chop and stir-fry in peanut oil.

Pak choi

'Early Jade Pagoda' Chinese cabbage

Chives are related to onions and garlic but are smaller and prettier. They grow in delicate-looking clumps, and in midspring produce clusters of rose-purple ball flowers. For something a little different, look for garlic chives, also known as *Chinese chives (gow choy)* or *Chinese leeks;* their straplike stems have a mild garlicky flavor.

BEST SITE Sunny or partially shaded, with fairly rich, well-drained soil.

PLANTING AND CARE Grow from seed in spring or from nursery plants. Sow seeds ⅛ to ¼ inch deep and 8 to 12 inches apart. Space nursery plants 8 to 12 inches apart.

Keep soil moist. Chives usually grow free of pests and diseases.

HARVEST Summer to first frost. If you start from seed, harvest lightly in the first year. Snip stems near base. Flowers are also edible; cut when still in bud. The yield from 3 or 4 plants is sufficient for most gardeners.

FOR THE TABLE Chop and add to cream cheese or use as a garnish on egg dishes.

tip Chives make a decorative edging plant for herb, vegetable, or flower gardens. Sow them in a container, and they will do well indoors on a sunny windowsill.

chives

Perennial herb; stems die back in winter, except in mildest regions.

Chives with boxwood, sage, and thyme.
DESIGN: KRISTIN HORNE.

cilantro, coriander

Cool-season annual herb; tender to frost.

Allowed to flower, cilantro produces coriander seeds.

The leaves are called *cilantro* or *Chinese parsley;* the seeds are coriander. If you like, you can start your crop with coriander seed from the grocery store. Cilantro is an annual—it's gone by the end of the year—but it self-sows, so expect to discover seedlings somewhere nearby the next spring.

BEST SITE Sunny, with well-drained soil.

PLANTING AND CARE Sow in early spring, after the last frost. Sow seeds ¼ inch deep. Thin seedlings to 3 to 4 inches apart. Water regularly.

Cilantro is sometimes troubled in spring by carrot rust flies. Cover the plants (see Floating Row Covers, page 56) from sowing until they are 6 to 8 inches tall to keep the egg-laying adults away.

HARVEST When a plant reaches about 8 inches tall, start to pick the outer leaves, which will encourage more leaves to grow. Harvest seeds as soon as they are ripe. The yield from 2 or 3 plants is sufficient for most gardeners.

FOR THE TABLE To make salsa, combine chopped cilantro with chopped onions and tomatoes. Season with salt and pepper.

tip If you live in a hot-summer climate, look for a slow-bolting variety, so your plants don't go to seed so quickly. In the South, start the seeds in fall.

citrus

Evergreen tree, 5 to 25 feet tall; trees are hardy to 22°F/–6°C, but fruit spoils during a light frost.

The glossy green tree hums with bees, the air is sweetly fragrant—a citrus in bloom is unforgettable. And as long as winter temperatures stay above 22°F/–6°C, you won't find a more obliging tree to grow. Citrus trees stay green year-round, need little or no pruning, and thrive in a wide range of soils. Heat makes the fruit sweet, but even if your summers are cool you can grow a lemon tree; choose 'Improved Meyer', a delicious-tasting lemon-orange hybrid.

BEST SITE Sheltered, sunny, with well-drained soil.

POPULAR VARIETIES *Lemon:* 'Improved Meyer', thin-skinned juicy fruit with less acidity than other lemons, bears year-round, dwarf tree can be kept at 5 feet tall. *Mandarin, satsuma:* 'Owari', nearly seedless, easy to peel, bears fruit December to April, can't tolerate intense heat but tolerates cold better than other citrus. *Orange:* 'Moro', blood orange, with burgundy-red flesh, bears fruit January to April; 'Valencia', the commercial juice orange, bears fruit from March to October; 'Washington', navel orange for peeling and eating, bears fruit December to May.

PLANTING AND CARE Plant in spring after all danger of frost is past and before summer heat begins. Remove any fruit before planting. Dig a hole (see page 54) that's twice the diameter of the rootball and mix in a controlled-release fertilizer. Position the tree so the graft union (the knobby ring around the trunk) is 3 inches above the soil surface. Build a water basin around the tree, wider than the spread of the branches.

In desert or hot inland areas, whitewash the exposed trunk of a young tree to protect the bark from sunburn. Use commercial whitewash or white latex paint.

Water deeply twice a week the first year, except during wet weather, and then weekly thereafter. Although citrus like consistent moisture throughout the root area, don't let the soil become soggy.

Feed with a fertilizer formulated for citrus; besides nitrogen, phosphorus, and potassium, it should contain the minor nutrients iron, manganese, and zinc. If the foliage turns chlorotic (yellow leaves with green veins), spray it with a foliar food containing chelated iron and the minor nutrients listed above. In freeze-prone areas, start feeding in late winter, and stop in late summer. In other areas, stop in fall. Make sure trees are well watered before feeding; spread the fertilizer over the soil, and then water deeply.

Pest and disease problems are usually minor. If scale insects (small, hard bumps on trunk and twigs) or greasy spot (starts as fungal blisters on lower side of leaves, and then forms black greasy splatterings on leaf surfaces) become a problem, treat with horticultural oil sprays during the growing season (see page 73), and remove and destroy fallen leaves. To control citrus scab (brown scabby growth on fruit), remove and destroy affected leaves, twigs, and fruit, and keep foliage as dry as possible in spring. For information on aphids and spider mites, see pages 74 and 76.

'Improved Meyer' lemon

zest in a pot

Citrus trees generally need hot summers and mild winters, but you can circumvent those requirements if you put them in pots. In cool-summer climates, place the pot where it gets reflected heat from a sunny south-facing wall or driveway, or grow a lemon (see main text). To avoid frost damage, move your pot indoors in fall, and keep it there until after the last frost; lemon is a good choice for an indoor-outdoor pot.

Settle on a dwarf tree and a container at least 18 inches in diameter. Use a high-quality potting mix. If you are not using automatically controlled drip irrigation, add soil polymers to the potting mix, to help retain moisture. Daily watering may be necessary in hot weather, especially if your pot is small.

In a cold climate, move your tree indoors to a cool, bright location before the first frost. Place the pot on a tray of wet pebbles to provide good humidity.

Vigorous trees may need repotting after 3 to 5 years. The signs are compacted roots and soil that dries out quickly between waterings. Slide the tree gently from the container, prune the roots, and repot in fresh potting mix.

Pruning is necessary only to remove twiggy growth, weak branches, and any suckers that grow from below the graft union; or, if the tree is young, to nip back wild growth and balance the shape of the tree. But you can prune your tree to reduce its size if you need to; you can also espalier citrus in an informal style. In freeze-prone areas, don't prune in fall or winter.

Help protect your tree against frost damage by keeping it well watered ahead of time. If a frost is predicted, wrap the tree with a string of Christmas lights, and then cover it with a frost blanket or a floating row cover (see page 56).

HARVEST Satsuma is highly perishable, so pick when ripe. Other citrus can be left on the tree and harvested over several months; up to a point, the longer a fruit hangs, the sweeter it gets. Pick lemons and other tart citrus before they become puffy. Yields vary depending on tree size.

FOR THE TABLE Peel oranges and Meyer lemons, and cut into cubes; mix with diced avocado, a little minced red chili, and fresh mint to make a salsa.

tip **If you need a small tree, be particular about what you are buying. Trees labeled "true dwarf" may be semidwarfs, which grow to 15 feet tall. The most reliably dwarf citrus trees available (slowly maturing to 5 to 7 feet) are those grafted onto the rootstock of 'Flying Dragon', which is a naturally dwarf form of trifoliate orange (*Poncirus trifoliata*). (A naturally dwarf form is sometimes called a *genetic dwarf*.) Ask your supplier about the tree's mature height if size is critical.**

collards

**Cool-season annual;
frost hardy and heat tolerant.**

'Vates' collards

corn

**Warm-season annual;
killed by frost.**

Leafy, headless relatives of cabbage, collards are best planted in summer for autumn and winter harvest. After light frosts, the mature leaves are sweeter. Collards tolerate heat well, unlike many greens, so you can also start a crop in early spring for plenty of nutritious early summer greens.

POPULAR VARIETIES 'Champion', standard, fast-growing; 'Green Glaze', resistant to cabbageworms; 'Vates', large-leafed.

BEST SITE Sunny or partially shaded, with rich soil; tolerates a slightly acid soil, to pH 5.5. Practice crop rotation (see page 77).

PLANTING AND CARE In cold-winter climates, set out plants in spring or late summer; sow seeds in late summer. In mild-winter climates, set out plants or sow seeds in spring and late summer.

Set plants 12 to 18 inches apart in rows 2 to 3 feet apart. Sow seeds ¼ inch deep, 1 to 2 inches apart, in rows 2 to 3 feet apart. Thin seedlings to 12 to 18 inches apart; stir-fry the thinnings.

Keep the stems and leaves tender and green by watering frequently. A well-watered plant in fertile soil can grow to 3 feet tall.

Collards are a little less prone to pests and diseases than cabbages, but watch for aphids, cabbage loopers, cabbageworms, and harlequin bugs (see pages 74–75).

HARVEST From 50 to 80 days after setting out plants. Cut off lower leaves, leaving the center of the plant to grow more, or harvest the whole plant at any time. Yields range from 3 to 15 pounds per 10-foot row.

FOR THE TABLE Chop and stir into bean or lentil soup.

tip **Collards are very healthful, rich in vitamin A, calcium, and iron.**

Home-grown corn does taste better than store-bought—it's not your imagination. If you pick corn at its prime and eat it right away, you'll taste the sugar in the kernels before it turns to starch.

Extra sweetness has been bred into new varieties. You can go for the supersweets (look for SH2 next to the variety name), which are at least twice as sweet as standard corn and a little too sweet for some people; or the less sugary sugar-enhanced (SE) and everlasting heritage (EH) varieties. The new extrasweet hybrids generally stay sweet longer after harvest than the older varieties.

To grow successfully, corn needs ample space, warm weather, and generous amounts of fertilizer and water. If your area has a long growing season, you can plant early, midseason, and late-maturing crops for a whole summer of fresh corn. Allow enough time for a late crop to ripen before the first frost date in autumn. In Florida, in the mildest areas, you can also sow in autumn and winter. In short-growing-season areas, choose early or extra-early varieties.

POPULAR VARIETIES *Early:* 'Early Sunglow', matures 63 days after sowing, grows well in cool weather, stalks grow just 4½ feet tall, yellow kernels; 'Polar Vee', 53 days, yellow kernels, cold tolerant. *Midseason:* 'Golden Bantam', 78 days, classic yellow variety; 'Honey and Cream', 78 days, bicolored white and yellow; 'Indian Summer SH2', supersweet, 79 days, long ears of multicolored kernels. *Late:* 'Country Gentleman', 96 days, old-time favorite with irregular "shoe-peg" white kernels, good for freezing; 'Illini Xtra-Sweet SH2', 85 days, four times sweeter than standard corn, yellow kernels; 'Iochief', 86 days, yellow kernels, large ears, wind-resistant stalks; 'Kandy Korn EH', 89 days, yellow flavorful kernels, reddish stalks; 'Silver Queen', 92 days, classic white variety, flavorful kernels.

tip If you want to grind flour for your own tortillas, look for "dent" corn varieties. For the best popcorn, try 'Strawberry', which produces small yields of pretty red kernels.

BEST SITE Sunny—8 hours or more of direct sunlight a day—with rich, well-drained soil.

PLANTING AND CARE Sow seeds in spring when the soil has warmed to at least 50°F/10°C. Sowing early in cold soil won't give plants a head start, and they will be more prone to pests. Generally, the warmer the weather, the faster corn grows (but in hot parts of the Southwest, plant corn as early as possible to harvest by June).

Choose a block of space for planting corn. Pollen in the male tassels at the plant tops must travel in the breeze to the green female silk at the tip of each emerging corn ear, to pollinate it, so that a full set of kernels forms. This process works much better if you grow at least four rows in a block than if you plant in a single row.

Mix compost or well-rotted manure into the soil 2 to 3 weeks before planting time.

In dry-summer climates, prepare irrigation ditches before sowing. Use string and stakes to line up straight rows 2½ to 3 feet apart. Scoop out trenches a few inches deep along the rows, and pile the excavated soil along the rim of each trench. You'll place the seeds in this shoulder of excavated soil.

Just before sowing, water the soil until it is thoroughly moist. Then you shouldn't have to water again until the seeds have sprouted and grown several inches. Seeds tend to rot if the soil is too wet.   *continued >*

corn, continued

Sow seeds 1 to 2 inches deep and 4 to 6 inches apart. Make at least 4 rows. When seedlings are 6 inches high, thin them to 12 to 18 inches apart. Don't skip the thinning; overcrowding results in fewer and poorer-quality ears.

tip **You can sow corn in hills (see page 55), instead of in rows. Make soil hills a few inches high, 3 feet apart. Sow a cluster of 5 or 6 seeds 1 to 2 inches deep in each hill. Thin seedlings to 3 plants per hill.**

Keep the soil moist during the growing season; it's especially important not to let the soil dry out once the ears start to form silks. Feed with a high-nitrogen fertilizer twice during the growing season: when plants are 12 to 15 inches tall and again when they are 24 to 30 inches tall.

Corn plants may be troubled by aphids, flea beetles, or damping off; for help, see pages 74–75, 77. More damage is usually done by the larvae of night-flying moths—corn borers, corn earworms, and armyworms. Handpick the caterpillars, release trichogramma wasps when you see moth eggs or catch moths in a monitoring trap, or spray with *Bacillus thuringiensis (Bt);* see pages 72–73. Covering the ears with pantyhose helps protect against borers and earworms.

RIGHT *White corn*

BELOW *'Indian Summer' corn, with silk and tassel.*

tip **If you are growing more than one variety of corn, keep them separate, or they will cross-pollinate. Alternatively, plant varieties that mature at different times, or plant in succession, so the different kinds do not mature at the same time.**

HARVEST From 60 to 100 days after sowing seeds, depending on the variety; usually about 20 days after silks appear. When silks turn brown, make a small slit in the outer husk on one or two ears. Ripe kernels will squirt milky white juice when pinched. The tradition is to harvest just before you are ready to cook, but some new hybrid varieties of corn hold their sugar for 10 days if refrigerated. Twist the ears off the stalks. Yield is about 10 to 12 ears per 10-foot row, or 1 or 2 ears per plant.

FOR THE TABLE Boil in salted water for just 3 minutes; then eat plain or smear with basil butter (¹/₂ cup chopped basil leaves mixed with ¹/₂ cup butter) and salt.

'County Fair' pickler

cucumbers

'Lemon'
cucumber

Cucumbers are categorized into two types: slicers and picklers. Slicers are generally smooth, dark green, slightly tough-skinned, and long. Picklers are shorter, tender-skinned, and more prickly or warty. You can actually use young slicers for pickling and picklers for slicing into summer salads. Some varieties grow like vines, others as bushes. There are also novelty cukes, like lemon cucumber, a bright yellow mild-flavored ball; and Armenian and Asian cukes 2 feet long.

All cucumbers love warm weather, long deep irrigation, and space. Vines may spread 6 feet before the plants stop bearing. You can curb their rambling by training them up sturdy trellises (see page 57), which helps keep long cukes straight, or confining them in containers. Or you can plant dwarf and compact bush varieties that are very productive but take less space.

Bitter-free varieties won't taste bitter or attract cucumber beetles, since the beetles are drawn to the chemical compound causing bitterness. Burpless varieties don't cause burping.

POPULAR VARIETIES *Slicers:* 'Bush Champion', compact, good for containers, 10-inch fruit; 'Salad Bush', small vines, 8-inch fruit, disease resistant, monoecious (see tip); 'Sweet Success', parthenocarpic (see tip), burpless, 12- to 14-inch fruit. *Picklers:* 'Pickalot', bush, gynoecious (see tip), bears over a long season, 5-inch fruit; 'Pioneer', medium-length vines, gynoecious (see tip), disease resistant. *Others:* 'Suyo Long', Asian slicing type, 14-inch spiny fruit, mild taste, burpless, bitter-free; 'Lemon', round 3- to 4-inch fruit, sweet taste, yellow skin, bitter-free, excellent for a container.

tip Standard (monoecious) varieties bear male and female flowers on the same vine. Insects pollinate the female flowers by carrying pollen from the male flowers (so avoid using pesticides, or at least those that kill bees, during flowering). Gynoecious hybrids bear only female flowers and are far more productive, but you must plant at least one male plant for pollination (a few color-coded seeds of male plants are included in each seed packet). Varieties described as parthenocarpic require no pollination; they are virtually seedless.

BEST SITE Warm, sunny, with rich, well-drained soil.

PLANTING AND CARE Sow seeds in spring, after the last frost date, when the soil temperature has warmed to at least 60°F/16°C. If you'd like to get a head start, start seeds indoors (see page 52) in a warm place 4 weeks before the last frost date. *continued >*

'Salad Bush'
slicer

cucumbers, continued

ABOVE *Armenian cucumbers are best harvested at 20 inches.*

RIGHT *An old 6-foot ladder keeps cucumbers off the ground.*

Choose whether to grow your crop in rows or in hills (see page 55). For rows, sow a cluster of 2 or 3 seeds 1 inch deep, 8 to 12 inches apart; space rows 3 to 6 feet apart; when seedlings are a few inches tall, thin to 1 per cluster. For hills, make soil mounds 4 to 6 feet apart in each direction and sow clusters of 4 to 6 seeds 1 inch deep in each hill; thin seedlings to 2 or 3 per hill.

Cucumbers are extremely thirsty plants. Keep the soil moist throughout the growing season; be especially vigilant about watering from the time the fruit begins to swell. Furrow or drip irrigation works best (see pages 62–63); sprinkling is not recommended, because it encourages downy mildew. Weed regularly. Mulch under the fruits to help keep them clean.

Cucumbers are subject to several pests and diseases: aphids, cucumber beetles, flea beetles, mites, squash bugs, squash vine borers, bacterial wilt, and downy and powdery mildew. For information on avoiding these problems, see pages 74–78. Squash vine borers and bacterial wilt also may cause problems. Squash vine borers enter the vine near soil level and cause sudden wilting; try slitting open the vine, removing the borers, and mounding soil around the slit area to encourage new rooting; or purchase parasitic nematodes (see page 73) and inject them into the stems. To help prevent bacterial wilt, which causes wilting and may cause the plant to die, control cucumber beetles, which transmit it.

HARVEST Cut from the vine when fruits are a usable size—6 to 8 inches long for slicing cucumbers (longer for extralong varieties), at least 2 inches long for sweet pickles, 5 to 6 inches long for dill pickles. Harvest 3 or 4 times a week to keep plants producing new fruit and to prevent ripe fruit from becoming seedy. Yields are 8 to 10 pounds per 10-foot row.

FOR THE TABLE Peel cucumbers to make them easier to digest. Slice thinly, and season with freshly ground white pepper.

tip Cucumbers taste bitter if the soil isn't kept constantly moist, so check the soil often. (Temperatures over 100°F/ 38°C also cause bitterness.) Seedy cucumbers have been left too long on the plant; harvest every few days to keep the seeds from growing in ripe cukes.

Purple, plump, and polished to an inky sheen, eggplants are as beautiful to look at in the garden as to taste. The plants are handsome too—little bush-trees, with big purple-tinged leaves and drooping violet flowers. Like its cousins, tomato and pepper, eggplant is an annual fruit but commonly called a vegetable. Violet, green, rose, and white varieties are available, as well as Asian, sometimes called *Japanese,* eggplants, which are long and slender.

Eggplant isn't for a cool-summer climate; to produce well, it needs 60 to 95 warm days and nights, with night temperatures above 65°F/18°C. If your season is short, choose fast-maturing varieties.

POPULAR VARIETIES *Oval fruits:* 'Black Beauty', classic purple-skinned variety, with large fruits, for long warm summers; 'Dusky', purple, fast-maturing; 'Rosa Bianca', heirloom, white skin with lavender streaks. *Asian eggplant:* 'Neon', dark pink, slightly bulbous; 'Pingtung Long', lavender-purple, very long fruits.

BEST SITE Sunny, warm location, with fertile, recently manured soil.

PLANTING AND CARE Start by setting out young nursery plants in spring when day temperatures reach 70°F/21°C and all danger of frost has passed, or by sowing seeds indoors (see page 52) in a very warm place 6 to 8 weeks before planting. Don't set out plants too early; they hate cold weather and are very tender to frost. Space them 2 to 2½ feet apart in rows 3 feet apart.

Keep the soil moist; mulch (see page 66) to maintain soil moisture and warmth. Weed regularly.

Stake varieties that bear large oval fruit (see page 57), or place tomato cages over the plants when they are young, to support the branches, which are brittle and prone to breaking if heavily weighted with fruit. Large oval-fruited varieties may grow 4 feet tall.

Aphids, Colorado potato beetles, cutworms, flea beetles, whiteflies, blights, and verticillium wilt are the hindrances. Keep plants well-fed and watered; for other strategies, see pages 74–78.

HARVEST In summer, when fruits are still firm and glossy (once they lose their sheen, they taste bitter). Use a knife or clippers to cut each fruit from the plant when it's ready. Oval-fruited varieties yield about 8 fruits per plants, Asian kinds up to 15.

FOR THE TABLE Bake baby eggplants on a bed of stewed onions, tomatoes, garlic, olives, and thyme.

tip Stuck for space? Plant one Japanese eggplant, which will grow to only about 2½ feet tall and yield from 8 to 15 fruits.

eggplant
Warm-season annual; very tender to frost.

'Farmers' Long' Japanese eggplant

fennel

Cool-season annual; tolerates light frost.

figs

Deciduous fruit tree, 10 to 30 feet tall; needs no frost protection above 20°F/–7°C.

The vegetable fennel produces a solid, crisp bulb above the soil line. It tastes slightly of anise, like the herb fennel, its cousin, but herb fennel has no bulb. In Italy, the vegetable is called *finocchio;* sometimes you'll see it here as *Florence fennel.*

Fennel takes up to 3 months to form a bulb, and in warm weather it bolts quickly into flower and stops growing. Unless you garden in a region with a mild winter or a long, cool spring, it's easier to get a good crop by sowing the seeds in summer and letting the plants mature during the cool weather in fall. If you want to try an early crop, you can get a head start by sowing the seeds in pots indoors (see page 52) 6 to 8 weeks before the last frost date, then planting outdoors when all danger of frost has passed.

POPULAR VARIETIES 'Herald', resistant to bolting, good for spring planting; 'Trieste', large bulbs, late maturing; 'Zefa Fino', tender fat bulbs.

BEST SITE Sunny, with rich, well-drained soil.

PLANTING AND CARE Sow seeds ¼ inch deep and 1 inch apart in rows 2 feet apart. Keep the soil moist until germination. Thin seedlings to 10 inches apart. Water and remove weeds consistently. Apply a mulch (see page 66) to keep the soil moist and cool. When bulbs start to form, mound soil around the base of each plant to blanch the bulb and keep it tender.

HARVEST Pull plants as needed, and cut off roots and tops of stems. To avoid damage, harvest all the plants before the first hard frost.

FOR THE TABLE Cut in half, brush with olive oil, and grill on the barbecue; or slice raw into a green salad.

tip Fennel foliage is light green, delicate, and ferny. The plant grows to about 2 feet tall. Make a place for it in a flower garden, or grow it with tall, bronze sweet fennel, the herb, which has pretty coppery foliage.

Figs are among the easiest fruit trees to grow. Unless freezes keep them to the size of a large shrub, they grow fairly fast to 15 to 30 feet tall, depending on the variety. You can make them smaller by pruning or by espaliering them against a wall or fence (see page 91). In a big container, you can hold them to 10 feet. Most varieties bear two crops a year (a small one in spring and a larger one in fall), and the fruits don't ripen on the tree all at once. Figs are also remarkably pest-free, although gophers find their roots delectable (see Planting and Care on the next page).

Most fig varieties need a long warm summer; if you live in a cool-summer area, plant the tree in the warmest part of the garden, for example, near a south-facing wall that reflects light and retains warmth.

Frost hardiness varies; no protection is needed if the temperature stays above 20°F/–7°C. Where hard freezes are common, the branches may freeze back severely, but the tree will continue as a big shrub. In cold-winter climates, protect container-grown trees by bringing them into a garage or storage area for the winter.

POPULAR VARIETIES 'Brown Turkey', brownish purple fruit with light red flesh, small tree, cold hardy, good for containers; 'Kadota', greenish yellow thick-skinned fruit with delicious amber-pink flesh, big tree, needs lots of heat; 'Mission', purple-black fruit with rosy pink flesh, large tree.

BEST SITE Warm, sunny, with fast-draining soil.

PLANTING AND CARE Container trees can be planted anytime except during extreme summer heat; for planting information, see page 54. Plant bare-root (dormant) trees in winter or early spring; for planting instructions, see page 88. Amend the soil with organic matter such as compost, and add a controlled-release complete fertilizer. If gophers are a potential problem, line the hole with wire mesh.

To train the tree during the first few years, see pages 88–89, 91 (use the open center system, or espalier).

Water regularly until the tree is established, then deeply every 2 weeks (some varieties are drought tolerant and need little water once they are established). Apply mulch around the tree, but not right up to it, to help keep the soil moist. Avoid cultivating under or near the tree, because the spreading roots are just beneath the soil. Apply a balanced fertilizer each spring; do not use high-nitrogen fertilizers, which promote growth at the expense of fruit. Before fruit begins to ripen, cover the tree with netting to keep birds away.

PRUNING Prune lightly each winter, removing any dead wood or crossed branches (see page 90). Pinch back runaway shoots in any season. If you live in a hot-summer region, whitewash the trunk to protect any newly exposed bark from sunburn; use commercial whitewash or latex paint.

HARVEST Pick the fruit when it is slightly soft and beginning to bend at the neck; figs picked before maturity won't ripen. If the milky white sap irritates your skin, wear gloves.

tip Fig trees are handsome. The large, bright green, lobed leaves give a tropical look to the garden; when they drop in fall, the branch structure is so pleasing (eventually it becomes beautifully gnarled) that garden designers often illuminate it from below.

ABOVE *'Brown Turkey'* fig
BELOW *'Kadota'* fig

garlic

Cool-season perennial; withstands frost.

STIR-FRIED GARLIC LETTUCE

(*SHOON CHOW SAANG CHOY*)

MAKES 6 SERVINGS

Stir-fried garlic lettuce is made from a classic yin-yang pair: lettuce is yin, with a cooling, soothing power, and garlic is yang, full of warmth and energy. It's perfect if cooked only lightly—it's like a wilted salad, and the lettuce retains some crunch.

Rinse and drain thoroughly 1 head **iceberg lettuce** *(1½ pounds). Cut out and discard the core. Separate the leaves, and tear them into 3- by 5-inch pieces. In a small bowl, mix 1½ teaspoons* **soy sauce,** *1½ teaspoons* **Asian** *(toasted)* **sesame oil,** *1 teaspoon* **Shao Xing rice wine** *or dry sherry, ¾ teaspoon* **sugar,** *¼ teaspoon* **salt,** *and ¼ teaspoon* **white pepper.** *Set a 14-inch wok or 12-inch frying pan over high heat. When it is hot, add 1 tablespoon* **salad oil** *and 3 cloves peeled and pressed* **garlic.** *Stir-fry until the garlic just begins to brown, about 30 seconds. Add the lettuce, and stir just until slightly limp but still bright green and somewhat crisp, about 2 minutes (if all the lettuce doesn't fit, add half, stir until slightly wilted, about 30 seconds, and then stir in the remaining leaves). Stir in the soy sauce mixture. Pour onto a platter, and serve immediately.*

PER SERVING: 56 CALORIES, 59% (33 CALORIES) FROM FAT; 1.6 G PROTEIN; 3.7 G FAT (0.5 G SATURATED); 5.1 G CARBOHYDRATE (1.1 G FIBER); 191 MG SODIUM; 0 MG CHOLESTEROL.

Garlic is easy to grow if you start with bulbs (sets) from a nursery and choose a variety suited to your climate. You might also have luck with bulbs from a grocery store. Break the bulbs up into cloves, and plant only the biggest ones, those with pieces of root attached.

POPULAR VARIETIES 'Inchelium Red', excellent sweet flavor; 'Polish White', good for cold regions; 'Silver Rose', rose-hued cloves, great for braiding; 'Spanish Roja', purplish skin, good for cold regions.

tip Giant, or elephant, garlic has unusually large (fist-size) bulbs and a mild garlic flavor.

BEST SITE Sunny, with rich, fluffy, well-drained soil.

PLANTING AND CARE Set out cloves in fall, for an early summer harvest. In cold-winter climates, choose the hardiest varieties; you might try setting out cloves in early spring for a fall harvest, but the bulbs will likely be smaller.

Plant the cloves with pointed ends up and tops 1 inch deep, 4 to 8 inches apart, in rows 16 inches apart. (Space cloves of elephant garlic 8 to 12 inches apart.)

Keep the soil moist, and weed regularly or mulch to keep weeds out. In cold-winter climates, mulch heavily at the onset of winter to help prevent soil heaving, which can force the cloves out of the ground.

Rake back the mulch in spring. Keep the soil moist. Pick a few of the green leaves when they are 12 inches tall for eating in salads if you like. Pinch off any blossoms that develop. When leaf tips start to turn yellowish brown, stop watering.

Smut fungus—black spots and streaks on leaves and between cloves—may develop in areas where summers are cool. Remove any affected plants.

HARVEST When the leaves are mostly brown. Lift bulbs out carefully with a garden fork; pulling by hand may crack apart the bulbs and decrease their shelf life. Dry the bulbs by hanging them in bundles in a dry, well-ventilated area until the skins are papery, about 3 weeks. Remove dirt, and cut off most of the roots; then store the bulbs in mesh bags in a cool, airy place out of direct sunlight. "Softneck" types can be braided.

FOR THE TABLE Mix minced garlic with olive oil and chopped parsley, spread on French bread, sprinkle with parmesan, and toast in the broiler.

Scented geraniums grow year-round in mild-winter climates. Elsewhere, they are popular as annuals or are grown in pots so they can be moved indoors before the first frost. Place one where you are likely to brush its leaves—and release its fragrance—as you move about the garden. It's hard to choose just one; there are so many aromatic species available, including apricot, nutmeg, and even coconut. Plant size varies from 6 inches to 3 feet tall; leaves from rough to felty, tiny to huge.

tip Peppermint geranium makes an unusual ground cover. All kinds of geraniums are great for herb gardens, edgings, and the front of flower beds. Look for trailing types for window boxes and hanging baskets.

POPULAR VARIETIES Apple geranium *(Pelargonium odoratissimum),* lemon geranium *(P. crispum* or *P.* 'Prince Rupert'), peppermint geranium *(P. tomentosum),* rose geranium *(P. capitatum, P. graveolens, P.* 'Lady Plymouth').

BEST SITE Sunny or, in hot-summer climates, lightly shaded, with well-drained soil; can also be grown indoors on a bright sunny windowsill.

PLANTING AND CARE Set out plants in early to midspring—even late winter in mild-winter areas. Keep them moderately well watered. Pinch growing tips while the plants are small to force side branches. Remove faded flowers to encourage new growth.

Scented geraniums have virtually no pest or disease problems. In mild areas, some are attractive to budworms, which nibble the leaves and drill holes into the flower buds; to control, spray with *Bacillus thuringiensis (Bt).*

In cold-winter regions, dig up the plants, pot them, and bring them indoors for the winter; or take cuttings from the plants anytime during the year, and pot these, for planting outdoors in spring.

HARVEST Pick leaves as needed.

FOR THE TABLE Use fresh leaves for flavoring iced drinks or jelly.

geraniums
(Pelargonium species)

Perennial, or annual in cold regions; edible leaves; tolerates light frost.

TOP *Peppermint geranium*
LEFT *Chocolate mint geranium*

Besides contributing to jelly jars and fruit bowls, table grapes (also called *dessert grapes*) bring beauty to the garden. The plants create a filigree of heart-shaped leaves, twisting vines, and curling tendrils. Their glistening fruit ranges from pale gold-green through shades of red and purple to deep blue-black. Fall color is another feature, and few other vines grow so fast—a single grapevine produces enough new growth each year to roof an arbor.

Grapes grow nearly everywhere in the United States, although different varieties are adapted to different regions. The vines are not quick to produce fruit—they'll need perhaps 4 or 5 years to yield a full harvest—but they live extraordinarily long, for 100 years and more.

Grapevines need plenty of sun and free air movement. Choose early-maturing varieties if your growing season is short; the earliest need at least 140 frost-free days, and European varieties need many more.

continued >

grapes

Perennial vine; frost-hardiness varies by type.

grapes, continued

training grapes on a wire

*During the **first summer** after planting, let the vine grow unchecked. Then proceed as follows: **First winter,** select the sturdiest shoot as the trunk, tie it to the support, and cut it back to three or four buds. Remove the other shoots. **Second spring,** once the buds have grown out to 6- to 8-inch shoots, select a vigorous upright one for the continuation of the trunk, and cut off the others. (To grow a grapevine on a double wire rather than a single one, choose another two strong shoots for side arms, and tie them to the lower wire.) **Second summer,** when the trunk reaches the wire, cut its tip so arms form. Choose the two strongest developing shoots for arms; remove the others. If any shoots develop from the arms, pinch them back to 10 inches long. **Second winter,** prune off all growth on the trunk and arms. **Third summer,** allow the vine to grow. Prune off any growth from the trunk. Training is now complete (see drawing). For cane and spur pruning, needed every year from now on, see the main text.*

POPULAR VARIETIES *American grapes* (for cold-winter areas): 'Canadice', red, seedless, early, ripens in very cool areas, excellent for fresh eating or juice, hardy to –20°F/–29°C if well pruned; 'Concord', blue-black, seeded, midseason, classic variety for juice, jelly, and jam; 'Reliance', red, seedless, early midseason, mild sweet flavor, good for fresh eating or juice, dependably productive.

European grapes (for mild-winter areas of California and Arizona): 'Flame', red, seedless, early midseason, very vigorous, water lightly to keep growth in check, good for fresh eating and raisins; 'Thompson Seedless', pale green, midseason, small sweet fruit, for fresh eating and raisins, does best in hot dry areas.

Muscadine grapes (for Southern regions where winter temperatures do not fall below 10°F/–12°C; if you choose a variety that is not self-fertile, be sure to purchase 1 vine with male flowers to pollinate up to 12 vines with female flowers): 'Cowart', black, seeded, early to midseason, for fresh eating or juice, self-fertile; 'Scuppernong', bronzy green, midseason, original variety, good for fresh eating and wine, needs a pollenizer.

TOP *'Steuben' is a seeded American grape with good disease resistance.*

LEFT *'Perlette' grapes need less heat than most other European varieties.*

tip **Avoid a site where grapes were grown within the past 3 years. A slope is ideal; stagnant air in a low-lying basin increases chances of frost damage and mildew.**

BEST SITE Sunny, with deep, fertile, well-drained soil.

SUPPORT Grapevines can be grown on a trellis, arbor, chain-link or rail fence, or wall strung with wire. Whatever your choice, it must offer sturdy support for the heavy bunches of fruit. For a custom single-wire trellis (see sidebar), set stout posts in the ground 15 to 20 feet apart (farther for the more vigorous grapes, such as muscadines). The posts should rise 5 feet above the soil. For spacing of rows, see Planting and Care, next. String sturdy wire—10- or 11-gauge—across the post tops. For a double-wire trellis, string a lower wire, at the 2 1/2-foot level.

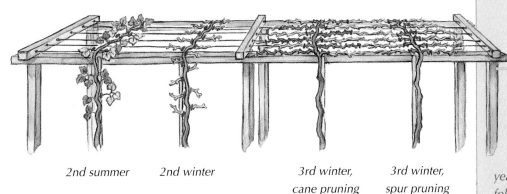

| 2nd summer | 2nd winter | 3rd winter, cane pruning | 3rd winter, spur pruning |

PLANTING AND CARE Purchase 1-year-old bare-root vines, and plant during the dormant season, before new growth starts—winter in mild-winter regions, early spring (about 3 weeks before the last frost date) in cold-winter regions. Before planting, set up supports for your vines; see Support, earlier.

At planting time, trim the vine roots to 6 inches, which forces feeder roots to grow. Dig holes (see page 54) wide and deep enough for the roots. Space the holes as follows: American and European grapes, 8 to 10 feet apart in rows 10 to 12 feet apart; muscadine grapes, 12 to 15 feet apart in rows 20 feet apart. If you are planting at an arbor or fence, position the holes about 1 1/2 feet away from the structure, and set the plants at a 45° angle, so they lean toward the support.

Cut top growth back to two or three buds. Place the vines as deep in the soil as they grew in the nursery, spreading the roots in all directions. In some areas, it's recommended that you plant grapes deeper than they grew in the nursery, leaving just one bud exposed; check with a local nursery.

Water and weed regularly. Grapes are prone to fungal diseases, so avoid splashing water on the leaves; drip irrigation is ideal.

Fertilize each spring when buds swell, with a balanced fertilizer (such as 10-10-10). Spread it in a band around the vine, 12 to 18 inches from the trunk at first, and then 2 to 3 feet from the trunk by the fourth year. In the first year, apply just 1/4 the amount recommended on the fertilizer bag; in the second year, 1/2; in the third year, 3/4 the recommended amount; and thereafter the full dose.

Grapevines are sometimes plagued by aphids, leafhoppers, and downy mildew; for controls, see pages 74–75, 77. In some regions, grape berry moth larvae feed on flower buds and fruits; be sure to discard leaf debris under the vines in fall, and if necessary, use a biological control or natural pesticide (see pages 72–73) when pests appear.

TRAINING AND PRUNING Grapevines are vigorous; they can grow to 100 feet long if left unpruned. To control the growth and harvest good crops, start training and pruning the vines in the first year (see sidebars).

After the third summer, the training will be complete, but you must continue to prune the vines each winter for good fruit production. The two most widely used pruning methods are spur pruning and cane pruning. When you purchase your vines, check the recommended pruning method

training grapes on an arbor

If all you want is a leafy cover for an arbor, you need only train a strong vine up and over its support and thin out tangled growth each year. For good fruit production, follow these steps:

First summer after planting, let the vine grow unchecked.

First winter, select the sturdiest shoot as a trunk, tie it to the arbor post, and cut it back to 3 or 4 buds. Remove the other shoots.

Second spring, once the buds have grown out to 6- to 8-inch shoots, select a vigorous upright one for the continuation of the trunk, and cut off the others.

Second summer, when the vine reaches the top of the arbor, bend it over, and secure it as it grows across the top. Remove the side shoots to encourage the tip to grow.

Second winter, cut back the main stem to the point just beyond where you want the last set of branches. Cut off all the side shoots.

Third spring, thin new shoots to 1 foot apart. Cane pruning and spur pruning differ from now on.

Third winter, for spur pruning, cut back each selected shoot (from third spring) to 2 buds. Now follow the spur pruning guidelines in the main text.

Third winter, for cane pruning, cut back branches alternately to long canes (12 buds) and spurs (2 buds). Now follow the cane pruning guidelines in the main text.

grapes, continued

for each variety. Of the popular varieties listed earlier, 'Concord' and 'Flame' can be pruned using either method, 'Thompson Seedless' needs cane pruning, and spur pruning is recommended for the others.

Spur pruning begins in the third winter. Remove weak side shoots from the arms. Leave the strongest shoots (spurs), spaced 6 to 10 inches apart, and cut each to two buds. Each spur will produce two fruit-bearing shoots during the next growing season. During the next winter and every winter thereafter, remove the lower shoot on each spur, and cut the upper shoot to two buds. Those buds will develop into shoots that bear fruit the following summer.

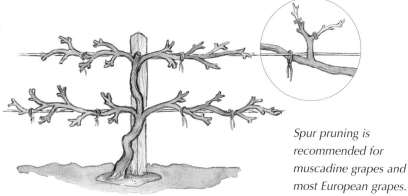

Spur pruning is recommended for muscadine grapes and most European grapes.

For cane pruning, in the third winter, select one strong lateral shoot near the trunk on each arm, and cut it back to 2 buds; these are the renewal spurs. Select another strong lateral near the trunk on each arm, cut it back to 12 buds, and tie it to the wire. Remove all other shoots. The 12 buds will produce fruiting canes in the summer; the following winter, remove the fruiting arms entirely, and replace them with the two longest and strongest shoots that grew from the renewal spurs; cut each to 12 buds and tie these shoots to the wire; select the two next-best shoots as renewal spurs, and cut each to 2 buds. Remove all other shoots.

Cane pruning is recommended for most American grapes and a few European grapes.

HARVEST Late summer to late fall, when the grapes are sweet and fully colored. Cut bunches from vines. Shake muscadine grapes from the vines onto a cloth. Yields vary, depending on the variety.

FOR THE TABLE Include grapes in salads with apples and nuts.

This arbor carries four different grape varieties that ripen in succession, starting in mid-August.

Johnny-jump-ups, as their name implies, turn up unexpectedly where you didn't plant them. They reseed themselves merrily year after year, but they are easy to pull or hoe if you want to corral them. Pansies are more mild-mannered, though equally irresistible—they have such friendly faces.

tip Johnny-jump-ups and pansies grow beautifully in containers and make a colorful edging for vegetable or herb gardens.

POPULAR VARIETIES Imperial hybrids and Majestic Giants pansy strains, extralarge flowers; Joker pansy strain, striking color combinations, such as orange, purple, and black.

BEST SITE Sunny or shady, with rich, well-drained soil.

PLANTING AND CARE In mild-winter areas, sow seeds in late summer or set out nursery plants in fall, for winter-to-spring bloom. In cold-winter areas, set out plants as early as possible in spring for summer bloom, or start seeds indoors (see page 52) 10 to 12 weeks before the last frost date, for flowers by early summer. Sow seeds 1/4 inch deep and 2 inches apart. Set plants, or thin seedlings to, 8 inches apart.

Water regularly through the growing season. To keep plants blooming, remove spent flowers. In cool-summer areas, trim the plants lightly when they get leggy in summer, to encourage a flush of flowers in fall. Replace pansies that are ragged.

FOR THE TABLE Mix pansy petals or Johnny-jump-ups with fruit (see page 160) or mesclun.

johnny-jump-ups, pansies
(Viola species)

Cool-season annual, perennial grown as annual; withstands frost.

Kale is easy to grow and generally isn't prey to the pests and diseases that afflict other cabbage-family crops. The "ornamental kale" varieties have edible, brightly marked and colored leaves, but the leaves of the regular kinds are also highly decorative: long, slender, and deep black-green, or emerald and frilly edged, or bluish, or stark red.

POPULAR VARIETIES 'Dwarf Blue Curled Vates', blue-green crinkled leaves, compact, very cold hardy; 'Dwarf Siberian', curly green leaves, compact; 'Lacinato', blue-green crinkled leaves, tall; 'Red Russian', red leaves in cold weather, leaves turn green when cooked, tall.

BEST SITE Sunny or lightly shaded, with fertile soil. Practice crop rotation (see page 77).

PLANTING AND CARE For a summer crop, sow seeds in early spring (get started early, because hot summer sun turns the leaves of many varieties bitter). For a fall and winter crop, sow seeds in late summer and fall. Sow seeds 1/4 inch deep, 1 inch apart, in rows 1 1/2 to 2 feet apart. Alternatively, broadcast the seeds (see page 55) in wide bands. When the seedlings are a few inches tall, thin them to 8 to 18 inches apart, and stir-fry the thinnings.

Keep the soil moist during the growing season, but stop watering after the first frost. For information on aphids, cabbageworms, damping off, and fusarium wilt, see pages 74, 77–78. *continued >*

kale

Cool-season annual; cold hardy.

lavender

(*Lavandula* species)

Shrub; species mentioned are quite cold hardy.

LINDA DOWLING'S LAVENDER LEMONADE

MAKES 6 CUPS, ABOUT 6 SERVINGS

'Hidcote' lavender turns lemonade rosy pink. Other varieties turn it a paler color. Avoid piney-smelling lavenders, such as spike.

*Combine 1 cup **sugar** with 2½ cups **water** in a medium pan. Bring to a boil over medium heat, stirring to dissolve the **sugar.** Add ¾ cup (a generous handful of) fresh **lavender blossoms** or 1 tablespoon dried lavender blooms stripped from stems. Cover, remove from the heat, and let stand at least 20 minutes (and up to several hours). Strain and discard the lavender. Pour into a glass pitcher. Add 1 cup freshly squeezed strained **lemon juice** and 2½ cups water. Stir well. Pour into tall glasses half-filled with ice, or refrigerate until ready to use. Garnish with fresh **lavender sprigs.***

PER SERVING: 139 CALORIES, 0% (0 CALORIES) FROM FAT; 0.2 G PROTEIN; 0 G FAT; 37 G CARBOHYDRATE (0.2 G FIBER); 0.7 MG SODIUM; 0 MG CHOLESTEROL.

HARVEST Start with the thinnings. Then either cut outer leaves as the plant grows, or wait until the plant is mature, 55 to 75 days after sowing, and pull it up entirely. Yields are 4 to 8 pounds per 10-foot row.

FOR THE TABLE Stir-fry with a little sliced onion and a shake of chili flakes.

tip Mature leaves taste sweeter—and ornamental varieties are most brightly colored—when they have been nipped by frost.

The best lavenders for cooking are those with the sweetest scent, such as English lavender and lavandin, the lavender used by French perfume makers. Grow several plants, maybe a hedge of lavenders around a vegetable or herb plot, so you have enough stems and flowers for summer savory dishes and desserts and plenty left over to dry. Lavender plants don't mind drought, but they struggle in steamy heat; lavandin is more tolerant of warm humidity than English lavender.

POPULAR VARIETIES English lavender *(L. angustifolia):* 'Hidcote', 1½ to 2 feet tall, deep violet-blue flowers; 'Munstead', 1½ feet tall, long blooming. Lavandin *(L. intermedia):* 'Grosso', 3 feet tall, very fragrant indeed; 'Provence', 3 feet tall, light purple flowers.

BEST SITE Sunny, sheltered from wind, with loose, well-drained soil.

PLANTING AND CARE Start with nursery plants in containers; set them out (see page 54) in spring or at any time except during summer heat. Space them 2 to 4 feet apart, depending on the size of the variety.

Water regularly during the first year while plants become established. Thereafter, water about once a month. No fertilizer is necessary or advisable. Prune back stems to about 6 inches immediately after bloom, to keep plants compact and neat. Lavender is not prone to pests or diseases.

English lavender

HARVEST Just as flowers open, in late spring and summer.

FOR THE TABLE Throw a handful of flowers and stems on barbecue coals that have turned to white ash for the last 5 minutes of cooking to give a mild floral fragrance to lamb, pork, or salmon. Chopped fresh or dried lavender combined with lemon juice and olive oil makes a fine marinade. Add 1 to 2 tablespoons of finely chopped flowers to a favorite sugar cookie or shortbread recipe.

tip To air-dry lavender, hang bunches upside down for a few days in a dark, cool place with good air circulation.

leeks

Cool-season annual; cold hardy.

Growing leeks takes patience—the regular thick leeks spend 4 to 7 months fattening up to prime size; the baby leeks, ½ inch in diameter, take about 3 months. Set leeks out in furrows so it's easy to mound soil around them, which increases the length of the white shanks.

POPULAR VARIETIES 'Blue Solaise', sweet-tasting large shanks, very cold hardy, good for overwintering; 'King Richard', early maturing, tall baby leeks for summer harvest.

BEST SITE Sunny (partially shady in hot climates), with rich soil.

PLANTING AND CARE To save time in the long growing cycle, start leeks from purchased plants. Set them out in spring around the time of the last frost date if your summers are cool; in hot-summer areas, set out plants in fall. You can also start seeds in pots indoors (see page 52) 6 weeks before spring planting.

LEFT *'Musselborough' leeks*
BELOW *'Selecta' leeks*

Make 5-inch-deep furrows spaced 4 to 12 inches apart. Set the plants in the furrow 2 to 4 inches apart.

Keep the soil moist during the growing season. As the plants grow, mound soil into the furrows and around the stalks to blanch them—which makes the stem bottoms white and mild. Feed with kelp or fish emulsion every few weeks.

Thrips may be a nuisance; for information, see page 76.

tip Mound the soil just short of the leaf joints (where the leaf joins the stem). If you pile it higher, the soil will work its way into the shanks.

HARVEST When the stems are ½ to 2 inches thick. Lift out of the ground with a spading fork. In cold-winter areas, harvest before the ground freezes. Yields are 4 to 6 pounds per 10-foot row.

FOR THE TABLE To make potato and leek soup, boil a pound of each in salted water, purée, and serve with a dollop of butter.

lettuces, salad greens

Cool-season annual (except chicory and radicchio, which are perennials, although usually grown as annuals); tolerates light frost.

'Oak Leaf' leaf lettuce

A browse through a seed catalog or seed display rack reveals an awesome assortment of modern lettuces and salad greens. If you've heard of mesclun, maybe you haven't heard of escarole or Batavian crisphead. Even good old-fashioned leaf lettuce is available with bronze or rose tints as well as plain green. The contemporary salad scene is a grand, diverse mix of easygoing, quick-growing leaves.

The main growing requirement for lettuces and salad greens is cool weather. Crisphead (iceberg) lettuce tolerates heat better than others, but generally in warm weather lettuce turns bitter and quickly bolts to seed.

For other salad greens, see Arugula, page 110, Mustard Greens, page 153, and Nasturtiums, page 154.

BEST SITE Sunny or partially shaded, with fertile, well-drained soil.

tip Because lettuce grows well in cool conditions, plant it in the shade of taller vegetables such as broccoli or corn. Or make a container planting that you can move into the shade in hot weather; lettuce has shallow roots, so you need a soil depth of just 9 inches.

PLANTING AND CARE Start sowing seeds or setting out nursery seedlings in very early spring; they will grow readily in cool soil. If you like, start seeds indoors (see page 52) 4 weeks earlier. Make repeat sowings outdoors at 2-week intervals until late spring or when temperatures are 75 to 80°F/ 24 to 27°C. Then wait to make additional sowings until the weather cools in late summer or fall (lettuce seeds won't germinate in hot soil); continue sowings until 6 to 8 weeks before the first frost—through the winter in mild climates.

Sow seeds ⅛ to ¼ inch deep, 1 to 2 inches apart, in rows 1 to 2 feet apart (1 foot for leaf lettuce, at least 1½ feet for butterhead, romaine, and crisphead). Or broadcast the seeds in a wide bed (see page 55). Cover the seeds with a thin layer of fine soil, and regularly spray the seedbed very lightly with water until the seeds germinate. Thin the seedlings as directed for the different types.

Keep the soil moist; if it dries out, growth will stop, and leaves may become bitter. Weed regularly. Watch for slugs (see page 76 for nontoxic controls). Other pests and diseases may also appear: aphids, cabbage loopers, cutworms, flea beetles, leafhoppers, leaf miners, snails, downy mildew, and fusarium wilt; see pages 74–78.

'Four Seasons' butterhead lettuce

FOR THE TABLE Delicate leaf lettuce takes a light dressing made with a champagne or white wine vinegar. Use stronger vinegars, such as balsamic, and heavier oils, such as olive oil mixed with nut oils, to tame spicy greens.

leaf lettuce

The lettuce that has the most varieties and is the easiest to grow is leaf lettuce. It produces bunches of leaves rather than a head. The leaves may be dark green, chartreuse, red, or bronze, and smooth, puckered, frilled, or ruffly. All types are exceptionally tender. They mature quickly, 4 to 6 weeks after sowing, which makes leaf lettuce a good choice for areas where hot weather follows closely on the heels of spring.

POPULAR VARIETIES 'Black Seeded Simpson', apple-green large leaves; 'Green Ice', superfrilly, sweet, slow to bolt; 'Lolla Rossa', edged with pink-red, deeply curled, heat tolerant; 'Oak Leaf', dark green, tender thick midribs; 'Red Sails', edged with red, heat tolerant; 'Salad Bowl', bright green and deeply lobed, heat tolerant.

HARVEST Start with thinnings (thin until plants are 4 to 8 inches apart). Thereafter you have three choices: pull off individual outer leaves when they are large enough to use; or cut off all the leaves 1 inch above the soil, and wait for new leaves to come again (see page 100); or pull up the entire head when it is mature.

butterhead lettuce

The butterhead type forms small, tender, rather open heads, with white-veined creamy or butter-yellow centers. They take a little longer to mature than leaf lettuce, from 50 to 65 days after sowing.

POPULAR VARIETIES 'Bibb', delicate taste; 'Buttercrunch', solid head, tolerates heat; 'Tom Thumb', tiny firm head, good for containers.

'Buttercrunch' (butterhead) lettuce

HARVEST Start with thinnings (thin until plants are 6 to 8 inches apart). Then wait until the head is mature, and pull up the entire plant.

romaine lettuce

The freshest Caesar salad starts in your own plot. Romaine, also called *cos* lettuce, has upright clusters of big leaves that are exceptionally crisp and flavorful. Some are slow to mature (up to 80 days from sowing), so you'll need a long stretch of cool-to-moderate weather to grow them. Get a jump start by sowing seeds indoors (see page 52) for early spring planting.

continued >

mesclun

Mesclun is a salad concept that originated in Mediterranean countries. French mesclun is usually a mix of young lettuces, arugula, chervil, and endive.

Italian mesclun is more likely to contain lettuces, chicory, curly endive, and escarole. American mesclun really mixes it up: you'll find mesclun seed packets that contain kale, mustard greens, cress, and dandelion, and other packets of just heirloom lettuces.

Most mixes provide a pretty combination of leaf colors. Pay attention to whether the mesclun is described as spicy or mild. If you choose spicy, perhaps also grow a mild mix or regular leaf lettuces, so you can blend your salads.

Grow mesclun as you would leaf lettuce, sowing a patch of seed every 2 weeks. Start harvesting when the leaves are 4 inches long; practice the cut-and-come-again method—cut off all the leaves 1 to 2 inches above the soil level, so new leaves will grow (see page 100). Some components of the mix, such as mustards, may grow so vigorously that they overwhelm the others; harvest those plants early.

lettuces, salad greens, continued

LEFT *'Rosy' Batavian lettuce*
RIGHT *'Sierra' Batavian lettuce*

POPULAR VARIETIES 'Blushed Butter Cos', romaine-butterhead, ruffled red-and-green, early maturing; 'Little Gem', dwarf, good for containers; 'Parris Island Cos', mild flavor, slow to bolt.

HARVEST Start with thinnings (thin until plants are 6 to 8 inches apart). Then pluck the outer leaves of maturing plants; or wait until the plants are mature, and pull them up entirely.

crisphead and batavian lettuce

Crisphead lettuce is marketed as *iceberg* lettuce; it takes the longest to mature, up to 90 days, which is too long for all gardeners except those in cool-summer regions, even though some varieties have good heat tolerance. Batavian lettuce, a form of crisphead, is easier to grow and combines the best characteristics of leaf and iceberg lettuces: young leaves are handsome and textured like leaf lettuce; later, small heads form, similar to iceberg but with more flavor.

POPULAR VARIETIES *Batavian:* 'Nevada', heat tolerant; 'Sierra', red-tinged, heat tolerant. *Iceberg:* 'Summertime', good for warm climates.

HARVEST Start with thinnings (thin until plants are 12 to 14 inches apart). Then, for iceberg, wait until the head is firm, and pull up the entire plant. Harvest Batavian lettuce when the leaves are young and tender; or wait for the head to form.

chicory, radicchio

Radicchio is a form of chicory, but it forms dense heads that become a deep rosy red (some varieties redden only in cold weather), whereas regular leaf chicory, green or red, grows loosely like leaf lettuce. Both taste bitter.

Grow leaf chicory as you would leaf lettuce, described earlier. Radicchio is a little trickier: it is more reliable if started in mid- to late summer, to mature in fall, but some varieties have good heat resistance and can be planted in spring—heat makes the plants bolt into flower and also increases the bitterness of the leaves. Heads form when the plants are reaching maturity, up to 90 days after sowing; if your plants fail to make a head, cut back (harvest) the leaves, and see if heads form then.

POPULAR VARIETIES *Chicory:* 'Sweet Trieste', green, fast growing. *Radicchio:* 'Giulio', heat tolerant, good for spring sowing; 'Red Verona', cut back for heads; 'Rossana', small, dark red, heat tolerant.

HARVEST Start with thinnings (thin leaf chicory until plants are 6 to 8 inches apart, radicchio until plants are 8 to 12 inches apart). Harvest leaf chicory as you would leaf lettuce. Harvest radicchio when heads are full; in mild-winter climates, cut off 1 to 2 inches above the soil level, and the plants may regrow in spring.

endive, escarole

Endive, sometimes called *curly endive* or *frisée,* has a rosette of lacy or ruffled leaves; escarole is a broad-leafed version with a creamy white

Radicchio

center. (Belgian, or French, endive is something else—the blanched heart of a kind of chicory.)

Grow endive and escarole as you would leaf lettuce. These are relatively slow growing, slightly bitter greens, maturing 65 to 90 days or more after sowing. They tolerate higher temperatures better than lettuce does, but hot weather tends to make them more bitter. To tone down the flavor, blanch the leaves for 2 to 3 weeks: draw up the outer leaves, and tie them together loosely to shield the interior from sunlight; avoid wetting the leaves while watering, or the insides may rot.

POPULAR VARIETIES *Endive:* 'Frizz E', very finely cut lacy leaves. *Escarole:* 'Broadleaf Batavian', thick tasty leaves.

HARVEST Start with thinnings (thin until plants are 6 to 12 inches apart). Then pluck the outer leaves of young plants; or wait until they are mature, and pull up the entire plant.

'Tres Fine' endive with beet.

melons, watermelons

Warm-season annual; damaged by frost.

Melons are juicy and delicious, but they are also a little demanding. They'll mature to full sweetness, two to five fruits per 10-foot-long vine, under these conditions: a spacious site in full sun, 2½ to 4 months of warm weather, rich soil, and generous amounts of water.

If the long period of warm weather is the sticking point, choose an early-ripening variety and a planting spot near a wall that reflects heat, or cover the planting area with black plastic, or use some of the other techniques to raise temperatures around plants (see pages 102–103). Another approach is to plant the seeds in your compost pile; decomposition creates the heat that melons thrive on.

To save space, choose a miniature melon, and plant it in a large container; or train the vines up a sturdy frame made of 2-by-2 lumber (see page 57) rather than letting them sprawl across the ground.

'Ambrosia' cantaloupe

POPULAR VARIETIES *Cantaloupe* (muskmelon), orange flesh: 'Alaska', matures early, in about 70 days, good for cool summers; 'Ambrosia', 86 days, thick flesh, resistant to powdery mildew; 'Minnesota Midget', very early maturing, small sweet fruits, good for small spaces; 'Sweet 'n' Early', matures early, great taste, resists powdery mildew. *Watermelon:* 'Crimson Sweet', medium size, oval; 'Moon and Stars', dark green skin spotted with yellow, medium size; 'Redball Seedless', small, very few seeds; 'Sugar Baby', early, small, round; 'Yellow Doll', early, small, oval, yellow flesh. *Other melons,* all early maturing: 'Earlidew', honeydew type, pale green flesh; 'Passport', Galia type, light green flesh, large fruits; 'Savor', French Charentais type, small fruit, deep orange flesh, resistant to powdery mildew.

BEST SITE Very sunny and warm, with well-drained soil high in organic matter.

continued >

melons, watermelons
continued

ABOVE *Charentais melon*
BELOW *Watermelon*

PLANTING AND CARE Set out plants or sow seeds in spring after the soil has warmed to 75°F/24°C. If you like, and many gardeners say you get the best vines if you do, start the seeds indoors in pots 3 to 4 weeks earlier (see page 52).

Before planting, prepare the soil with well-rotted manure and organic soil amendments (see page 50). Melons are very sensitive to fertilizer burn. If you use conventional fertilizers, mix them well with the soil before planting, and apply them sparingly.

Melons can be grown in hills or raised rows. To plant in hills, form the soil into flat-topped mounds 3 to 4 inches high and 2 to 3 feet in diameter, with irrigation ditches encircling them. Space the hills 4 to 8 feet apart (the largest spacing for watermelon varieties). Sow four or five seeds 1 inch deep in each hill. When seedlings begin to grow, thin to two.

To plant in rows, make mounds of soil 3 to 4 inches above the soil surface and 12 to 15 inches wide. Make irrigation ditches along both sides of the row. Space the rows 5 to 7 feet apart. Set out plants 2 to 3 feet apart; or sow seeds 1 inch deep and 12 inches apart; thin to 2 to 3 feet apart when seedlings are a few inches tall.

Keep the soil moist. When the seedlings are small, apply water near enough to them so that it reaches the tiny roots. When the plants are established, fill the ditches with water, keeping the foliage and fruit dry to prevent downy mildew and rot. Leaves may wilt slightly on hot days even when the soil is moist; water deeply if they are still limp by evening.

To make melons taste sweeter, hold off watering a week or so before you expect to harvest the ripe fruit, but don't let the vines wilt. Resume watering after the first harvest, so the next crop of fruit will continue to put on size.

Place a clean brick or piece of wood under each developing fruit to keep it clear of the wet soil and prevent disease. If you are growing melons on a trellis, when the fruits reach 2 inches in diameter, support them in slings made of netting (see page 101) or old nylon stockings: slip the melons inside the stockings, knot the stocking toes, and tie the open ends to the trellis.

Melons are subject to aphids, cucumber beetles, mites, and downy and powdery mildew; see pages 74–78. To help prevent bacterial wilt, which may cause the plant to die, control the cucumber beetle, which transmits it. For information on squash vine borers, see page 136.

HARVEST From 70 to 115 days after sowing seeds. Lift cantaloupes until they separate from the vine; cut other melons from the vine with a knife or shears. Expect two to five fruits per vine.

FOR THE TABLE Marinate melon chunks with mint leaves and citrus juice, and serve with feta.

tip A watermelon is probably ripe if it makes a dull "thunk" when thumped and its underside has turned from white to pale yellow. Cantaloupe is ripe when the rind looks like netting and the fruit slips off the stem with a gentle tug. Harvest other types of melons when they have a strong, sweet aroma and slight softening at the blossom (not stem) end or when the rind turns from shiny to dull.

Mint spreads rapidly by underground stems and can be quite invasive in a kitchen garden. To keep it in bounds, grow it in a pot. Peppermint and spearmint are most popular, but you can also grow lemon mint, orange mint, pineapple mint, and apple mint. Mints grow from 1 to 3 feet tall.

BEST SITE Sunny or partially shaded, with average soil; mint is not fussy.

PLANTING AND CARE Set out young nursery plants in spring, spaced at least 6 inches apart. For best growth, keep the soil moist. Mint is usually free of pests and diseases. After 3 years, plants become bare in the center; replace them, or dig up and divide each plant, and replant a few of the pieces with roots.

HARVEST Snip sprigs of new growth.

FOR THE TABLE Stir whole peppermint leaves into a glass of black tea, and serve with sugar. Chop mint into salad dressings or yogurt. Or serve sprigs of mint and cilantro with feta cheese, olives, and warm pita bread.

tip To keep fresh growth coming, snip off old, ragged stems and any flower shoots that form.

mint

Perennial herb;
goes dormant in cold regions.

Tangy hot mustard greens are enjoying a new popularity. You can grow them as a cut-and-come-again crop and harvest them small for tasty salad greens; spoon-shaped tatsoi leaves and feathery mizuna are particularly in favor as raw greens. Tall, crinkly, purple-leafed mustard varieties can double as handsome foliage plants in a container or flower bed. Green broad-leafed mustard greens are traditionally cooked with fatback.

Mustard greens spring up quickly and thrive in cool weather; too much heat makes the leaves tough and their flavor strong. They mature quickly, though, just 35 to 40 days after sowing.

POPULAR VARIETIES 'Florida Broad Leaf', large smooth leaves, mild flavor; mizuna, long feathery leaves, mild flavor; 'Osaka Purple', large frilly deep-purple-tinted leaves, pungent flavor; 'Red Giant', very large red-purple leaves, tall plant, slow to bolt; tatsoi, dark green spoon-shaped leaves that grow in a rosette.

BEST SITE Sunny or partially shady, with fertile, well-drained soil. Practice crop rotation (see page 77).

PLANTING AND CARE Sow seeds early in spring as soon as you can work the soil, even as early as 6 weeks before the last frost date. You can sow a second crop in fall, for late fall or winter harvest. Sow seeds ¼ inch deep and 1 inch apart in rows 15 to 30 inches apart.

Keep the soil moist. When seedlings are 4 to 5 inches high, thin them to 4 to 6 inches apart, and enjoy the thinnings

mustard greens

Cool-season annual;
tolerates light frost.

ABOVE *'Red Giant' mustard greens*
LEFT *'Osaka Purple' mustard greens*

Tatsoi

mustard greens,
continued

in a salad. Weed regularly. Watch for cabbage loopers, flea beetles, and downy mildew; see pages 74–75, 77.

HARVEST Snip young leaves, leaving the stems to regrow, or cut just the outer leaves when they are 6 to 8 inches long (see page 100); continue until hot weather. Or pull up the entire plant when it is mature. Yields are 3 to 6 pounds per 10-foot row.

FOR THE TABLE Braise with kale, chard, beet greens, and escarole.

nasturtiums
(Tropaeolum majus)

Warm-season annual, perennial in mild climates; frost sensitive.

Nasturtiums with lettuce.

While 'Empress of India' still reigns as the favorite nasturtium, with its brilliant reddish orange flowers among deep blue-green, lily-pad leaves, nasturtiums, all easy to grow, come in a range of colors now, including pastels. Grow some in a container, or to cover a fence—or a scarecrow (see page 27)—superfast, and pick the leaves and petals to add a peppery, watercress taste to a salad.

POPULAR VARIETIES Dwarf Jewel Mix, yellow, orange, and color blends, rich green leaves, mounds to 15 inches tall, good for containers; 'Empress of India', vermilion flowers, blue-green leaves, makes small cascading mounds; 'Moonlight', primrose-yellow flowers, bright green leaves, rambles to 6 feet tall or taller; Whirlybird strain, rich cherry-rose, cream, gold, mahogany, scarlet, tangerine, and mixed-color upward-facing blossoms, mounds to 15 inches tall.

BEST SITE Sunny or partially shaded, with well-drained soil.

PLANTING AND CARE Sow seeds when soil has warmed in spring. Place seeds $1/2$ to 1 inch deep and 4 to 8 inches apart (8 inches for the large rambling varieties). Keep the soil moist until seedlings emerge. Thin to 12 to 18 inches apart, half that distance in containers. Once established, plants do best with only moderate watering. Too much water and fertilizer prompts luxuriant foliage but fewer flowers.

HARVEST Pick leaves and flowers while they are young and fresh looking.

FOR THE TABLE Chop leaves and flowers with herbs such as chives and basil, and stir into cream cheese.

tip Besides being edible, nasturtiums are useful for garden bouquets. They can last a week or more if you snip off the lower leaves before immersing the stems in water.

▶ For nectarines, see Peaches, Nectarines, page 159.

Okra grows straight and tall, to 6 feet, with attractive tropical-looking leaves and lovely ivory hibiscus-like flowers. It grows well under the same conditions as sweet corn. If you have a small space, plant a dwarf variety—perhaps one with red pods—in a large tub. Keep okra plants away from paths and seats, because the prickly pods can irritate the skin.

POPULAR VARIETIES 'Burgundy', 2 to 4 feet tall, red pods and stems, handsome in a container; 'Cajun Delight', early, good for a short growing season.

BEST SITE Sunny and very warm, with well-drained soil.

PLANTING AND CARE Sow seeds in spring, but wait until the soil is warm (higher than 70°F/21°C); if your growing season is short, start seeds indoors in pots 4 to 6 weeks earlier (see page 52), or choose an early-maturing variety. Sow seeds ½ to 1 inch deep, 6 inches apart, in rows 2½ to 4 feet apart. Thin seedlings to 12 to 18 inches apart.

Keep the soil moist during germination, but thereafter on the dry side. Watch for aphids, mites, and nematodes (see pages 74, 76–79); corn earworm may also be a problem (see page 134).

HARVEST From 55 to 65 days after sowing seeds, when pods are 2 to 4 inches long. To keep plants producing, cut off pods every 2 days, as they mature. Wear gloves when harvesting. Yields are 5 to 10 pounds per 10-foot row; one plant in a warm spot yields enough to make it worth growing.

FOR THE TABLE For a crisp texture, quickly sauté or batter-fry the pods.

tip To speed germination, soak seeds for 24 hours before planting; use only seeds that are swollen.

okra

Warm-season annual; killed by frost.

ABOVE *'North-South' okra*
LEFT *'Burgundy' okra*

Since bulbs don't take much space, you can grow onions in a container if that's all the garden you have. There are all sorts of onions (storage, bunching, sweet Spanish, and torpedo, for example), but basically you either pull them while they are young and mild-tasting, when they're called *scallions,* for salads; or let them mature into big onions for slicing and cooking.

Onions can be started from seeds, nursery plants, or sets (which are miniature, dormant onions). Sets are the easiest, and they produce quick results, but they may bolt into flower before the bulbs have had much chance to develop. If you decide on sets, select the smallest ones available, because they are less likely to bolt than large ones. Most of the sets sold are for long-day varieties (discussed next).

What's fascinating about onions is that you choose a variety depending on your latitude; the amount of daylight affects the development of onion bulbs. Call a local nursery or Cooperative Extension Office for the best varieties in your area, or follow these guidelines: choose short-day varieties in

onions

Cool-season bulb; most kinds tolerate frost well.

shallots, the multipliers

Shallots are prized for their flavor—a combination of mild onion and pungent garlic. Like potato onions, which are stronger tasting, shallots are a perennial or "multiplier" onion; they grow from single cloves (sections of bulbs) into clusters. They are easier to grow than standard onions, and you can save the largest cloves of your harvest for replanting.

Purchase cloves by mail order or from seed stores, or buy bulbs at a grocery store and separate them into cloves. Place the cloves in the ground with the fat base downward and the tip covered with 1/2 inch of soil. Space them 4 to 8 inches apart in rows spaced 2 to 4 feet apart.

If you like, pull up some clumps before the bulbs swell, and use them as you would scallions. Harvest the mature bulbs when the shoots turn yellow and die. Separate the bulbs. Let the outer skin dry for about a month before using the bulbs. Store for as long as 8 months in a cool, dry place.

southern areas, such as the Deep South, the Southwest, and Southern California; short-day varieties tend to be sweet and are poor keepers. Choose long-day varieties, which tend to be pungent and store well, in northern areas. Intermediate-day types are suited to all growing areas.

tip *Bunching onions and green onions are other names for scallions; use thinnings of other onions for scallions, or plant a scallion variety such as 'Evergreen Hardy White'. Potato onions are perennials; plant these heirloom onions once, and you can harvest the offsets for years to come.*

POPULAR VARIETIES *Long-day:* 'Early Yellow Globe', early, mildly pungent, good for winter storage; 'Sweet Spanish', yellow, large, mild flavor, tolerates mildew and thrips; 'Walla Walla Sweet', yellow, mild and sweet, doesn't store for long. *Intermediate-day:* 'Candy', yellow, large, sweet, stores fairly well; 'Stockton Red', red, mild tasting; 'Superstar', white, large, sweet; *Short-day:* 'Granex' or 'Vidalia', classic sweet yellow, large.

BEST SITE Sunny (onions tolerate light shade), with fine-textured, loose, rich, well-drained soil.

PLANTING AND CARE Before planting, rake the soil free of stones and clods; work in soil amendments (see page 50) and a complete fertilizer (see page 64), and then rake the soil fine and smooth.

For a spring and summer crop, set out nursery plants or sets in spring, 4 to 6 weeks before the last frost date. Sow seeds when the soil temperature has warmed to at least 35°F/2°C and preferably 50°F/10°C. In mild-winter climates, you can start a second crop in fall, for spring harvest.

'Alisa Craig' onion

Plant sets in one of two ways: for scallions, place them 1 to 2 inches apart in furrows 1 to 2 inches deep and 1 to 1 1/2 feet apart. For big cooking bulbs, simply push the sets under the soil surface, aligning their pointed ends with the soil level, and space them 3 to 4 inches apart.

Plant nursery plants so that the tops of the bulbs are about 1 1/2 inches deep and 4 inches apart, in furrows 1 1/2 to 2 feet apart.

Sow seeds 1/2 inch deep, 1/2 inch apart, in rows 1 1/2 to 2 feet apart. Thin seedlings to 1 inch apart for scallions, 3 to 4 inches apart for large bulbs.

To help plants grow fast during the cool months, keep the soil moist, and weed regularly but carefully, because the bulbs are easily damaged. Thrips, wireworms, and downy mildew may trouble onions; see pages 76–77 for information.

HARVEST Start pulling scallions as soon as they are large enough to use. For mature onions, first prepare the crop for harvest: when half of the onions have dropped their foliage naturally (it yellows and dries up), push the rest of the foliage flat to the ground with the back of a rake. This procedure, called *lodging,* forces the bulbs into their final maturing stage and ensures longer-lasting storage after harvest. About 3 weeks later, dig up the onions; or just leave them in the ground until needed, but use them before you see any new growth, such as a flowering stalk. Lay the harvested onions on news-papers in a dry, shady spot protected from dew and rain; keep them there for about 10 days. Then brush off the dirt, and trim away most of the stems and roots. Yields are about 7 to 10 pounds per 10-foot row.

tip Some red and white onions don't store well, but most yellow onions keep for at least several months if you hang the cleaned bulbs in mesh bags in a dark, indoor place where temperatures remain between 35 and 50°F/2 and 10°C.

oregano, marjoram

Perennial herb; marjoram is damaged by frost, oregano is much more cold tolerant.

Oregano and marjoram are closely related and can be substituted for one another in cooking, but marjoram generally tastes milder and sweeter than oregano. Of the many varieties available, Greek oregano and Italian marjoram are considered the best for flavor.

POPULAR VARIETIES Greek oregano, *Origanum vulgare hirtum,* to 2 ½ feet tall, purplish pink flowers, gray-green leaves; Italian, or Sicilian, marjoram, *O. × majoricum,* to 2 feet tall, inconspicuous white flowers, milder bright green leaves.

BEST SITE Sunny, with especially well drained soil; or indoors on a sunny windowsill.

PLANTING AND CARE Purchase nursery plants in spring and plant them 9 to 18 inches apart, the closer spacing for marjoram.

Keep the soil moist, not soggy, until plants are established; then water less. Mature plants thrive on little water.

Replace plants every 3 years, when they become woody.

LEFT: *Sweet marjoram*
BELOW: *Oregano*

HARVEST For a strong flavor, cut stems when they are in bud. Two or three plants yield enough for most gardeners.

tip To encourage fresh growth and prevent plants from flowering, cut them back to 4 inches tall in late spring, summer, and fall.

parsley

Cool-season biennial herb, often grown as an annual; fairly cold hardy.

Flat-leafed parsley (left) *and curly parsley* (right).

Curly-leafed French parsley is decorative both in the garden and on the dinner plate. But chefs prefer flat-leafed Italian parsley for cooking, because it has a little more flavor. Either looks great in the garden, mixed with flowers or vegetables or planted as an edging.

POPULAR VARIETIES 'Extra Curled', curly, good as a garnish; 'Giant Italian', best for cooking.

BEST SITE Sunny or partially shaded, with moderately rich soil.

PLANTING AND CARE Parsley is biennial—it flowers the second year—but most gardeners treat it as an annual, starting anew from seeds or plants each year. In cold-winter areas, sow seeds in spring after the average last frost date; where winters are mild, sow in fall or early spring. To speed germination, which can take 3 weeks, soak the seeds in warm water for 24 hours before planting. Sow seeds $1/4$ inch deep and $1/2$ inch apart in rows 12 to 30 inches apart. Thin plants to 6 to 18 inches apart, the greater distance for flat-leafed parsley, which grows much larger than curly parsley. Or start with nursery plants, and set them out 6 to 18 inches apart. Water plants regularly.

HARVEST When a plant is about 8 inches tall, start picking the outside leaves, so the center continues to grow. Three plants of each type produce enough for most gardeners.

FOR THE TABLE Pound chopped parsley with crushed garlic, and use as a garnish for soup. It's an excellent source of vitamin C and iron.

parsnips

Cool-season biennial grown as an annual; cold hardy.

Carrot relatives from Siberia, parsnips are among the most cold hardy of vegetables. And they taste better if exposed to cold. After the first frost, the sugar content increases in mature parsnips, so they taste extra sweet.

POPULAR VARIETIES 'Lancer', sweet, smooth long roots.

BEST SITE Sunny or partially shady, with deep, fertile, fine-textured soil.

PLANTING AND CARE A few weeks before sowing, prepare the soil. Break up lumps, remove stones, and till to at least 18 inches, because parsnips grow as long as 15 inches. Work sand and well-rotted compost into the soil, to improve its texture.

In early spring or fall, sow seeds $1/2$ inch deep, 1 inch apart, in rows $1^{1}/2$ to 3 feet apart. Thin seedlings to 3 inches apart.

Keep the soil moist, and weed regularly. Watch for armyworms (see page 134), cabbage root maggots, flea beetles, leafhoppers, and nematodes (see pages 74–76).

HARVEST From 90 to 130 days after sowing. Dig up roots with a spade or spading fork, and store in a cool, damp place for up to several months. Or leave them in the ground until needed (see page 83). Yields around 10 pounds per 10-foot row.

FOR THE TABLE Roast parsnips to bring out their delicately sweet and creamy flavor.

'Pineapple' nectarine

peaches, nectarines

Deciduous tree, 5 to 12 feet tall if kept well pruned, depending on type and whether dwarf or standard.

Dry, hot summers and chilly winters make the ideal climate for growing peaches and nectarines. The trees grow rapidly, and you'll be busy keeping up with them—cutting back the branches hard every winter; religiously thinning the fruit, which is naturally excessive; and, at harvest, canning or making huge quantities of pies and jam, because all the fruit matures at once.

For a small garden, look for a single dwarf tree grafted with two or three varieties of peaches and nectarines. Or plant two to four bare-root trees in the same hole, trunks angled outward, which dwarfs the trees. You can choose varieties to provide crops over a couple of months instead of all at once. At planting time, prune each tree in the hole so that it retains just one primary branch, and point those branches outward. Peaches and nectarines can also be grown in large pots; choose natural or genetic dwarf trees, which grow to 6 feet tall and bear medium-size fruit. Or you can espalier the trees on a fence or wall, using a fan or Belgian fence pattern (see page 91).

Extrahardy varieties are available for cold-winter areas. For mild-winter regions, choose varieties that have a low winter-chill requirement (the number of hours needed at temperatures below 45°F/7°C). Avoid early-blooming varieties if late frosts are common in your area. Most peaches and nectarines are self-pollinating, so you don't need different varieties to pollinate one another. For the best advice on which varieties suit your region, consult a local nursery or your Cooperative Extension Office.

tip The flesh of clingstone peaches adheres to the pit; in freestone peaches, the pit is easily separated. Freestone varieties are more common and generally preferred for fresh eating, but most are not as good as clingstone types for canning.

POPULAR VARIETIES *Nectarines:* 'Arctic Star', early, large fruit, white flesh, semifreestone, sweet, one of the best for mild-winter areas; 'Mericrest', midseason, yellow flesh, freestone, very cold hardy, good resistance to brown rot. *Peaches:* 'Frost', midseason to late, yellow flesh, freestone, tangy flavor, resistant to peach leaf curl; 'Redhaven', early, yellow flesh, freestone, good flavor, long ripening season, good for freezing and canning; 'Reliance', early, soft yellow flesh, freestone, good flavor, outstanding cold hardiness; 'Santa Barbara', midseason, large fruit, freestone, flavorful, low chill requirement; 'Tropic Snow', early, red skin, white flesh, freestone, superb flavor, low chill requirement.

BEST SITE Sunny, with well-drained soil.

continued >

'Springtime' peach

'Redhaven' peach

peaches, nectarines
continued

NECTARINE-BLUEBERRY SALAD
MAKES 6 SERVINGS

Fruits and flowers combine to make a beautiful simple salad. If you don't grow your own organic

Johnny-jump-ups and roses, buy some at the produce section of a food market; florist flowers can be harmful if eaten. Rose flower water is available in liquor stores, Middle Eastern food markets, and fancy supermarkets.

Arrange 3½ cups sliced nec-tarines and 1½ cups blueberries on a platter. Sprinkle ¼ cup Johnny-jump-ups and ¼ cup rose petals over the fruit. In a small bowl, mix 2 tablespoons raspberry vinegar with 1½ teaspoons rose flower water. Spoon the mixture evenly over the salad. Season to taste with salt (optional).

PER SERVING: 61 CALORIES, 7.4% (4.5 CALORIES) FROM FAT; 1 G PROTEIN; 0.5 G FAT (0 G SATURATED); 15 G CARBOHYDRATE (2.1 G FIBER); 2.3 MG SODIUM; 0 MG CHOLESTEROL.

PLANTING AND CARE Container-grown trees can be planted anytime except during extreme summer heat; for planting information, see page 54. Plant bare-root (dormant) trees in winter or early spring; for planting information, see page 88.

To train a tree during the first few years, see pages 88–89; use the open-center system, or espalier the tree (see page 91).

If your tree is coming into bloom or blooming and a late frost is forecast, you can help protect the blossoms by throwing a light sheet over the tree.

Water consistently; deep soakings are best. Feed with a balanced complete fertilizer in early spring. To get a good crop of large fruits and prevent branches from breaking under too heavy a load, thin fruits after the natural fruit drop in June but when they are still small, leaving one fruit approximately every 8 to 10 inches along the branches. Be especially careful not to let a new tree bear a heavy crop; severely thinning the fruit will allow the tree to establish more strongly.

Prune every year during the dormant season or in early spring (see page 90). Peaches and nectarines need heavy pruning, more than other fruit trees. Thin out two-thirds of the previous season's growth by removing two of every three branches formed that year; or head back each branch to one-third its length; or, best of all, head back some and thin out others. Fruit is produced on 1-year-old branches; severe annual pruning not only renews fruiting wood but also encourages fruiting throughout the tree rather than at the ends of sagging branches that can easily break. Genetic dwarf trees need less pruning than standard ones, but prune to keep the center of the tree open; otherwise it will become crowded and prone to disease. To restrict tree growth in a small area, practice summer pruning (see page 67).

Brown rot and peach leaf curl are among the most serious diseases of peaches and nectarines. Both are fungal diseases. Brown rot causes flowers to wilt and decay, while twigs crack and ooze sap. When peach leaf curl occurs, new leaves thicken and pucker, infected leaves become tinged with red, pink, yellow, or white, and leaves usually fall in midsummer. To control both diseases, clean up well in fall, so fungal spores do not overwinter on fallen fruit or leaves. Apply lime sulfur dormant spray once after autumn leaf drop and again as buds begin to swell but before they open.

tip To reduce peach leaf curl in wet climates, grow genetic dwarf peaches and nectarines in pots, and move them to a covered location during rainy weather.

HARVEST Between June and September, depending on the variety, when the fruit is firm and twists off easily from the stem. Yields vary, depending on the size, age, and variety of the tree.

FOR THE TABLE Glaze peach halves with melted butter and sugar; then grill them until they are warm but still hold their shape. Serve with whipped cream and raspberry sauce.

'Midpride' peach

Decked with glossy, bright green leaves and pretty clusters of white flowers in early spring, pears trees are handsome additions in a garden plot or fanned against a south-facing wall. Unless they get fireblight (discussed later), pear trees are altogether easier to grow than many other fruit trees; some live for a hundred years.

Pear trees need at least 600 hours of winter chill (45°F/7°C or lower), and most varieties do better with 900 hours. In the warmest-winter climates, choose low-chill varieties; some of these are Asian hybrids, crosses between European and Asian pears with fruit similar to that of European varieties.

Pears are generally not self-pollinating. Plant two or more varieties so they cross-pollinate one another and produce a heavy crop. Choose dwarf or semidwarf trees for small gardens. A standard pear tree grows to 40 feet.

tip Asian pears are a different species of pear, round in shape, with a crisp, gritty texture. Grow Asian pears as you would the European species (the regular pear, described here), but thin them to one pear per fruiting spur, and pick them when ripe. They have a lower chill requirement than European pears and a greater resistance to fireblight; they generally bloom later, so you can't use them to pollinate European pears.

POPULAR VARIETIES *Asian pears:* 'Chojuro', ripens late midseason, russeted brown-green skin, keeps for many months; 'Hosui', early, golden brown fruit, juicy, sweet flavor, resists fireblight; 'Ya Li', late, green skin, low chill requirement, stores very well, resists fireblight. *European pears:* 'Comice', late, large fruit, russeted greenish yellow skin, superb flavor; 'Moonglow', early midseason, yellow skin, juicy, heavy crop, high resistance to fireblight; 'Seckel', early midseason, yellow-brown skin, very small fruit, very sweet, a favorite for canning, big crop, fairly resistant to fireblight; 'Warren', late, pale green skin, buttery flesh, excellent flavor, stores well, cold hardy, extremely resistant to fireblight.

BEST SITE Sunny, with well-drained soil, but pears tolerate heavy soil. Choose a sheltered site if late frosts are common.

PLANTING AND CARE Container-grown trees can be planted anytime except during extreme summer heat; for planting information, see page 54. Plant bare-root (dormant) pear trees in winter or early spring; for planting information, see pages 88–89.

To train the tree during the first few years, see pages 89–90. Pears naturally grow upright; you can train them to a central leader if your trees are dwarf (the fruit grows out of reach on larger trees) or to an open center. The open center design is a good choice in areas where fireblight is a problem, because a tree with several main limbs has a better chance of survival if seriously infected. Pears may also be espaliered (see page 91).

Water consistently; water stress makes the tree vulnerable to fireblight. Profuse new growth from fertilizer or too much pruning at one time also

pears

Deciduous tree, 8 to 20 feet tall, depending on whether dwarf or semidwarf.

'Shinko' Asian pear

'Comice' European pear

pears, continued

'Bartlett' European pear

increases the risk of fireblight, so feed pear trees sparingly and avoid pruning heavily in any one season.

Pear crops do not need thinning.

During winter, remove any weak, dead, or crossed branches (see page 90) to create a healthy, well-shaped tree; if necessary, remove branches or twigs growing toward the center of the tree, because crops are heavier and disease incidence lower when some sunlight can reach the middle.

To restrict tree growth in a small garden area, practice summer pruning (see page 67).

Fireblight can be a serious problem; in areas prone to it, plant fireblight-resistant varieties. The disease causes entire branches to die back quickly. As soon as you see blackened growth, cut it back to a growth bud or stem with green, healthy tissue, and disinfect your pruning tools after each cut. Codling moth larvae can be a serious pest and ruin a fruit crop; as a control, use pheromone traps (see page 107).

HARVEST July to late October, depending on the variety. Yields vary, depending on the size, age, and variety of the tree. Pick when the pears are green and firm and the stem snaps free from the branch when you lift the fruit to a horizontal position. Handle pears gently, or they'll bruise.

tip Don't wait for pears to ripen on the tree—they'll turn mealy and be ruined. Pick them unripe, when they are full-size but still green and firm. Put most pears in a cool, dark place to ripen. 'Anjou', 'Bosc', and 'Comice' pears, however, need to be put in cold storage (32 to 40°F/0 to 4°C) for about a month after picking and then in a warm room to ripen.

FOR THE TABLE Serve sweet ripe pears with Stilton cheese and freshly cracked walnuts.

peas

Cool-season annual; tolerates frost.

'Oregon Sugar Pod II' snow pea

So delightful is the taste of the first sweet, tender garden peas—as long as they are served almost straight off the vine. Like sweet corn, peas begin to convert their sugars to starch the moment they are picked, which is why peas should be home-grown.

There are two types of green peas: shelling, also called *English peas;* and edible-pod, which include sugar peas (also called *sugar snap peas*) and snow peas. Shelling peas are removed from the pod, and only the peas are eaten; the entire pod of sugar and snow peas is eaten. Both types are grown the same way.

Peas climb by sending out tendrils that curl around a support. Dwarf (sometimes called *bush*) varieties range in height from 1½ to 2 feet and stand best with some support but can be grown without support if you plant them close together in double rows. The tall varieties grow 6 to 8 feet high and need a string, netting, or chicken wire trellis (see page 57) to climb. Tall varieties have longer harvest periods than dwarf kinds; dwarf peas mature more quickly, which makes them a good choice for a fall crop.

tip Sugar peas are versatile: you can eat the immature pods, or eat pods and peas together, or wait for the peas to mature and shell them.

'Cascadia' snap pea

POPULAR VARIETIES *Shelling peas:* 'Alderman' ('Tall Telephone'), very
sweet, big crop, 5 to 6 feet tall; 'Green Arrow', old favorite for flavor,
2½ feet tall; 'Little Marvel', early, 1½ feet tall. *Sugar peas:* 'Sugar Snap',
sweet, large pods, 5 feet tall. *Snow peas:* 'Dwarf Gray Sugar', bush type,
1½ feet tall; 'Mammoth Melting Sugar', long pods, vines 4 to 5 feet tall.

BEST SITE Sunny, with rich, loose, well-drained soil.

PLANTING AND CARE Peas like cool weather, so make them one of
the very first crops you sow in spring. For late spring crops, sow early
in spring, 6 to 8 weeks before the last frost date. For autumn crops,
which are trickier unless you have a long mild fall, sow in late summer
about 12 weeks before the first frost date. If you live in a mild-winter
area, you can sow through autumn for winter and early spring crops.

Peas thrive in soil that is rich in organic matter but limited in nitrogen. (Too much nitrogen results in mostly foliage.) If your soil is low in
organic matter, dig a trench 1 or 2 feet deep, and mix in large amounts
of compost, leaf mold, bonemeal, and manure before planting (see page
50). Buy inoculated seeds, or inoculate them yourself (see page 84).

Put up poles or trellises if necessary. Sow seeds 1 to 2 inches deep,
1 inch apart, either in single rows 2 to 4 feet apart or in double rows
6 inches apart, with 2½ to 3 feet between double rows. Keep the soil
moist while the seeds are germinating, but avoid overwatering, which
in cold soil causes the seeds to rot. Thin seedlings to 2 to 4 inches apart.
Keep the soil moist during the growing season. Weed regularly. Watch
for aphids, cucumber beetles, and powdery mildew (see pages 74, 78).

HARVEST From 55 to 70 days after sowing, when peas for shelling
are full size and the pods are bright green, or when peas in edible
pods are just beginning to form. Pick from the lower parts of vines as
peas mature. For the freshest taste, harvest every 2 days. This also
keeps the plants producing. Yields are 2 to 6 pounds per 10-foot row,
depending on whether the plants are dwarf or tall.

FOR THE TABLE Young pea shoots (tips of stems) are delicious raw
in salads or stir-fried.

'Mr. Big' shelling pea

peppers

Warm-season annual; killed by frost.

'Lilac Belle' bell pepper

peppers in pots

Small-fruited peppers grow well in large pots (18 inches or more in diameter). Fill your container with good potting soil amended with a complete organic or controlled-release fertilizer. During the growing season use fertilizer formulated for tomatoes, applied lightly. Water whenever the top inch of soil dries out. For a hot pepper, consider 'Tabasco', 'Serrano', or a Thai pepper. A miniature bell pepper, 'Jingle Bells', is a good sweet pepper for pots.

You can choose peppers that are short and chunky, long and skinny, cone-shaped, round, or crumpled—in nearly any color imaginable, including lilac and chocolate. Select a flavor from mild to sweet to sizzling hot and pungent. A huge variety of peppers is available, but as garden plants they are somewhat demanding about conditions. Sweet peppers grow best when daytime temperatures range between 70 and 75°F/21 and 24°C. Hot peppers thrive at slightly warmer temperatures, 70 to 85°F/21 to 29°C. For both types, if night temperatures fall below 60°F/16°C or stay above 75°F/24°C, blossoms often fall off, and fruit set is poor.

Hot peppers generally ripen later than sweet peppers and like slightly warmer weather, but otherwise they require the same care as sweet peppers. Both kinds grow on attractive bushy plants, ranging from 1 to 4 feet high, depending on the variety.

The best-known sweet peppers are bell peppers. Often these are harvested when green, which makes for a bigger crop. When left on the plants to mature, bell peppers turn different colors, depending on the variety. There are numerous other sweet peppers, and they generally have more flavor than bells.

tip Some hot peppers, such as 'Hungarian Wax Hot' and hot cherry peppers, look just like their sweet counterparts, but they contain capsaicin, the fire in hot peppers. Read labels carefully at planting time to avoid confusing hot and sweet peppers.

POPULAR VARIETIES *Hot peppers:* 'Anaheim', fairly mild, but a hot form is available, 7 inches long, good for frying and chiles rellenos; 'Habanero', searing hot, lantern-shaped small fruit; 'Jalapeño', mild and hot forms are available, 2 1/2 inches long, thick flesh; 'Serrano', extremely hot, small cylindrical fruit. *Sweet peppers:* 'Ace', standard bell pepper, early harvest, big crop, tolerates cooler weather than most bell peppers; 'Giant Marconi', red, smoky-sweet flavor, 7 inches long, fleshy, great for grilling; 'Gypsy', yellow or red, mild taste, more tapered than a bell, prolific; 'Large Sweet Cherry', red, round, about 1 1/2 inches across, good for pickling whole; 'Sweet Banana', light yellow, 7 inches long, good for cooking; 'Sweet Pimento', scarlet, heart-shaped, 4 inches long, good for fresh eating, pasta salad, and dips.

BEST SITE Sunny, warm, and sheltered from wind, with fertile, well-drained soil rich with organic matter.

PLANTING AND CARE Set out nursery plants in spring, 1 week or more after the last frost date, when the soil temperature has warmed to 65°F/18°C. If you like, raise your own plants by sowing seeds in a warm place indoors (see page 52) 6 to 8 weeks before planting time.

Space plants 18 to 24 inches apart in rows 2½ to 3 feet apart. Keep the soil moist, especially during flowering and fruiting. Weed regularly. Stake tall plants if necessary (see page 57). Watch for aphids, Colorado potato beetles, and mites; see pages 74, 76 for help. Other pepper pests include corn borers and armyworms (see page 134).

If plants stop bearing fruit during hot weather, don't pull them up. Keep them watered and tended, and they should produce again when the weather cools.

HARVEST From 60 to 95 days after planting. Cut peppers from the plant gently with pruning shears, being careful not to break the plant stems. Pick sweet peppers when full size; allow pimientos to turn fully red on the plants, but harvest other kinds at any color stage (flavor typically becomes sweeter as the fruit ripens). Pick hot peppers when full size and still green, or wait until they turn yellow or red for richer flavor; if you are growing very hot peppers, wear rubber gloves, and avoid touching your eyes. Yields vary from 5 to 18 pounds per 10-foot row.

'Jingle Bells' miniature bell pepper

plums

Deciduous tree, 10 to 15 feet tall if kept pruned.

Plums come in many colors—both inside and out. The skin may be yellow, red, purple, green, blue, or almost black; the flesh may be yellow, red, or green. Japanese plums are the largest and juiciest of the lot, and they are mainly eaten fresh. European plums have firmer flesh, are generally sweeter, and can be cooked or eaten fresh.

Choose European varieties, which are hardier and bloom later, if your winters are cold, your spring weather is cool and rainy, or late frosts are common in your region. In a mild-winter area, choose Japanese varieties; most European varieties need a lot of winter chill.

Semidwarf trees are only slightly smaller than standards; no truly dwarfing rootstocks are available for plums. Where space is limited, train a tree against a fence or wall (see page 91). In very cold-winter regions, try one of the hardy American hybrid plum varieties, which are crosses between native plums and Japanese plums; some are tree size, others are 6-foot-tall bushes.

Many plum varieties are self-pollinating, but others need cross-pollination by another plum variety to produce good crops; consult a knowledgeable local nursery for effective pollenizers.

POPULAR VARIETIES *European plums:* 'Green Gage', mid-season, greenish yellow skin, amber flesh, very rich sweet flavor, good fresh and for canning and jam, self-pollinating; 'Stanley', midseason, large fruit, purplish black skin, yellow flesh, sweet and juicy, good for fresh eating and for canning. *Hardy hybrids:* 'Pipestone',

'Stanley' European plum

'Purple Heart' Japanese plum

PLUM RELISH
MAKES 2¼ CUPS

Plum relish makes a gourmet meal of barbecued duck breasts. Use a red-skinned plum, such as 'Santa Rosa'.

When the meat is cooked, transfer it to a platter, let it stand for 5 minutes, and then thinly slice it crosswise. Mix any accumulated juices into the relish. Serve the relish beside the meat—with mu shu wrappers or flour tortillas if you like.

*Pit and finely chop 1 pound **ripe plums**. In a bowl, mix the plums, 2 tablespoons thinly sliced **scallions** (including tops), 1½ tablespoons firmly packed **brown sugar**, 2 teaspoons **rice vinegar**, 1 teaspoon **Asian** (toasted) **sesame oil**, 2 teaspoons minced **fresh ginger**, and 1½ teaspoons minced **garlic**. Season to taste with **salt** and **pepper**.*

PER SERVING: 92 CALORIES, 17% (16 CALORIES) FROM FAT; 1 G PROTEIN; 1.8 G FAT (0.2 G SATURATED); 20 G CARBOHYDRATE (2.3 G FIBER); 2.8 MG SODIUM; 0 MG CHOLESTEROL.

early midseason, large fruit, tough red skin, greenish yellow flesh, a little stringy but juicy and sweet, very good for fresh eating and jam, vigorous tree. *Japanese plums:* 'Burbank', midseason, large fruit, red skin, amber flesh, excellent sweet flavor; 'Santa Rosa', early, purplish red skin with blue bloom, yellow flesh, pleasingly tart flavor, self-pollinating, weeping form that grows 6 to 8 feet high is available; 'Shiro', early midseason, yellow skin and flesh, mild but good flavor, heavy crop, good for eating fresh and cooking, self-pollinating.

tip Pluots and apriums are hybrids between plum and apricot. They combine characteristics of both fruits in varying degrees. Pluots taste very sweet and mostly of plum; grow them as you would Japanese plums. Apriums taste like juicy apricots with a touch of plum flavor (see page 109).

BEST SITE Sunny, with fertile, well-drained soil, but plums tolerate many soil types.

PLANTING AND CARE Container-grown trees can be planted anytime except during extreme summer heat; for planting information, see page 54. Plant bare-root (dormant) plum trees in winter or early spring; for planting information, see page 88.

To train the tree during the first few years, see pages 88–89. European plum trees are usually trained to a central leader. Japanese plum trees can be trained to a central leader or to an open center. Plums may also be espaliered (see page 91).

Water moderately but consistently. Feed lightly to moderately. In small gardens especially, do not overfeed Japanese plum trees, because they are naturally vigorous.

European plum crops generally do not need thinning, unless the trees produce a particularly large amount of fruit. Thin Japanese plums to 4 to 6 inches apart as soon as the fruit is large enough to see; Japanese varieties bear very heavily, and, if the entire crop is allowed to ripen, its weight may damage the tree.

During winter or spring, remove any weak, dead, or crossed branches (see page 90) to create a healthy, well-shaped tree. European plum trees need little additional pruning. Japanese plum trees are much more vigorous.

Each year, prune shoots that are much longer than the others: head them back to lateral shoots or thin them out if they are badly placed and crowding. Japanese plum trees also tend to produce excess upright growth; shorten the vertical shoots to outside branchlets. On bush-form American hybrid trees, cut the oldest shoots back to the ground every few years.

To restrict tree growth in a small garden area, practice summer pruning (see page 67).

In humid climates, plum trees are susceptible to plum curculio (which infests the fruit) and the diseases bacterial canker (which causes open wounds on the trunk and branches) and brown rot (see page 160). You may be able to control curculio with traps (see page 107). To reduce the risk of bacterial canker, prevalent in the South, don't leave stubs when pruning, and remove dead or broken branches right away.

HARVEST June to September, depending on the variety, when plums have turned color and are starting to soften. Pick carefully, so as not to damage the fruiting spurs. Yields vary, depending on the size, age, and variety of the tree.

'Santa Rosa' Japanese plum

Potatoes have all the virtues: easy to grow, long-lasting if properly stored, nutritious, and heartily satisfying to eat—especially with butter or sour cream. They are also popular with children, but be aware that all parts of the plants are poisonous except the tubers. Start with certified disease-free seed potatoes; do not use potatoes from the supermarket, as these are often chemically treated to prevent sprouting. Most varieties take about 3 to 4 months to mature.

potatoes

Cool-season annual, not frost hardy.

POPULAR VARIETIES 'All Blue', midseason, novelty, blue skin and flesh, big crop, good boiled or baked; 'Butte', late, brown skin, white flesh, classic large baking potato, high in vitamin C; 'Butterfinger' ('Swedish Peanut'), early, long slender fingerling type, light tan skin, yellow flesh, good for salads or sautéing; 'Kennebec', midseason, white skin, white flesh, high yield, all-purpose big potato, resists blight, stores well; 'Red Norland', early, red skin, white flesh, flavorful, good for boiling; 'Yukon Gold', early to midseason, yellow skin and flesh, good for baking, boiling, or frying, stores well.

'All Blue' potato

BEST SITE Sunny, with fertile, fast-draining soil that is high in organic matter and has a pH below 5.5 (if the pH is higher, potatoes may get scabby).

PLANTING AND CARE Plant in spring, 4 to 6 weeks before the last frost date; choose early-maturing varieties if warm weather comes quickly, because potatoes stop growing when the soil warms up. You can plant a second crop later: in cold-winter climates, plant a late-maturing variety in late spring for a fall crop; in mild-winter

potatoes, continued

barrel potatoes

You can produce quite a few potatoes in a half wine barrel. Any variety will grow this way, but red ones such as 'Buffalo' and 'Red La Soda' are especially good. Fill the bottom of the barrel with about 6 inches of soil, add three seed potatoes, evenly spaced, and cover with 3 or 4 more inches of soil. As the foliage appears, fill the barrel with more soil until just the tips show. Continue to fill the barrel as the potatoes grow, until the soil level is 1 to 2 inches below the rim of the barrel. Water and fertilize the plants regularly. Harden and harvest when the tops start to die down (see main text).

Potato skins may be red, brown (russets), blue, or white (actually most of those are pale yellow).

climates, plant in late summer or early autumn for crops through winter into spring.

Two days before planting, cut the seed potatoes into chunks about 1½ inches square, each with at least two "eyes," from which sprouts will emerge. Allow them to dry a bit (callus) for 2 days before planting, which helps prevent rotting.

Set the chunks 12 to 18 inches apart in furrows 6 to 8 inches wide and 4 inches deep, spaced 2½ to 3 feet apart. (The closer spacing will result in higher yields of smaller potatoes.) Cover the chunks with 2 inches of soil.

After sprouts emerge, add another 2 inches of soil to the furrow, leaving the foliage tips exposed. As the vines grow, continue adding soil, mounding a ridge of soil up and over each row, until the ridges are about 4 inches high and 18 inches wide. Keep the ridges formed as the plants mature, since the soil cover helps ensure the best temperature and moisture for the tubers growing below. It also protects the tubers from the sun, which would turn any exposed areas green; the green areas of a potato are poisonous, so cut them off before cooking.

TOP *Cut seed potato into chunks.* **BOTTOM** *Keep soil ridges mounded around the plants.*

Keep the soil uniformly moist during the growing season. Weed regularly. Watch for aphids, Colorado potato beetles, flea beetles, leafhoppers, wireworms, and blights; see pages 74–78 for help.

When most of the foliage has turned yellow to brown, water the plants for the last time; then wait 7 to 10 days, and cut away the vines. This sets or hardens the potato skins, so they won't peel or bruise too easily.

tip New potatoes are so deliciously sweet straight from the garden because their skin is still thin and tender and their sugar hasn't yet converted to starch, as it has in mature potatoes.

HARVEST If you like, harvest a few tender "new" potatoes from around the edge of each plant when the vines start to flower (or about 8 weeks after planting for varieties that don't flower). Harvest mature potatoes 90 to 120 days after planting. About 5 to 7 days after you have cut away the vines, preferably when the weather is cool and overcast, dig up the plants carefully with a spading fork: keep the fork 10 inches away from the plants to avoid injuring the potatoes; lift the plant gently, shake off loose soil, and pull the potatoes

from the vines. Gather them in burlap bags or baskets; keep them out of strong sunlight. Yields range from 10 to 20 pounds per 10-foot row.

To store potatoes, first heal any injuries by placing them for 2 weeks in a dark place with high humidity and a temperature of 50 to 60°F/10 to 16°C; loosely cover the bags or baskets with burlap. Keep only healed potatoes for further storage; choose unblemished potatoes for the longest storage. Then store them in a well-ventilated, dark, dry location, such as a basement, where the temperature is about 40°F/4°C. In these conditions, potatoes should keep well for 3 to 6 months.

Fingerling-type potatoes.

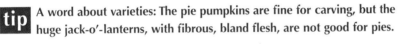

Pumpkins are fun. You can carve their shells, cook their flesh, and snack on their nutritious seeds. But the vines take lots of room; even the "bush" type, with its shorter vines, can spread to 20 square feet. The fruits range in size from miniatures to giants weighing more than 100 pounds. Some have ghostly white skin.

tip A word about varieties: The pie pumpkins are fine for carving, but the huge jack-o'-lanterns, with fibrous, bland flesh, are not good for pies.

POPULAR VARIETIES 'Atlantic Giant', gigantic champion-size fruit, large plant; 'Baby Bear', 2 pounds, fine flesh for pies, tasty edible seeds; 'Bushkin', 10 pounds, 6-foot vines, good carving pumpkin for small spaces; 'Jack Be Little', miniature orange fruit for decorative use, 6 or 7 per plant; 'Lumina', novelty, white fruit, 10 to 12 pounds, stores well; 'Small Sugar', traditional favorite, 6 to 8 pounds, fine-grained sweet flesh, great for pies; 'Triple Treat', 8 pounds, easy-to-eat hull-less seeds.

BEST SITE Sunny, with fertile soil high in organic matter.

PLANTING AND CARE Sow seeds outdoors in late spring when the soil has warmed to 65°F/18°C. In areas with a short growing season, give plants a 2- to 3-week head start by sowing seeds indoors (see page 52).

continued >

pumpkins

Warm-season annual; killed by frost.

For vining pumpkins, make hills (see page 55) 6 to 8 feet apart. Sow five or six seeds 1 inch apart in each hill; thin seedlings to two plants per hill. For "bush" pumpkins, sow a cluster of three or four seeds 1 inch deep, 2 feet apart, in rows 3 feet apart; thin seedlings to one or two plants per cluster.

Water the plants generously, but keep the leaves dry to prevent diseases. Weed regularly. Apply fertilizer after the blossoms appear. Keep watch for cucumber beetles, squash bugs, and powdery mildew; see pages 74, 76, 78 for help. Squash vine borers may also be a problem; see page 136. In late summer, slide wooden shingles or pieces of plywood or plastic foam under the fruits to protect them from wet soil and rot.

colossal pumpkins

Prize-winning pumpkins aren't special varieties; they are ordinary full-size pumpkins grown in a special way (though gardeners aiming for gigantic fruits do have favorites, such as 'Atlantic Giant'). Start with warm, fertile soil that is rich in organic matter (see page 50). To focus the energies of the plant into producing one or two grand pumpkins, as it develops cut off all but two main stems. Then, after the blossoms fade and you see the fruits swelling, remove all but one fruit on each stem. Feed your plants, starting when the flowers appear, and keep them well watered. To increase the uptake of water and nutrients, mound a 4-inch-wide hill of soil every 2 feet along the length of each stem; additional roots will form there.

A young 'Atlantic Giant' pumpkin.

tip To grow a mono-grammed jack-o'-lantern, scratch a name onto the fruit in mid- to late summer, before the shell has hardened. As the pumpkin matures, the inscription will callus over and become easily readable.

HARVEST From 90 to 120 days after sowing seeds, when the shells are hard and the color is strong and even, before the first frost. Cut the stems with pruning shears. Handle the fruits carefully to avoid bruising. To store, first cure the pumpkins by placing them in a well-ventilated, warm (75 to 80°F/24 to 27°C) location for 1 to 2 weeks, or leave them in warm sunshine; then store at a lower temperature—around 50°F/10°C is ideal. Yields vary from one to four pumpkins per plant.

A 'Small Sugar' pumpkin raised off the soil on plastic foam.

'Small Sugar' has been grown for pies for more than a century.

radishes

Cool-season annual; withstands light frost.

Radishes are a surefire success with children because they germinate in a few days and produce bright, crunchy bouquets for eating just 3 weeks later. Grow short-season radishes (the common small ones) in a container if you like. The seed mix 'Easter Egg' includes purple, lavender, pink, rose, scarlet, and white radishes. You can also find black radishes and gold ones. Radish shapes range from small and round to carrotlike roots 1 foot long; some radishes look like turnips or cucumbers; Japanese radish (daikon) can be gargantuan. (The big radishes take longer to mature, up to 150 days for the very largest varieties.) Flavors vary widely, too, from delicate and mild to sizzling hot.

LEFT TOP *Daikon radish*
BELOW *'Round Black Spanish' radish*

POPULAR VARIETIES 'April Cross', white, daikon type, 18 inches long; 'Cherry Belle', red, classic small round; 'Easter Egg', multicolor mix, small round or short oblong; 'French Breakfast', red and white, 4-inch oblongs; 'Long Black Spanish', black, 10 inches long, very cold tolerant; 'Sakurajima', very large daikon, takes 150 days to mature.

BEST SITE Sunny, with loose, well-drained, rich soil. Practice crop rotation (see page 77).

tip For mild-tasting great radishes, keep the plot well and evenly watered, and harvest as soon as the radishes are plump.

PLANTING AND CARE Radishes need cool weather, so start sowings in early spring, 3 weeks before the last frost, and make successive sowings every 10 days for a steady crop until summer. Start sowings again in late summer, 4 to 6 weeks before the first fall frost, and continue into winter if your climate is mild. The slow-maturing radishes are easier to grow in fall; you can start daikon, which is more heat tolerant than common radishes, about 8 weeks before the first frost.

A few weeks before sowing, prepare the soil. Break up lumps, and remove stones to at least the depth the radishes will grow. Work aged compost and well-rotted manure into the soil, to improve its texture.

Sow seeds ½ inch deep, 1 inch apart, in rows 8 to 18 inches apart, the larger spacing for large varieties. Alternatively, broadcast seeds (see page 55) in wide beds. Thin out every other plant when the roots start to swell.

Keep the soil consistently moist. Weed regularly. Cabbage root maggots and flea beetles sometimes bother radishes (see pages 74–75 for help).

HARVEST As soon as the radishes mature, before they become too peppery, tough, or hollow inside. Pull up small radishes; pull or dig up large ones. Yields range from 2 to 5 pounds per 10-foot row.

FOR THE TABLE Serve daikon as a condiment, grated or sliced raw, with other condiments such as vinegar and hot mustard.

raspberries

Deciduous perennial with biennial canes; very cold hardy, to –35°F/–37°C.

Raspberries generally bear their soft, delicate, red, yellow, purple, or black fruit in the summertime, but one group of red and yellow raspberries, the fall-bearing (or everbearing) kind, gives an autumn crop as well as a summer one.

Cool summers, cold winters, and rainfall during the growing season make a perfect climate for raspberries. Heat—both humid and dry—is their enemy. ('Bababerry' is an exception; it produces well in warm-summer, mild-winter areas.) Results may be erratic in an unfavorable climate; check with your local Cooperative Extension Office for the best varieties for your area. To avoid disease problems, purchase only certified virus-free plants.

tip Red raspberries are the most common; yellow types are mutations of red ones. Black raspberries have blue-black fruit that is firmer and seedier than that of red and yellow types, with a more pronounced flavor. Purple raspberries are crosses between black and red kinds.

POPULAR VARIETIES 'Bababerry', everbearing red, needs little winter chill, stands heat well; 'Cumberland', large black, old flavorful variety, heavy crop; 'Fallgold', everbearing yellow, large fruit, good flavor; 'Heritage', everbearing red, tasty smallish berry; 'Jewel', large black, early crop, vigorous, good disease resistance; 'Latham', summer-bearing red, late crop, large berries, mildews in humid summers, very cold hardy.

BEST SITE Sunny, with good air circulation and rich, well-drained soil. In hot climates, choose a site with afternoon shade. Because of verticillium wilt, avoid sites planted with other cane berries, tomatoes, strawberries, potatoes, peppers, or eggplants in the last 3 years.

SUPPORT Raspberry canes are easier to manage if trained on supports. Set up a sturdy, 5-foot-tall trellis with two or four wires (see drawings). You'll need to tie the canes to the two-wire trellis; no tying is necessary with the four-wire, or hedgerow, system. Use 3-by-3s or 4-by-4s for the posts or round posts 3 or 4 inches in diameter, made of rot-resistant wood such as redwood or cedar. Anchor the posts well. Then string 10- or 11-gauge smooth galvanized wire between them. Red and yellow raspberries need some support; black and purple raspberries can be grown either freestanding or with support.

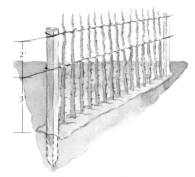

Two-wire trellis

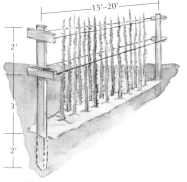

Four-wire hedgerow system

PLANTING AND CARE Set out dormant, bare-root plants in early spring and container-grown plants anytime except during summer heat. Put plants into the ground 1 to 2 inches deeper than they grew at the nursery (look for the soil mark). For information on planting a bare-root plant, see page 88; for a container-grown plant, see page 54.

Set out red and yellow raspberries 2 to 3 feet apart in rows 6 to 10 feet apart. Plant purple and black raspberries in slightly raised mounds 2 to 3 feet apart in rows 6 to 8 feet apart. Don't stint on the spacing; the more sunshine the canes receive, the more fruit they'll produce and the lower the risk of disease. After planting, cut back all canes to 5 to 6 inches tall.

At the end of winter, before the new buds swell, mulch around the plants with compost or well-rotted manure. Keep the soil moist, especially during flowering and fruiting; avoid overhead watering, which can encourage diseases. Remove weeds regularly, but cultivate no deeper than 2 inches. If the soil is rich, you won't need to fertilize, but if plants grow poorly or their foliage is not deep green, apply a complete fertilizer during flowering or the next spring before new growth starts. Tie new canes to the wires, or confine them inside the hedgerow.

Watch for cane borers—larvae boring through the canes (the first indication of trouble is wilting cane tips); cut off canes 6 inches below the dying tips and discard them. Pruning out and discarding infected canes is the best way to control leaf spot *(anthracnose),* a fungal disease that causes small red-edged spots on leaves and stems; it can also be reduced by avoiding overhead watering. Aphids, mites, and verticillium wilt (see pages 74, 76, and 78) may also trouble raspberries.

Red and yellow raspberry plants produce suckers; dig or pull out any canes that grow more than 1 foot away from your trellis or outside the hedgerow.

PRUNING SUMMER-BEARING RED AND YELLOW RASPBERRIES The canes of summer-bearing raspberries grow to full size their first year and bear fruit in their second year.

During the first summer, leave the canes unpruned. Early in the second spring, after frost danger is past but before buds begin to swell, cut any weak, broken, or diseased canes to the ground. Keep thinning canes until

raspberries, continued

the healthy canes are 6 to 8 inches apart at the wire. Prune the tops of those remaining canes, as necessary, to a height of 5 to 5 1/2 feet for standard rows, 4 feet for a hedgerow system (see drawing at right).

After you have harvested in summer, cut to the ground all the canes that bore fruit. The remaining canes will bear fruit the next summer; tie them to the wires or confine them within the hedgerow.

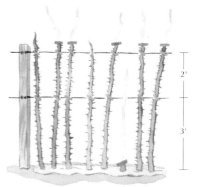

Early in the second spring, before growth begins, thin weak canes, and top vigorous ones.

PRUNING FALL-BEARING RED AND YELLOW RASPBERRIES The canes of fall-bearing raspberries produce a crop of fruit on the top third of the cane in the fall of their first year and on the lower part of the cane in the summer of their second year.

Let the first year's canes come up and bear fruit in autumn. After the harvest, cut off the top third of each cane that bore fruit (see drawing below left).

During the second year, after the 1-year-old canes have borne a summer crop on the lower parts of the canes, cut those canes to the ground. As new canes emerge during summer, tie them to the trellis or confine them in the hedgerow. After you harvest the fall crop, cut off the top third of all canes that bore fruit (see drawing below right).

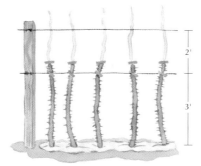

For fall-bearing red and yellow raspberries, after harvesting first year's autumn fruit, remove top third of canes.

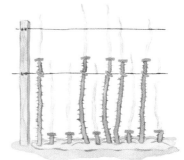

After the summer crop in the second year, cut to the ground the canes that bore summer fruit. After the fall crop, cut off the top third of the canes that bore fruit.

There's an alternative way to prune fall-bearing red and yellow raspberries, and it works particularly well for plantings in containers: simply cut all canes to the ground each year in fall after fruiting is finished (in cold regions wait until late winter); you'll sacrifice the summer crop in the second year, but get an extended harvest for the fall crop.

PRUNING PURPLE AND BLACK RASPBERRIES Purple and black raspberries grow in clumps, and their canes arch instead of growing straight.

During the first summer, "top" the canes to force them to grow lateral (side) branches. For freestanding plants, top the black varieties down to 2 feet tall and the purple varieties down to 2¹⁄₂ feet tall. For plants grown on a trellis, top black varieties to 2 to 2¹⁄₂ feet tall, purple ones to 2¹⁄₂ to 3 feet tall (see drawing below left).

Early in the second spring, before new growth starts, remove all weak canes, as well as any dead, diseased, or broken ones. Leave up to eight sturdy canes in a hill, or canes spaced 6 to 8 inches apart in a row. (If they are all less than ¹⁄₂ inch thick, remove all but the two strongest from each plant.) Also shorten the lateral branches to 8 to 10 inches for black raspberries and 12 to 14 inches for purple raspberries (see drawing below right). The side branches will bear fruit.

After harvest, in summer, cut to the ground all the canes that bore fruit. Top all the new canes.

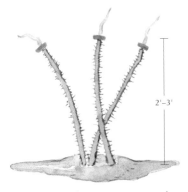

During the first summer, top the canes to encourage lateral branches.

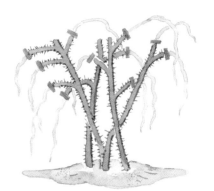

During the second spring, remove weak canes and shorten lateral branches.

HARVEST Gently pull ripe berries from their short stems; they are ripe when they slip off the stems easily.

rhubarb

Herbaceous perennial; frost hardy; sometimes grown as a cool-season annual.

If you're dreaming of having enough of your own rhubarb for a pie, plant it and be patient—it can take 3 or 4 years to produce the first full harvest. However, in the meantime, the plant is handsome to look at—the leaves are broad, crinkled, and pink-veined, atop tall, smooth, red or green stalks; one plant could fill a large spot in a flowerbed.

Rhubarb does best in areas where the ground freezes in winter, but it can be grown as a cool-season annual in mild-winter climates.

POPULAR VARIETIES 'Valentine', long vivid red stalks that retain their color when cooked; 'Victoria', lots of large thick stalks that are pink at the base fading to green at the top.

BEST SITE Sunny, with fertile, well-drained soil rich in organic matter; partial shade in hot-summer areas.

continued >

rhubarb, continued

To make stalks grow earlier and longer, place a forcing pot over the dormant crown in winter.

PLANTING AND CARE Plant in late winter to early spring, when dormant crowns (clumps of roots with growth buds) are available. To grow rhubarb as an annual in mild climates, plant in fall for a late winter and spring harvest.

Prepare the ground by digging in plenty of well-rotted manure or compost. Make low mounds 3 to 4 feet apart. Set the crowns in the soil so the tops are 1 inch below the soil surface.

Keep the soil moist. Feed the plants twice every spring, once when the first stalks emerge and again after harvest; use a high-nitrogen complete fertilizer. Watch for aphids, flea beetles, and leafhoppers (see pages 74–75). Remove any flower stalks that appear. In fall, when the foliage dies back, cover the crowns with a compost mulch.

HARVEST In the spring of the second year after planting, a few stalks may be thick enough to harvest; starting in the third or fourth year, expect a big harvest that lasts for 8 to 10 weeks. Using a sideways twist, gently pull off the stalks near their base when they reach 10 to 15 inches long. Harvest no more than a third of the stalks at any one time. Stop harvesting when the stalks start to become thin. Yields are about 1 to 1½ pounds per plant.

!!! Don't eat rhubarb leaves. They are poisonous.

FOR THE TABLE Remove and discard the leaves, chop the stalks into 1-inch lengths, and stew them in a little water with slivers of orange peel; add sugar to taste and serve with strawberry ice cream.

rosemary

Shrubby perennial herb; hardiness varies; upright kinds are often hardy to 10°F/–12°C; can be grown as an annual or indoors.

Some varieties of rosemary grow as ground covers; others are upright, and you can clip them like hedges. The flowers, usually delicate blue, appear among the dark, glossy green needlelike leaves. Rosemary is an excellent plant for containers, and it does well indoors on a sunny windowsill. Some rosemary species are mild tasting, others distinctly resinous.

POPULAR VARIETIES 'Arp', hardy to –15°F/–26°C, to 4 feet tall; 'Blue Boy', pleasant fragrance and flavor, small dome-shaped plant, good for pots; 'Blue Spires', strong upright growth to 6 feet tall, makes a fine hedge, attractive in the landscape, excellent flavor.

BEST SITE Sunny, with especially well-drained soil; tolerates poor, dry soil.

PLANTING AND CARE Set out small nursery plants in early spring. Space upright types at least 2 feet apart and spreading types at least 3 feet apart. In cold-winter climates, choose hardy varieties or plant rosemary in a container so that you can bring it indoors in fall.

Water regularly until the plants are established, then only to keep them from drying out—rosemary often fails in soggy soil.

'Tuscan Blue' rosemary

Prune the tips of the branches regularly to keep the plants tidy and compact and to encourage new growth. Prune older plants lightly and regularly; cut back branches to side branches or shear the plant with clippers.

HARVEST Snip branch tips. One or two plants are sufficient for most gardeners.

FOR THE TABLE Rub meat or vegetables with rosemary branches before grilling or lay several branches on the grill and place the food on top of them.

tip **Rosemary flowers are also edible; add them to salads, or use them as a garnish.**

herb garden in a pot

This two-tiered container garden holds a selection of basic culinary herbs, including rosemary and sage, which stay small in a pot. Trailers and fillers—chives, oregano, rosemary, and thyme—tumble over the edges of the bottom pot, which is about 24 inches wide. The top pot, which is about 16 inches wide, contains 'Tricolor' sage and purple, dwarf, and sweet basils, with thyme filling in around the edges. Use a high-quality potting mix. Place the container garden in an area that receives 6 hours of full midday sun. Water regularly. Fertilize occasionally with fish emulsion.

Garden sage, or common sage, is the traditional culinary sage, but some other *Salvia* species have a pleasant sage aroma also. The lavender-blue flower spikes in late spring and summer are reason enough to grow it. Some varieties of garden sage have beautiful leaves, too. Find a dryish, exceptionally well-drained place for sage; its roots rot where drainage is less than perfect.

POPULAR VARIETIES 'Aurea', compact, to 18 inches tall, green leaves rimmed with chartreuse-yellow, pretty edging plant; 'Berggarten', compact, to 16 inches tall, dense foliage, musky pungent flavor, few flowers, favorite for culinary use; garden sage (*Salvia officinalis*), 1 to 3 feet tall, gray-green leaves, blue flowers; 'Purpurascens', new leaves flushed with red-violet; 'Tricolor', to 3 feet tall, gray-green leaves with irregular cream border, new leaves flushed with purplish pink.

BEST SITE Sunny, with good air circulation and especially well-drained soil; afternoon shade in hot climates.

PLANTING AND CARE Set out small nursery plants in spring. Space them 2 to 3 feet apart, depending on the variety.

Water regularly until the plants are established; then keep the soil on the dry side, soaking it deeply just once a month. Avoid overwatering. Watch

sage
Shrubby perennial herb; garden sage is fairly cold hardy.

'Tricolor' sage

'Purpurascens' sage

for powdery mildew (see page 78). Cut back flower stems after they bloom.

Prune the tips of the stems regularly to keep the plants tidy. Prune older plants lightly and regularly; cut back branches to just above fresh growth. Replace plants every 3 to 4 years when they become woody or leggy.

HARVEST Snip branch tips. One or two plants are sufficient for most gardeners.

FOR THE TABLE White beans are delicious when cooked with a few chopped sage leaves.

southern peas

Warm-season annual; damaged by frost.

Southern, or field, peas—cowpeas, crowder, black-eyed, cream, lady, and purple hull—can be long or round, smooth or wrinkled, solid color or speckled. Although they are called peas, these plants grow and look much like bush snap beans; asparagus bean, or yard-long bean (*dow gauk*), is a variety of cowpea. Southern peas are packed with vitamins and protein.

Southern peas prefer a long, warm growing season. They thrive in the South and Southwest. You can grow them in cooler climates, but the yields will be paltry. Where the growing season is short, plant early-bearing dwarf or bush varieties.

POPULAR VARIETIES 'Calico Crowder', tan with maroon markings, flavorful favorite; 'Pinkeye Purple Hull', early, semibush, heavy yields, good resistance to disease; 'Queen Anne', black-eyed, compact plants, good pest and disease resistance; 'Zipper Cream', easy to shell.

BEST SITE Sunny and warm, with average, well-drained soil; some varieties grow in poor soil.

PLANTING AND CARE Sow seeds in successive batches starting in spring, but wait until nights are warm, at least 2 to 4 weeks after the last frost. Sow the last batch 11 weeks before the first frost date in fall.

Sow seeds 1 inch deep, 1 inch apart, in rows 2 to $3^{1}/_{2}$ feet apart. When seedlings are a few inches tall, thin them to 6 inches apart.

Water regularly, soaking the soil, but don't overwater—southern peas can tolerate some drought—and keep the water off the leaves. Watch for aphids, nematodes, thrips, and powdery mildew (see pages 74, 76, and 78). Mexican bean beetle is a common pest in some areas; it looks like a ladybug, yellow when young, then coppery with dark spots. Remove the yellow larvae and clusters of yellow eggs on the undersides of leaves in spring; in summer, shake the adults off the plants onto a cloth, and remove them. If plants become infested, apply a natural pesticide (see pages 72–73), following the directions on the label.

HARVEST From 50 to 120 days after sowing, depending on whether you pick the pods green, when the peas are fully grown but still soft to the touch, or let them dry on the vine, for hard, dry peas. Handpick the pods,

Asparagus (yard-long) bean

Lady peas

or cut them with pruning shears. Store shelled dry peas in jars. Yields range from 5 to 8 pounds per 10-foot row.

FOR THE TABLE Simmer dried southern peas with a slab of bacon in three times their volume of water until they are tender (1 to 1¼ hours); serve with rice or ham, or top each portion with a sweet tomato-and-green-pepper salsa.

A favorite today among flavorful greens, spinach has only one irksome tendency—it bolts quickly into flower if the weather gets too warm (above 75°F/24°C) or if days lengthen too much before harvest. Spinach thrives in the cool of spring or fall, or even winter in places where the climate is mild and nearly frost-free. To prolong harvests as long as possible into warm weather, choose bolt-resistant varieties. For a summertime crop, or if you live in a hot region, try the spinach taste-alikes (see sidebar).

tip Smooth, flat-leafed spinach varieties are the most tender; grow them in spring. The savoyed, crinkly-leafed kinds, which hold up better in frosty weather, are a more reliable choice for fall.

POPULAR VARIETIES 'Bloomsdale Long-standing', savoyed leaves, bolt resistant, good for winter crops; 'Indian Summer', savoyed leaves, high yields, great flavor; 'Space', smooth leaves, upright, productive, slow to bolt.

BEST SITE Sunny or lightly shaded, with rich, well-drained soil.

PLANTING AND CARE For a late spring crop, sow seeds in spring, 6 to 8 weeks before the last frost date; to prolong the harvest, make successive sowings at 2- to 3-week intervals. Stop sowing when the weather begins to warm, not much later than the last frost date. For a fall crop, sow seeds 4 to 6 weeks before the first frost date. In a mild-winter climate, you can also sow seeds through the winter, for a spring crop.   *continued >*

New Zealand spinach

spinach

Cool-season annual; withstands frost.

warm-season "spinach"

New Zealand and Malabar spinach aren't true spinach, but they have a similar taste and are useful for the warm months, when true spinach bolts into flower.

Give them rich soil. Sow seeds in late spring to early summer. Thin seedlings to 12 to 18 inches apart. When Malabar spinach plants are about 1 foot tall, train them on wires or a trellis; the vines will reach about 4 feet tall. New Zealand spinach is a vigorous, low, spreading plant. To encourage both kinds to branch and form more stems, pinch out a few inches of stem tip. Pick leaves individually. Neither plant can survive frost.

spinach, continued

Sow seeds ½ inch deep, 1 inch apart, in rows 1 to 2½ feet apart. When seedlings are well established, thin them to 3 to 4 inches apart. As the plants grow larger and begin touching, thin out every other plant, and eat the thinnings.

Keep the soil moist, and weed regularly. Watch for aphids, cabbageworms, and leaf miners (see pages 74–75).

HARVEST From 40 to 50 days after sowing seeds, or earlier if you pick just a few leaves. Either pull up the entire plant, or cut or pinch off just enough outer leaves for a meal, or cut all the leaves 1 inch above soil level and let the plant regrow (see page 100).

'Oriental Giant' spinach

FOR THE TABLE To wilt a spinach salad, heat olive oil in a small frying pan over high heat; when it's very hot, pour it over the salad, and mix quickly.

squash

Warm-season annual; killed by frost.

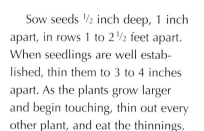

'Yellow Scallop' summer squash

Squash is a rewarding crop for both beginning and experienced gardeners. Few other vegetables produce such a bountiful harvest for so little effort; your biggest job, especially for zucchini, will be keeping the crop picked.

The two basic types are summer squash and winter squash. The major differences between them are in the stage at which the fruits are harvested and in their ability to last well in storage.

Summer squashes are planted for a warm-weather harvest and are eaten when the fruits are small and tender—skins, immature seeds, and all. Winter squashes, with fruits that are slower to mature and usually bigger, are grown for late summer harvest and winter storage, although some can be harvested when immature and eaten like summer squashes. The skin of the mature fruits is hard and inedible. Ordinarily, you scoop out the seeds and pulp before baking the squash. The seeds may be saved, dried, and roasted to eat.

BEST SITE Sunny, with rich, well-drained soil.

PLANTING AND CARE Get started in spring. Sow seeds indoors in a warm place (see page 52) 1 week or so before the last frost date; or wait until the soil has warmed, at least 2 weeks after the last frost date, and sow seeds outdoors. In the garden, sow seeds of vining squash 2 to 3 inches deep, 12 to 18 inches apart, in rows 6 to 8 feet apart. Alternatively, sow them in hills (see page 55), 4 or 5 seeds per hill, 5 to 6 feet between the hills, in rows 7 to

12 feet apart; once the seedlings are established, thin them to 2 per hill. Sow seeds of bush squashes 2 to 3 inches deep, 12 inches apart, in rows 3 to 5 feet apart; thin seedlings to 2 to 4 feet apart.

Water deeply by flooding or soaking (see page 63) to keep the soil moist. Avoid splashing water on the leaves, stems, and flowers. Weed regularly. Watch for aphids, cucumber beetles, mites, nematodes, squash bugs, and powdery mildew (see pages 74, 76, and 78 for help on controlling these pests). Squash vine borers may also be a problem (see page 136).

To prevent rot in winter squash, raise the fruits off the ground onto pieces of plywood, bricks, or scraps of plastic foam.

tip Squash plants depend on bees to pollinate the flowers; for better pollination and fruiting, plant two rows side by side instead of one long row. In small plantings, use a little paintbrush to brush pollen from the male flowers, which appear first, into the centers of the female flowers.

summer squash

Summer squash yields prodigious crops from just a few plants and continues producing for several weeks. The vining types can grow to 4 feet across at maturity, but most varieties are "bush" types, which have shorter vines. Summer squashes include zucchini (green and golden, many shapes), pattypan (scalloped), yellow crookneck, and straightneck squash.

POPULAR VARIETIES 'Cocozelle' and 'Costata Romanesco', zucchini, green, favorites for flavor; 'Eight Ball', zucchini, round, dark green; 'Sunburst', pattypan, bright yellow; 'Sundance', crookneck, early, bright yellow, smooth skin; 'Zephyr', straightneck, yellow with green tip.

HARVEST From 50 to 65 days after sowing. Cut stems close to the fruits with a sharp knife. Harvest the ordinary and golden zucchini and straightneck squashes when they are 4 to 6 inches long, or even smaller; harvest the round zucchini when it's 3 to 4 inches wide; harvest crookneck and scallop squashes when they are 2 to 3 inches wide.

tip If your summer squashes become large and tough (a thumbnail doesn't pierce the skin easily), hollow them out and make stuffed squash, or shred them for zucchini cake or bread. Regular harvesting keeps the plants producing new fruits.

winter squash

Winter squash, like pumpkin (a type of this squash; see page 169), needs plenty of space and plenty of water. It comes in an array of colors, shapes, and sizes. The smallest kinds are acorn squash and buttercup squash, which is shaped like a turban. Medium-size types include smooth-skinned butternut squash and warty hubbard squash. Banana squash can grow up to 20 inches long; and melon

ABOVE *'Zephyr' (straightneck) summer squash*

LEFT *Orange hubbard winter squash*

*'Queensland Blue'
winter squash*

squash, which looks like an extralarge butternut, grows to 30 inches long. Melon squash has a particularly sweet flavor, more like a yam than a melon, but it takes a long time to mature. Spaghetti squash, which looks like a fat, yellow-skinned zucchini, has flesh made up of long strands. Some winter squashes are big sprawlers; to save space, grow them on a frame (see page 57).

POPULAR VARIETIES 'Blue Hubbard', 15-pound ridged blue fruit, sweet yellow flesh prized for freezing; 'Buttercup', turban-shaped, blackish green skin, deep orange flesh, rich taste, excellent keeper; 'Early Butternut', tan-skinned sweet fruit, compact vines; 'Table King', acorn, bush type, dark green with golden flesh.

HARVEST From 60 to 110 days after sowing, when the vines have dried but before the first heavy frost. The skin should be hard and unscratchable. Cut the stem with a sharp knife, leaving a 2-inch stub on the fruit. To store, keep the squash warm and dry, and handle it gently. It keeps from 8 to 24 weeks, depending on the variety.

FOR THE TABLE Cut crookneck or pattypan squash, eggplant, red bell peppers, and red-skinned potatoes into big chunks, drizzle olive oil over them, and roast with a couple of sprigs of rosemary.

strawberries

Perennial, sometimes grown as an annual; goes dormant in winter; frost tolerant.

June-bearing strawberries produce one crop in late spring or early summer; generally they are the highest-quality strawberries you can grow. Everbearing varieties peak in summer and continue to produce into fall, often until the first frost. Though they bear for a longer time, they tend to be less vigorous than June-bearing strawberries and may produce fewer fruits; for a single, large fall crop, you can remove the summer blossoms.

Varieties do not perform predictably in different climates; for the best selection for your area, consult a regional nursery or your local Cooperative Extension Office. Buy certified disease-free plants. The plants decline in vigor after 2 or 3 years and need replacing. Some growers in mild-winter areas replant every year, in fall.

tip Strawberries are attractive plants. Grow them in containers, tuck them into a flowerbed or herb garden (alpine strawberries, which have tiny, delectable berries, make a lovely bed edging), or use them as a ground cover in front of shrubs. To plant a strawberry jar, see page 59.

POPULAR VARIETIES *June-bearing:* 'Benton', firm flavorful berries, virus tolerant, mildew resistant, excellent for the Northwest; 'Chandler', large juicy berries, excellent flavor, good for Southern California or as an annual elsewhere; 'Sequoia', very tasty, long crop, good disease resistance, developed for coastal California. *Everbearing:* 'Alexandria', small red-fruiting alpine type, grows from seed, reseeds, no runners; 'Fort Laramie', very cold hardy, excellent flavor, good for warm and cold climates; 'Ozark Beauty', large long-necked berries, mild sweet flavor, good cold hardiness and climate adaptability; 'Tristar', large berries, excellent flavor, mildew resistant, widely adapted.

BEST SITE Sunny, with rich, well-drained, acid soil (most varieties need a pH no higher than 6.5); in areas with late frosts, plant on a slope, so cold air will drain away from the fragile blossoms; because of verticillium wilt, avoid sites planted with strawberries, tomatoes, raspberries, potatoes, peppers, or eggplants in the last 3 years.

PLANTING ARRANGEMENTS Choose a planting system—hills or matted rows—before you purchase plants. Hills result in a smaller yield but produce big, beautiful berries from large, vigorous plants; it's a more costly setup, because you'll need more plants, but the harvest may seem well worth the price. Everbearing varieties are usually grown in hills; they produce fewer runners. In a matted row system, you place the plants farther apart and allow runners to root within the boundaries of the row.

PLANTING AND CARE In cold-winter climates, set out plants in early spring, 3 or 4 weeks before the last frost date. In mild-winter climates, you can set out the plants at any time of year. Before planting, keep the roots moist, and, just before planting, trim them to 6 inches for easier management.

For a hill system, set out plants 12 to 14 inches apart on mounds that are 5 to 6 inches high and 5 to 6 inches wide, spaced 28 inches apart at the centers (see drawing above right).

For a matted row system, set out plants 18 to 24 inches apart in rows spaced 4 feet apart (see drawing at right).

As you plant, be sure to position the base of the crown at soil level; a buried crown will rot. Firm the soil around the roots; they must be completely covered.

During the first year, pinch off the early blooms, to strengthen the plants. If the plants are in hills, also trim off all runners as soon as they appear. Weed regularly.

If you plant in matted rows, cultivate shallowly once a week for the first 6 weeks (2 weeks for everbearing varieties) to loosen the surface soil and allow the runners to root easily. Decide on a row width of 18 to 24 inches, and allow runners to root anywhere within the row. Trim off any runners that extend beyond the row (see drawing below right).

Water regularly, at least 1 inch per week for prime fruit, more in dry weather. Fertilize June-bearing plants very lightly when growth begins in spring and more heavily after harvest. Give everbearing plants consistent light feedings. Do not overfertilize in spring. Watch for mites, slugs, snails, powdery mildew, blight, and verticillium wilt (see pages 76 and 78). Strawberry root weevils can be a problem in some regions; the larvae feed on the roots, and the adults chew holes in the leaves and crown. Keep the rows free of debris, and quickly remove any affected plants. Promptly removing diseased foliage and ripe or rotting fruit will also reduce fruit rots.

continued >

PLANTING STRAWBERRIES

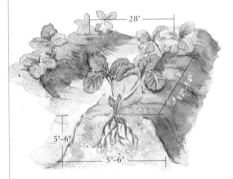

Hill system

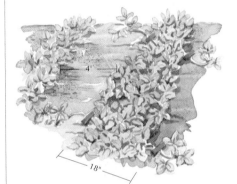

Matted row system

'Sequoia' strawberries

strawberries, continued

tip Strawberries are a treat for birds as well as people. Protect emerging berries from avian attacks with plastic netting.

A straw mulch helps to keep the fruit clean and discourages weeds. In areas with very cold winters, straw mulch is vital in fall: sift straw over the plants, covering them completely, in late November. The following spring, brush the straw off the leaves, but keep it as a mulch. If you expect a late frost when the plants are in bud or bloom, heap the straw over the plants, and remove it again the next day.

After harvest, choose whether to dig up the plants or to renovate the rows for another season's crop. To renovate, remove and destroy any plants that show signs of insect infestation or disease; clip or mow the leaves of the remaining plants to within 1 inch of the crowns; if plants are crowded, thin out the older ones so those left are 6 inches apart. Apply a high-nitrogen complete fertilizer.

HARVEST When berries are fully red and ripe. To avoid bruising the fruit, cut the stems. Yields are from 5 to 10 quarts per 10-foot matted row.

FOR THE TABLE To poach strawberries, simmer together for 12 minutes 2½ cups Merlot or another dry red wine, 1 teaspoon lemon juice, ½ cup sugar, and a vanilla bean split lengthwise and with seeds removed. Remove from the heat, stir in 6 cups of strawberries, and let cool. Remove the vanilla bean. Serve with whipped cream.

sunflowers

Warm-season annual; killed by frost.

Every garden, especially a garden visited by children, should have sunflowers; they're so easy to grow and so beautiful. You can always find room for at least one—at the end of a row, or wherever there's a sunny moist spot. The seeds are handy for nutritious snacks or for winter bird food.

tip Cut-flower varieties often have lemon-yellow, orange, mahogany, deep red, and multicolored blooms. Many of these bear multiple flowers and are usually not grown to harvest the seeds.

POPULAR VARIETIES 'Mammoth Russian', to 10 feet tall, 10-inch flower heads; 'Sunspot', 3 to 6 feet tall, 10-inch heads.

BEST SITE Sunny, with rich, well-drained soil.

PLANTING AND CARE Sow seeds in spring when the soil has warmed to at least 60°F/16°C. Place seeds ½ inch deep, 6 to 12 inches apart, in rows 2½ to 3 feet apart. Thin seedlings to 12 to 18 inches apart.

Water plants generously. Watch for aphids, cucumber beetles, and mites (see pages 74 and 76). If you plan to harvest the seeds, cover the flower heads with cheesecloth or paper bags as the seeds ripen, to keep birds from eating them.

HARVEST From 68 to 80 days after sowing, when the seeds are mature and fairly hard. Cut the flower heads with 1 foot of stem. Dry them in a warm, well-ventilated spot. Remove the seeds when they are thoroughly dry; store them (roasted for people, unroasted for birds) in a cool, dry place.

sweet potatoes

Perennial, grown as a warm-season annual; frost sensitive.

One of the few vegetables that thrive in hot weather, sweet potatoes keep growing until the first frost—the attractive vines will run all over the garden. There are two types: those with soft, sugary, orange flesh and those with firm, dry, whitish flesh. If you have a small space, choose a compact variety.

POPULAR VARIETIES 'Beauregard', light purple skin, dark orange flesh, uniform shape, high yields; 'Centennial', smooth skin, deep orange flesh, high yields; 'Vardaman', orange flesh, compact, attractive deep-red-and-green foliage.

BEST SITE Sunny, with loose, well-drained soil.

PLANTING AND CARE Buy certified disease-free slips (rooted cuttings). Plant them in spring when the soil has warmed to 70°F/21°C. Set them out 10 to 18 inches apart, on rows mounded 10 inches high and 12 inches wide, spaced 3 to 4 feet apart. Keep the soil moist until the plants are established. In cool-summer areas, you can increase the heat around the plants with plastic mulches and other techniques (see pages 66 and 102–103).

Once the plants are established, water regularly, but allow the soil to dry slightly between waterings. Do not fertilize (too much nitrogen reduces yield and lowers quality). Let the vines sprawl. Watch for aphids, flea beetles, leafhoppers, nematodes, and wireworms (see pages 74–76).

HARVEST From 110 to 120 days after planting, before the first frost. Dig potatoes up carefully, and dry them in the sun. After curing (see tip), store them in a cool, damp place (not below 55°F/13°C). Yields are from 8 to 12 pounds per 10-foot row.

tip Uncured sweet potatoes taste musty. To cure them, after harvest put them in a warm (about 85°F/29°C), humid place for several weeks. Then store them; the flavor improves with storage.

FOR THE TABLE Mash baked sweet potatoes with milk, fresh goat cheese, and thyme.

thyme

Shrubby perennial herb; withstands light freezes.

Common thyme, also called *English thyme,* is the popular choice for culinary purposes. It makes a little shrub about 1 foot high, suitable for a low hedge around a vegetable, flower, or herb garden; and bees are very attracted to the white-to-lilac flowers in late spring and early summer. Other thymes, some sprawling or creeping, have good flavors, too.

POPULAR VARIETIES Caraway-scented thyme *(Thymus herba-barona),* dark green leaves, rose-pink flowers, caraway flavor, creeping mat 4 inches tall; common thyme *(T. vulgaris),* gray-green leaves, classic flavor, 12 inches tall; lemon thyme *(T. × citriodorus),* dark green foliage, lemon flavor, 12 inches tall.

BEST SITE Sunny, with light, well-drained soil; tolerates poor, dry soil.

PLANTING AND CARE Set out small nursery plants in early spring, 8 to 12 inches apart. Water regularly until the plants are established, then only to keep the plants from drying out completely.

Prune the tips of the branches regularly to keep the plants tidy and compact and to encourage new growth. Keep the flowers cut back so that the plants keep growing new shoots. Replace the plants every 2 to 3 years when they become too straggly.

HARVEST Snip branch tips (the flowers are edible too). Three or four plants are sufficient for most gardeners.

tomatoes

Warm-season annual; killed by frost.

'Black Krim', 'Supersteak', 'Big Rainbow', and 'Brandywine' tomatoes.

Real old-fashioned tomato flavor ripened on the vine is the reason gardeners grow their own tomato crop. No commercially grown tomato tastes better than a juicy one plucked from the vine, rinsed with the garden hose, and eaten right on the spot.

Tomatoes range in size from pop-in-the-mouth cherry types to 2-pound beefsteak slicers. Besides the usual round, red tomatoes, you can grow small yellow ones shaped like pears or plums. There are orange ones, pink ones, and heirloom tomatoes with stripes on their shoulders. To decide which varieties of each kind to grow, take advice from your local garden center, Cooperative Extension Office, and neighboring gardeners; no tomato does well in every climate and soil type.

If your growing season is short, be sure to choose a determinate variety. These are shorter plants—3 to 5 feet, compared to the indeterminate types at 12 to 14 feet—and they produce an earlier (though smaller) crop over a shorter harvest period. Where summers are very short or chilly, you'll need an early maturing variety; or you can extend your growing season by using plastic mulches and other techniques (see pages 66 and 102–103).

tip Beefsteak-type tomatoes, the giants, usually thrive in the South, Midwest, and East but flop in the West because they need long, humid summers and warm night temperatures (65 to 70°F/18 to 21°C).

POPULAR VARIETIES 'Brandywine', indeterminate, pink, beefsteak slicer, superb flavor, also available in red, black, and yellow versions; 'Dona', indeterminate, early, classic red, medium size, premium flavor, good yield; 'Isis Candy', indeterminate, gold-red marbled, cherry, very sweet; 'Stupice', indeterminate, early, red, modest size, cold tolerant, good for mild-summer climates; 'Sun Gold', indeterminate, yellow-orange, cherry, sweet as candy; 'Viva Italia', determinate, red, paste tomato, very sweet, disease resistant.

> **tip** Check the seed packet to find out if a variety has inbred resistance to one or more of the big four tomato troublemakers. The code is "V" for verticillium wilt, "F" for fusarium wilt, "N" for nematodes, and "T" for tobacco mosaic virus.

BEST SITE Sunny and warm, with fertile, well-drained soil, rich in organic matter.

STAKES AND WIRE CAGES Wise gardeners support tomatoes on stakes or in wire cages. Supports keep the plants neat and prevent rot by lifting the fruits off the soil; they also allow better air circulation through the plants, which helps prevent foliage diseases. In extremely hot areas, don't use metal supports, because they may burn your plants.

If you use stakes, choose sturdy ones at least 1 inch thick and 6 feet tall. Hammer the stakes into the ground 1 foot from the plant at the time of planting. To avoid any damage to stems, tie the tomato vines to the stakes or other supports with strips of cloth or other soft ties. For other ideas for tomato supports, see page 57.

PLANTING AND CARE Start in spring by sowing seeds indoors or buying young plants from a garden center. Sow seeds indoors in a warm place (see page 52) 5 to 7 weeks before you plan to set them out (at least 10 days after the last frost date, when the soil has warmed). If you are purchasing plants, choose the sturdiest ones; reject ones that are weak, spindly, or too mature. Harden off your plants or your home-grown seedlings (see page 53) before planting them in the garden.

Unlike most other plants, tomatoes prefer deep planting. Bury $\frac{1}{2}$ to $\frac{3}{4}$ of the stem after removing the leaflets (see photo). Roots will form along the buried part of the stem and strengthen the plant. *continued >*

Plant tomatoes deeper than they grew in pots.

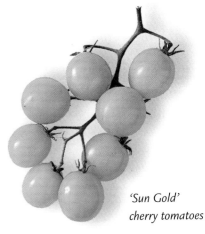

patio tomatoes

Standard tomatoes need a container with a capacity of 3 cubic feet, but you can grow dwarf and miniature tomatoes in pots or large hanging baskets with a capacity of 1 cubic foot. Put a stake or wire cage in the pot at planting time, and tie 1 to 3 main stems to the support as the plant grows. 'Sun Gold' (see Popular Varieties) is a great-tasting choice for a large container.

'Sun Gold' cherry tomatoes

tomatoes, continued

RIGHT *A cornucopia of tomatoes shows an array of colors, shapes, and sizes.*

husky tomatillos

A tomatillo is a large green tomato relative with a husk. It's tough, prolific, and easy to grow—not as bothered by pests and diseases as regular tomatoes are. The flowers also set earlier, and the fruits can be harvested sooner, so in many regions you can sow seed directly in the ground outdoors once all danger of frost has past. If your growing season is short, start seeds indoors (see page 52). Care for the plants just as you would regular tomato plants. Harvest the fruits when they fill the husks and are still firm and green. Remove the husks when you are ready to use the fruits—raw in salads or cooked in salsa verde.

If you're staking the plants, set them out 2 feet apart in rows 3 to 4 feet apart, the farthest spacing for indeterminate varieties. If you are not staking them, set them out 1½ to 4 feet apart in rows 3 to 4 feet apart.

Water often enough to keep the soil in the root zone damp but not soggy; keep the water off the leaves to help prevent foliage diseases. You may need to water seedlings every 1 to 2 days until they become established. During dry spells, water well-established plants deeply about every 10 days. Mulch the plants to conserve moisture; try to not let the soil dry out, because wide fluctuations in soil moisture are associated with blossom-end rot (discussed later).

To get earlier, larger tomatoes, pinch off the suckers that form at the notch between a branch and the main stem. To get more fruit and greater protection against sunscald, let a few suckers develop.

Feed the plants with a low-nitrogen fertilizer when the fruit starts to develop; too much nitrogen encourages leaves instead of fruit. Where summer nights are

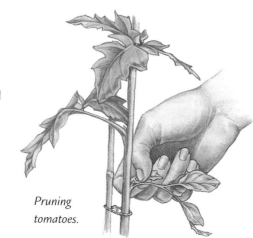

Pruning tomatoes.

cool, encourage pollination by tickling the blossoms once or twice during the warmest part of the day (pollination occurs reliably only in warm temperatures). If temperatures are likely to go over 100°F/38°C, drape nursery shade cloth over stakes to bring down the temperature a few degrees, or the plants will stop setting fruit.

Watch for aphids, Colorado potato beetles, cutworms, flea beetles, leaf miners, nematodes, whiteflies, blight, fusarium wilt, and verticillium wilt (see pages 74–76, 78). Blossom-end rot—a leathery spot on the blossom end of the fruit—is a potential problem; the cause of it is unclear, but keeping moisture steady and using a fertilizer that contains calcium may help.

tip Tomato hornworms—fat, green, 4-inch worms—eat leaves and fruit. Handpicking them is the best strategy, but they don't show up well against the leaves. Put an ultraviolet bulb in a fluorescent-bulb flashlight, and shine it on the plants at night; the worms then glow in the dark.

HARVEST From 50 to 90 days after setting out plants. Cut or gently pull the fruit from the stem. Complete the harvest before the first fall frost.

FOR THE TABLE To make a simple cherry tomato and mozzarella salad, halve the tomatoes, halve *bocconcini* (the small balls of fresh cheese), tear fresh basil leaves, and mix together. Drizzle with olive oil, and sprinkle lightly with coarse sea salt.

'Tiger' tomato

turnips

Cool-season annual; withstands frost.

Most kinds of turnips you can eat from top to bottom—the greens when they're young and the roots when they reach maturity; some varieties you eat only the greens. Turnips like cool weather. A sowing in late summer or fall usually yields the most tender and flavorful turnips.

POPULAR VARIETIES 'Hakurai', sweet-tasting white roots, excellent harvested small; 'Purple Top White Globe', classic for roots, stores well; 'Shogoin', excellent tender mild greens.

BEST SITE Sunny or lightly shaded, with rich soil. Practice crop rotation (see page 77).

PLANTING AND CARE Sow seeds in early spring and, for a second crop, mid- to late summer (fall in mild-winter climates). Place seeds 1/2 inch deep, 1 inch apart, in rows 1 to 3 feet apart for root crops (6 to 12 inches apart for greens). Water the soil well to ensure germination. Thin seedlings to 2 to 6 inches apart for root crops (1 to 4 inches for greens).

Water moderately but regularly to keep growth steady. Watch for cabbage root maggots and wireworms (see pages 74 and 76).

HARVEST Pick the greens when the leaves are 2 to 10 inches long. Periodically pinch off a few leaves at the base, or cut them all off at once 1 inch above the ground, and wait for new leaves to grow (see page 100); harvest only a few leaves if you want a good root crop. Pull up roots 30 to 60 days after sowing, when they are 2 to 3 inches in diameter. Store roots in a cool, damp place.

'White Lady' turnip

tip Turnips protected with a foot of straw can stay in the ground in fall until you're ready to use them, but harvest them before the ground freezes solid.

▶ *For Watermelon, see Melons, page 151.*

▶ *For Zucchini, see Squash, page 180.*

Melanie Acevedo/Picture Arts/Botanica: *5 top, 7 right, 24, 60, 171 bottom, 191 bottom;* **Curtis Anderson:** *86 right;* **Max Badgley:** *73-4, 73-6;* **Maryellen Baker/ Picture Arts/ Botanica:** *4 bottom, 40, 182 bottom right;* **Bill Beatty/Visuals Unlimited:** *74-5;* **Paul Bousquet:** *21 top left, 136 right;* **Marion Brenner:** *9 bottom left, 15 bottom right, 22 right, 32 bottom, 35 top right, 38 top;* **Roger Brooks/A–Z Botanical Collection Ltd.:** *23 top;* **Karen Bussolini:** *6, 7 middle top left, middle bottom left, 10 bottom, 17 top, 19 right, 27 bottom right, 29 top, 30 bottom, 39 top left, 93 bottom middle left, 100 top, 129 bottom, 141 top right;* **Ralph S. Byther:** *77 middle right;* **Rob Cardillo:** *2, 13 bottom right, 16 bottom, 41 top middle left, 61 right, 101 middle left; 105 bottom middle left, 116 left, 121, 127 bottom, 132 bottom, 134 right, 135 top left, 137 top, 149 top, 178 bottom, 180 bottom, 186 bottom, 189;* **James Carrier:** *112 middle left, 118 left, 160 left, 166 left, 172,* **David Cavagnaro:** *39 middle right, 56, 70-3, 71 middle left, bottom left, 86 left, 126 left, 111 top, 131, 132 top, 145 bottom, 149 middle, 155 right, 158 top, 163 top, 164 top, 171 top left, top right, 181 middle, bottom, 190 top;* **Jennifer Cheung/Picture Arts/Botanica:** *3, 25 right, 36 top;* **Connie Coleman:** *146 left;* **Crandall & Crandall:** *72 top, 167 top;* **Grey Crawford:** *156 left;* **Rosalind Creasy:** *15 top left, 17 bottom, 21 bottom, 29 right, 33 bottom right, 35 bottom left, 108 top, 110 top right, 115 bottom, 126 right, 128 right, 139 right, 146 right, 151 bottom, 176 bottom, 183;* **Claire Curran:** *188 right;* **Robin B. Cushman:** *79-2, 144, 177 bottom, 187 bottom right, 188 left;* **Francois De Heel/GPL:** *138;* **Arnaud Descaut/Mise au Point:** *91, 124 top, 147 bottom, 153 top, 175;* **Alan & Linda Detrick:** *19 top left, 113, 141 top left, 156 right, 162 bottom, 163 middle, bottom, 180 top;*

Frederic Didillon/ Mise au Point: *82 bottom right, 112 top, 122, 127 top, 133, 161 bottom;* **Miki Duisterhoff/ Picture Arts/Botanica:** *116 right;* **Laura Dunkin-Hubby:** *108 bottom, 169 middle, 185 left, 186 top;* **Wally Eberhart/Picture Arts/Botanica:** *25 middle top left;* **Clyde Elmore:** *70-4;* **Macduff Everton/Picture Arts/ Botanica:** *80;* **Rob Fiocca/Picture Arts/ Botanica:** *81 bottom middle left;* **Derek Fell:** *50 top right;* **Thomas E. Fitzroth:** *141 bottom;* **Roger Foley:** *19 bottom left, 32 top, 37 top left; 92, 94 left, 97;* **Gardener's Supply Co.:** *68 middle left bottom;* **John Glover:** *34 bottom, 35 middle right, 117 bottom, 120, 130 bottom;* **David Goldberg:** *53 left, 70-1, 70-6, 169 bottom;* **Alexandra Grablewski/Picture Arts/ Botanica:** *105 right, 182 bottom left;* **Steven Gunther:** *21 top right;* **Jamie Hadley:** *81 top left, 83;* **Jerry Harpur:** *11 top, 12, 13 bottom left, 29 bottom left, 33 bottom left, 93 top left, 94 right;* **105 top middle left;** **Marcus Harpur:** *34 top, 36 left, 123 bottom, 128 left, 147 middle, 167 bottom right;* **Sunniva Harte/GPL:** *150 bottom;* **Fred Hirschmann:** *43;* **Saxon Holt:** *4 top; 7 top left, 8, 106 top right, 109 right, 114, 136 left, 139 left; 142 bottom, 147 top; 155 left;* **Dency Kane:** *4 middle; 14, 25 top left, 26 bottom right, 27 top right, 101 bottom right; 124 bottom, 145 top, 154 top, 164 bottom, 178 top;* **Diana Koenigsberg/Picture Arts/ Botanica:** *25 middle bottom left, 30 top;* **A. M. Leonard:** *68 top left, middle top left;* **Marianne Lipanovich:** *187 top;* **Janet Loughrey:** *16 top, 61 top middle left, 66, 109 left; 154 bottom, 173;* **Jim McCausland:** *102 top, 176 top;* **Ericka Mcconnell:** *174;* **Jack McDowell:** *125 bottom;* **Allen Mandell:** *7 bottom left, 107;* **Charles Mann:** *41 bottom left:* **Ells W. Marugg:** *135 top right;* **Diana Miller/Picture Arts/Botanica:** *125 top;* **N & P Mioulane/ Mise au Point:** *5 middle right, 22 left, 82 left, 93 top middle left, 96;* **M Yan Monel/ Mise au Point:** *101 top right;* **Gary Moss/ Picture Arts/Botanica:** *37 top right;* **Amy Neunsinger/Picture Arts/ Botanica:** *81 bottom left;* **Clive Nichols/ GPL:** *9 bottom right, 11 bottom, 28 bottom;* **NOUN/Mise au Point:** *148 top, 152 top;* **Katie O'Hara-Kelly:** *18;* **Jerry Pavia:** *15 bottom left, 26 bottom left, 93 right, 179 bottom;* **Victoria Pearson/ Picture Arts/Botanica:** *1, 5 middle left, 25 bottom left, 41 right, 61 top left, 81 right, 105 bottom left;* **Pamela K. Peirce:** *70-5, 71 top right, top left, 74-1, 74-4, 75-1, 75-2, 78-3, 158 bottom;* **Ben Phillips/Positive Images:** *181 top;* **Norman A. Plate:** *20, 28 top, 31 top right, 42 right, 46 top, 52, 53 right, 55, 59, 67, 77 top left, 81 top middle left, 84, 85 left, 99, 106 left, 115 top, 117 top, 135*

bottom, 162 top, 167 bottom left, 168, 184 top, 187 bottom left ; **Rob Proctor:** *48;* **Ian Reeves:** *69 left;* **Howard Rice/GPL:** *105 top left, 118 right, 159 top, 182 top;* **Cheryl R. Richter:** *170 bottom;* **Christel Rosenfeld/ GPL:** *140;* **Susan A. Roth:** *10 top, 33 top, 35 top left, 36 bottom right, 37 bottom right, 38 bottom, 70-2, 76-1, 76-5, 76-6, 78-4, 79-4, 87, 91 bottom left, 95, 100 bottom, 102 bottom, 111 bottom, 119, 123 top, 129 top, 142 top, 148 bottom, 151 top, 153 bottom left, 159 bottom, 165 bottom, 166 top, 170 top left, 184 bottom;* **Janet H. Sanchez:** *82 top right;* **Science Vu/Visuals Unlimited:** *77 top right, bottom right;* **Thomas A. Seiter:** *78-2;* **Malcolm C. Shurtleff:** *78-5;* **J. S. Sira/ GPL:** *9 top, 153 bottom right;* **Evan Sklar/ Picture Arts/Botanica:** *179 top;* **Southern Progress Corporation:** *72 bottom;* **Thomas J. Story:** *5 bottom; 26-27, 42 left, 49, 58, 61 bottom middle left; 64, 79-1, 79-3, 85 right, 104, 110 bottom left, 112 middle right, bottom, 137 bottom, 157 bottom left, bottom right, 170 middle right, 177 top;* **F. Strauss/ Mise au Point:** *169 top;* **Michael S. Thompson:** *61 bottom left, 62 bottom, 161 top;* **E. Spencer Toy;** *41 top left, 46 bottom, 98, 149 bottom;* **Mark Turner:** *13 top;* **Union Tools, Inc.:** *50 top left, bottom, 68 bottom left, right, 69 right;* **Dierdre Walpole:** *31 top left;* **Darrow M. Watt:** *63, 150 top, middle;* **Jonelle Weaver/Picture Arts/Botanica:** *41 bottom middle left;* **William J. Weber:** *76-2;* **Rick Wetherbee:** *39 bottom left, 134 left, 152 bottom, 157 top, 165 top;* **Ron West:** *73-1, 73-2, 73-3, 73-5, 74-2, 74-3, 75-3, 75-4, 75-5, 75-6, 76-3, 76-4, 76 right, 78-1;* **Dave Wilson Nursery:** *159 middle, 160 right;* **Craig D. Wood:** *62 top;* **Tom Woodward:** *130 top;* **Shane Young:** *31 bottom right.*